Starck, dibujos secretos
4.000 croquis desvelados

Starck, Secret Drawings
4,000 Sketches Unveiled

Starck, dibujos secretos
4.000 croquis desvelados

Starck, Secret Drawings
4,000 Sketches Unveiled

Centre Pompidou   Centre Pompidou Málaga   **T** TURNER

Francisco de la Torre Prados
Alcalde de Málaga

Francisco de la Torre Prados
Mayor of Málaga

Es una de las características más obvias y por ello menos advertidas de la vida moderna, el hecho de que no solo estamos rodeados de tecnología y técnica, sino que estas están revestidas de formas que facilitan el uso pero a la vez tienen una dimensión estética que, sin darnos la perturbadora sensación de estar manejando objetos artísticos, sí aportan una comodidad visual, formal, nos reconcilian con el incesante progreso y nos confortan con la vida cotidiana. Es algo que ya supo William Morris y desarrolló el movimiento Arts and Crafts, que más tarde asumirían los Talleres Omega a la sombra del grupo de Bloomsbury, la Bauhaus de Walter Gropius o la escuela nórdica de diseño. Así, al llegar a nuestro tiempo, nos encontramos con el hecho de que el diseño industrial es omnipresente y a la vez casi invisible, y que entre todos los creadores han dotado de nuevas formas a las invenciones de siempre y también a las más nuevas, hay uno que se ha convertido, por su versatilidad y por la amplitud de ámbitos a los que extiende su actividad, en un referente y guía del diseño contemporáneo, que ahora acogemos en nuestro Centre Pompidou Málaga: Philippe Starck.

No hay ámbito en el que Philippe Starck no haya mostrado su capacidad de aportar al diseño una dimensión estética y, al mismo tiempo, emocional. Así, ha sido y es diseñador de interiores y de páginas web, arquitecto naval, arquitecto, diseñador gráfico e industrial, decorador, diseñador de lámparas, muebles, gafas, motocicletas o utensilios domésticos. Desde una perspectiva creativa, en la que combina elegancia, ironía, y sentidos utilitarios y orgánico, Starck es alguien con quien el mundo ha convivido desde hace décadas, haciendo que nuestra realidad cotidiana sea no solo más elegante, sino también seductora. Es esa capacidad para el asombro y para la atracción la que acogemos y saludamos en Málaga.

One of the most obvious and at the same time least perceived aspects of modern life is that we are not only surrounded by technology and technique, but that they are distinguished by forms that facilitate their use while still being physically attractive. Without giving us any sort of perturbing sensation that we might be handling artistic objects, they are comfortable on a visual and formal level, reconciling us with relentless progress and reassuring us in our daily life. This is something William Morris perceived in developing the Arts and Crafts Movement, which would later lead to the Omega Workshops, founded by the Bloomsbury group, Walter Gropius's Bauhaus and the Nordic school of design. In our day and age, we find that industrial design is everywhere, though it is equally invisible. Yet among all those creative designers who have given new forms to common and more novel inventions alike, there is one who, for his versatility and breadth of scope in everything he does, has become a leading reference point and guide to contemporary design: Philippe Starck, now exhibiting in the Centre Pompidou Málaga.

There is no area of activity where Philippe Starck has not shown his capacity to enliven design both aesthetically and emotionally. He has been (and still is) an interior designer and a web designer, a naval architect and an architect on land, a graphic and industrial designer, a decorator, and a designer of lamps, furniture, glasses, motorcycles and domestic implements. Working from a creative approach combining elegance, irony, utilitarian logic and organic good sense, Starck is a man the world has been living with for decades, making our everyday reality even more elegant and seductive. We are pleased to welcome him to Málaga, saluting his extraordinary capacity to surprise and entice us.

6

José María Luna
Director de la Agencia Pública para la gestión
de la Casa Natal de Pablo Ruiz Picasso y otros equipamientos
museísticos y culturales

José María Luna
Director of the Public Agency for the Management
of the Casa Natal de Pablo Ruiz Picasso and Other
Museum and Cultural Facilities

En los primeros compases de su trayectoria, el Centre Pompidou Málaga ha apostado claramente por ampliar el espacio de las disciplinas susceptibles de exposición. Fotografía, arquitectura, imágenes en movimiento o danza filmada han formado parte de la programación con tanta frecuencia o más que pintura y escultura.

El diseño, en este contexto, estaba llamado a formar parte de nuestra oferta expositiva tarde o temprano. La oportunidad de incorporarlo ha resultado ser inmejorable: Philippe Starck es uno de los nombres imprescindibles en su disciplina, pero también una marca, un concepto de autoría que rebasa la filiación de obras concretas para acabar encarnando un modo, un estilo propio y reconocible con independencia de formatos y materiales.

Frente a aproximaciones como las de Sottsass y el grupo Memphis, más cercanas al vocabulario y las intenciones del arte, Starck representa el diseño puro, la búsqueda de soluciones particulares para cada necesidad y una cierta ascesis conceptual atemperada por las gotas de ironía que convierten sus objetos en generadores de referencias infinitas. Y es en calidad de buscador de soluciones como lo presenta esta muestra: los objetos por todos conocidos se exhiben rodeados de 4.000 dibujos preparatorios que revelan una disciplina de trabajo sin concesiones cara a la galería ni veleidades artísticas, ideas que transitan entre la mano y el cerebro, y toman forma en el trayecto.

Es motivo de orgullo para el Centre Pompidou Málaga exponer la obra de un autor que, por voluntad propia, se ha prodigado tan poco en museos, pero, antes que la excepcionalidad de la ocasión o el carácter de primicia en España, es la calidad extraordinaria de la muestra lo que verdaderamente importa.

Through the first stages of its history, the Centre Pompidou Málaga has chosen to emphasize a wide range of disciplines for exhibition. Photography, architecture, moving images and filmed dance have been just as much a part of the programming as painting and sculpture.

Design, in this context, was always going to be part of our exhibition programme, sooner or later. This opportunity for showcasing it could not have been better, for Philippe Starck is one of the discipline's leading lights. Yet he is also a brand, a concept of authorship going far beyond his relationship with concrete works to become a way of being, a unique, recognizable style, regardless of the formats and materials brought into play.

In contrast to the approach of Sottsass and the Memphis Group, whose work was nearer to the vocabulary and intentions of art, Starck represents pure design, a search for specific solutions for each and every necessity. He is also typified by a certain conceptual asceticism, tempered in turn by a dose of irony, turning his objects into generators of the widest array of references. He appears in this exhibition in his role as a seeker of solutions: objects we are all familiar with are surrounded by some 4,000 preparatory drawings, testifying to his working discipline, his insistence on making no concessions and going off on fewer artistic flights, the ideas moving between hand and brain while taking shape along the way.

The Centre Pompidou Málaga is immensely proud to be exhibiting this creator, someone who by his own choice has been seen little in museums. However, even more important than the exceptional nature of the occasion, or the chance to see his work for the first time in a major show in Spain, is the extraordinary overall calibre of this Philippe Starck exhibition.

BON JOUR.

AU MILIEU DU CERVEAU, ONT DIT QUE SE CACHE L'INCONSCIENT, PEUT ETRE.

MAIS EN FAIT ET SURTOUT IL Y A LE MAGMA. LE MAGMA, MON MAGMA EST UNE PÂTE MOLLE, COMME UNE PÂTE A PAIN OU UNE PÂTE A PAPIER. CETTE PÂTE VIT, GRANDIT, SE CONVULSE DANS UN MILIEU CHAUD ET HUMIDE.

QUAND ON PARLE, QUAND ON EXPLIQUE, DES FRAGMENTS DU MAGMA SONT EXPULSÉS DANS L'AIR, PAR LA BOUCHE. AU CONTACT DE L'AIR CES FRAGMENTS SECHENT, SE DELITENT, SE DESQUAMENT EN FEUILLES TRANSLUCIDES ET LAITEUSES, COMME DES FEUILLES DE PAPIER.

C'EST LÀ QUE LES RÊVES, LES INTUITIONS, LES FULGURANCES, PEUT ETRE MEME LES CREATIONS ONT LAISSÉ DES TRACES, DES MESSAGES.

C'EST INTIME, C'EST SECRET.

POUR VOUS, QUATRE MILLE DE CES PAILLETTES VERRONT LE JOUR.

C'EST PEUT-ÊTRE INTERRESSANT.

D'Y VOIR QUE SEUL LE PROJET EXISTE ET QUE LE PRODUIT N'EST QU'UN DOMMAGE

PH.S

Bonjour

Philippe Starck

Hola,

Dicen que, tal vez, en el centro del cerebro se esconde el inconsciente.

Pero, de hecho y sobre todo, lo que hay es magma. El magma, mi magma, es una pasta suave como una masa de pan o una pasta de papel. Esa masa vive, crece, se convulsiona en un ambiente cálido y húmedo.

Cuando hablamos, cuando nos explicamos, arrojamos al aire, a través de nuestras bocas, fragmentos de magma. En contacto con el aire, estos fragmentos se secan, se desintegran, se descaman en hojas translúcidas y lechosas, como hojas de papel. Es allí donde los sueños, las intuiciones, las ideas brillantes, tal vez incluso las creaciones, han dejado sus vestigios y sus mensajes.

Es algo íntimo, secreto.

Ahora, aquí, verán la luz cuatro mil de esos destellos.

Quizá sea interesante.

Ver que solo existe el proyecto y que el producto no es más que un perjuicio.

Ph. S.

Bonjour

Philippe Starck

Hello,

They say that the unconscious is perhaps found in the middle of the brain.

As a matter of fact, and above all, that is where we find magma. Magma, my magma, is a soft paste, like bread dough or paper pulp. This living, growing paste convulses in a warm, humid milieu.

When we speak, when we explain ourselves, magma fragments are expelled into the air through our mouths. Coming into contact with the air, these fragments wither, split and peel off into translucent, milky flakes, like sheets of paper. It is here that dreams, intuitions, fulgurations and perhaps even creative acts leave behind their traces and messages.

This is something intimate and secret.

For you, four thousand of these little specks will make their appearance.

That might be interesting.

From this we see that only the project exists, and that the product is but collateral damage.

Ph. S.

Starck o la ubicuidad intranquila

Marie-Ange Brayer

1. Su primer hinchable, expuesto en el Salón de la Infancia en el Grand Palais de París, en 1969, había sido construido por la asociación Perce-Neige.

Philippe Starck es quizá el único diseñador cuyas obras pueden considerarse omnipresentes, tanto en nuestros hogares como en nuestro imaginario. Estandarte del «diseño democrático», Starck ha trabajado en más de diez mil proyectos, desde un cepillo de dientes hasta un yate revolucionario. Desde sus inicios, a finales de los setenta, con su estudio Ubik cuyo nombre está inspirado en una novela del autor de ciencia ficción Philip K. Dick, hasta sus actuales creaciones, inteligentes y tecnológicas, Starck no ha dejado de fascinarnos. Es capaz de promover la lógica y la economía del objeto y, al mismo tiempo, defender una dimensión poética y llevar a cabo una «arquitectura demostrativa», hiperbólica y surrealista. Si algo define a Starck es la paradoja. Su creación es el resultado de un pensamiento global que supera las cuestiones de forma y estilo con una manera única de transgredir los códigos a través del humor, la poesía, la subversión. «Todo proyecto debe tener justificada su existencia, porque es inútil aportar material adicional a un mundo que ya tiene demasiado»: la exigencia de Starck en el diseño del objeto es absoluta, lo que lo lleva a lidiar continuamente con una tecnología de vanguardia unida a una profunda consciencia de los cambios contemporáneos. Esta exigencia encuentra su correspondencia en la «precisión» del objeto y en el «servicio» que este debe prestar, un servicio tanto emocional como funcional. El objeto solo verá la luz si responde a otra forma de necesidad, más misteriosa e incandescente, que le otorgue una carga existencial propia.

El comienzo de la década de los ochenta estuvo marcado por un «diseño de crisis» que el Studio Alchimia y el grupo Memphis en Italia, con Ettore Sottsass y Alessandro Mendini a la cabeza, transformaron en un crecimiento vitalista y liberador. En Inglaterra, NATØ (Narrative Architecture Today), de Nigel Coates, desplegaba una arquitectura narrativa en la estela de Archigram. Tras sus primeros proyectos experimentales de hinchables con Quasar,[1] Philippe Starck llevó a cabo varias creaciones icónicas, tanto en el ámbito del diseño como

2. Franco Bertoni, *Philippe Starck. L'architecture*, Lieja, Mardaga, 1994, pp. 10-11.

3. Jean Baudrillard, *Pour une critique de l'économie politique du signe*, París, Gallimard, 1973 [trad. cast.: *Crítica de la economía política del signo*, Madrid, Siglo XXI, 2010].

4. Paul Virilio, *Esthétique de la disparition*, París, Balland, 1980 [trad. cast.: *Estética de la desaparición*, Barcelona, Anagrama, 2003].

2. Franco Bertoni, *Philippe Starck. L'architecture (The Architecture of Philippe Starck)*, Liege: Mardaga, 1994, pp. 10–11.

3. Jean Baudrillard, *Pour une critique de l'économie politique du signe (For a Critique of the Political Economy of the Sign)*, Paris: Gallimard, 1973.

4. Paul Virilio, *Esthétique de la disparition*, Paris: Balland, 1980.

en el del interiorismo, entre ellas la butaca *Costes* (1983), la silla *Mister Bliss* (1980), la butaca *Richard III* (1983) o la lámpara *Ara* (1986). Starck pone a sus objetos nombres ocurrentes o intrigantes, que cuentan una historia, lo que suscita un vínculo afectivo con ellos. Recurre al tubo de acero, a las estructuras trípodes en objetos negros con formas arquitectónicas y gráficas; combina la tela y el tubo metálico en asientos transformables, como en la silla plegable *Miss Wirt* (1980). En la misma época, Shiro Kuramata, a quien Starck considera uno de los diseñadores más importantes, experimentaba la desmaterialización en *Sing Sing Sing* (1985), una silla de rejilla metálica. Como Kuramata, Starck renovó el lenguaje del diseño a través de objetos transgresores, abriendo la puerta a nuevos modos de percepción gracias a los cuales el objeto se dota de un comportamiento simbólico y expresivo.

Starck encontró en la arquitectura una dimensión orgánica y energética con la que hacer frente a la frialdad metálica del *high-tech* del momento. La arquitectura de Starck va más allá de las tipologías y recurre a «un lenguaje diferente: sombra-luz, blando-duro, subir-bajar, cerrar-abrir. Se trata de palabras relacionadas con el movimiento o las acciones que Starck trata de restituir [...]. Nada es definitivo ni evidente, todo puede recrearse: desde los objetos hasta las actitudes».[2] Al ensamblaje y al *collage* posmoderno de los años ochenta opuso una forma monolítica primitiva, incluso zoomórfica, con sus primeros proyectos de arquitectura en Japón: el concurso para el proyecto de la Ópera de Tokio (no realizado, 1986) junto con Jean Nouvel; el edificio Nani Nani (1989), de cobre oxidado, en Tokio; el Baron Vert (1992), en Osaka, con la fachada hermética tallada con aperturas orgánicas; el Asahi Beer Hall (1990) y su llama dorada desafiando al cielo nipón. Si bien las teorías de Jean Baudrillard sobre el objeto como signo[3] resuenan en los planteamientos de Starck, este parece más cerca de Paul Virilio, autor de la *Estética de la desaparición*.[4] El filósofo de la inmediatez había retratado en los años sesenta los búnkeres

we find *Mister Bliss* (1980), the *Costes* armchair (1983), the *Richard III* armchair (1983) and the *Ara* lamp (1986). Starck tagged his productions with quirkily intriguing names, telling a story and with it awakening an emotional connection. He made use of steel tubing, tripoidal bases with black objects in architectural or graphic shapes; he combined canvas and metallic tube on his changeable chairs, such as with the folding *Miss Wirt* chair (1980). It was in this same period that Shiro Kuramata (who Starck holds in high esteem) experimented with dematerialization, with *Sing Sing* (1985), made with steel mesh. Like Kuramata, Starck renewed the language of design by means of transgressive objects, opening up new modes of perception, thanks to which the object is made to behave symbolically and expressively.

Contrasting with the then-prevalent metallic coldness of high-tech, Starck found in architecture a way of working with an energetically organic dimension. Starck's architecture lies beyond the realm of typologies, making use of "a different language: shadow-light, supple-hard, go up-go down, close-open. It deals with words connected to movement or actions that Starck seeks to realize... Nothing is either definitive or evident, everything is subject to being redone, from objects to attitudes."[2] Unlike the post-modern assemblage and collage of the 1980s, he set up contrasts with primitive (even zoomorphic), monolithic shapes with his first architectural projects in Japan: the competition entry for the Tokyo Opera (not executed, 1986) with Jean Nouvel; the Nani Nani building in Tokyo (1989), in oxidized copper; the Baron Vert (1990) in Osaka, with its hermetic facade marked by organic slits; the Asahi Beer Hall (1990) and its golden flame, jutting into the Japanese sky. While Jean Baudrillard's theories regarding the object as a sign[3] can be matched with Starck's approach, it was with the author of *The Aesthetics of Disappearance* (1980),[4] Paul Virilio, that Starck seemed to bond most closely. In the 1960s the philosopher of velocity had photographed the

5. Paul Virilio, *Bunker Archéologie (1958-1975)*, París, Galilée, 1975.

6. Francis Ponge, *Le Parti pris des choses*, París, Gallimard, 1942.

5. Paul Virilio, *Bunker Archéologie (1958–1975) (Bunker Archaeology)*, Paris: Galilée, 1975.

6. Francis Ponge, *Le Parti pris des choses (The Nature of Things)*, Paris: Gallimard, 1942.

del muro del Atlántico.[5] Su reflexión sobre el brutalismo y el monolito en la arquitectura, al igual que la «inquietante extrañeza» de esos búnkeres, pudieron influir en la visión de Starck. Posteriormente, la Alhóndiga (2010) de Bilbao, el Port Adriano (2012) en la isla de Mallorca y el complejo deportivo Le Nuage (2014) en Montpellier serán otros ejemplos de arquitectura orgánica y demostrativa, concebidos como ágoras, «plazas públicas» accesibles a todo el mundo. Starck propone escenarios y situaciones cotidianas que cada cual pueda hacer suyos.

La arquitectura de Starck atraviesa todos los ámbitos, como el del objeto, desde el exprimidor *Juicy Salif* (1988), de forma invertida, hasta *Blade Runner* (2011), un disco duro para LaCie. Al igual que la hoja de cuchillo sobredimensionada fabricada por Laguiole (1980), la flecha orgánica del Asahi Beer Hall provoca un efecto de inestabilidad, como el hervidor de agua perforado *Hot Bertaa* (1988). El mismo efecto produce el taburete *W.W.* (1988), que Starck diseñó tras una conversación con el director de cine Wim Wenders. Este asiento en forma de trípode, cuyas líneas fluidas se extienden en el espacio como vegetales en crecimiento, aparece como una metáfora de la creación en la que el espíritu se libra «al borde de los mundos», en un estado de emulsión entre el sueño y la realidad. La fabricación de objetos a la vez funcionales e irracionales como las lámparas *Gun* (2003), con el pie en forma de arma de fuego se inscribe en la estela de los «objetos de funcionamiento simbólico» del surrealismo, en el seno del juego o del «cadáver exquisito». Lo importante es el juego mental instaurado por el objeto, la percepción semántica plural que lo transformará en el *objeu* (objuego) de Francis Ponge.[6] La fantasmagórica Maison Heler, un hotel que abrirá sus puertas en Metz en 2018, es un edificio monolítico símbolo de modernidad, sobre el cual se ha colocado la réplica de una casa burguesa de la ciudad de Metz del siglo XIX. Como si de un oxímoron se tratara, la Maison Heler representa el improbable encuentro entre la abstracción y la hiperfiguración, el ornamento y el funcionalismo, el sentido y el sinsentido.

bunkered pillboxes of the Atlantic coast.[5] This study of brutalism and the monolith in architecture, as well as the "troubling strangeness" of these bunkers, had had their impact on the way Starck set about working. At a later stage, the Alhondiga (2010) in Bilbao, Port Adriano (2012) on the island of Majorca, and the Le Nuage sports centre (2014) in Montpellier would be equally valid examples of organic, demonstrative architecture, conceived as they were as *agoras*, "village squares" accessible to all. With these projects Starck proposed scenarios, everyday life situations open to be assimilated by all.

Starck's architecture runs through every domain possible, whether through the object, from the *Juicy Salif* citrus squeezer (1988), featuring inverted topography, to *Blade Runner* (2010), the hard drive done for LaCie. Like the knife blade that came oversized from the Laguiole factory (1980), the organic arrow at the Asahi Beer Hall sets off an effect of instability, which is also seen in the pierced-through *Hot Bertaa* kettle (1988). Imbalance is there as well with the *W.W.* stool (1988), conceived after a conversation with filmmaker Wim Wenders. This tripoidal seat, with its fluid lines stretching out in space like rapidly growing plant shoots, is used here as a metaphor of creation, where the spirit comes apart "at the edge of the world" in an emulsified state between dreams and reality. The making of objects that are both functional and irrational – like the *Gun* lamps (2003), their bases shaped like firearms – follows in the wake of Surrealism's "symbolically functional objects", related to play or to the *cadavre exquis*, the exquisite corpse. What really matters is the mental game instigated by the object, its perception as pluralistic and semantic, transforming it into Francis Ponge's "objeu" (play object).[6] The phantasmagorical Maison Heler, a hotel that will open its doors in 2018 in Metz, is a monolithic building symbolizing modernity, topped by a replica of a bourgeois Metz nineteenth-century mansion. Like an oxymoron, the Maison Heler represents an improbable re-encounter between

7. «Entretien Philippe Starck–Marie-Laure Jousset», en *Connaissance des arts,* separata, 2002, p. 8.

8. Ibíd., p. 24.

7. "Entretien Philippe Starck – Marie-Laure Jousset" in *Connaissance des arts,* supplement, 2002, p. 8.

8. Ibid., p. 24.

13

Starck condena el «prejuicio de la forma». Uno de sus primeros objetos, *Easy Light* (1977) —una línea de luz ambulante—, es un no-objeto que transforma la percepción del espacio. La silla *La Marie* (1996) representa para Starck la quintaesencia de su búsqueda del «menos es más», «menos materia, menos presencia, menos coste». Esta silla, de una «extrema honestidad» y una «profunda modernidad», se presenta como un «objeto de segunda mirada», de ahí su fuerza.[7] Realizada en una sola pieza de policarbonato, es también una proeza tecnológica. La lámpara *Miss Sissi* (1988), de plástico inyectado, que se aleja del funcionalismo austero de objetos como la *Tizio* de Richard Sapper, responde al deseo de Starck de «crear un arquetipo»[8] y señala el «inicio de un trabajo basado en la memoria colectiva» que alcanza su punto álgido con *Louis Ghost* (2000), la butaca fantasma, una sombra transparente surgida de los prófugos arcanos de la memoria colectiva. La colección *Generic* para Kartell (2014) explora por su parte la estructura misma de la silla, su ADN; al conservar únicamente «la raíz cuadrada del objeto», Starck lo reduce a su expresión esencial. El objeto es llevado a la disolución; simplemente está allí, en su inmanencia, despojado de todo artificio inútil y disponible para los usuarios.

Creador comprometido, confrontado con las mutaciones del mundo contemporáneo, Philippe Starck fue uno de los primeros en reivindicar una consciencia ecológica de la creación. De 1990 en adelante ha colaborado con 3 Suisses, para quien diseña casas prefabricadas. Entre 1996 y 1997 elaboró, junto con La Redoute, *Good Goods*, un catálogo de no-productos para no-consumidores con vistas a un futuro mercado ético. En 2012, idea el proyecto P.A.T.H. (Prefabricated Accessible Technological Homes), casas prefabricadas de madera que combinan la ingeniera y la ecología. En los albores del nuevo siglo, la silla *Hudson* (1998) para Emeco se reivindica como un producto ético; Starck apela aquí a la protección del trabajo y los conocimientos. En 2009 diseñó la silla *Zartan* a partir de materiales reciclados y de bioplásticos éticos. En 2010, con la silla *Broom*,

Starck revolucionó la producción industrial a partir de residuos reciclados en origen. El coche eléctrico *V+* (2010), la bicicleta con asistencia eléctrica *Starckbike* (2012) o las sandalias *Ipanema with Starck* (2013), 100% reciclables y compuestas en un 30% de plástico reciclado, responden a esta misma exigencia de sostenibilidad. Junto con el estudio TOG-AllCreatorsTOGether, en el que ejerce de director artístico, Starck creó la silla *Misa Joy* (2012), con un asiento compuesto de tiras elastoméricas intercambiables, cuya simplicidad se conjuga con la personalización gracias a un diseño participativo. El diseño de *Misa Joy* busca resolver la paradoja de la producción en masa, combinando la alta calidad y la alta tecnología con una visión artesanal capaz de responder a las necesidades individuales. Las creaciones de Starck incluyen hoteles, restaurantes o barcos, los más emblemáticos de los cuales son el yate *A*, nacido de las olas (2004), o *Venus* (2008), el yate que perteneció a Steve Jobs y que cuenta con un diseño minimalista, sin olvidar los veleros *Bénéteau*, de perfiles orgánicos.

Starck, que se define a sí mismo como un «utopista naíf», no ha dejado de dar, una y otra vez, con usos portátiles e innovadores, ya sea mediante los auriculares conectados por Bluetooth *Zik (Parrot)* en 2010 y sus versiones *Zik 2.0* y *Zik 3* o, más recientemente, mediante objetos cotidianos inteligentes como el termostato *Netatmo* (2011) y el *Mimix* (2014), un teléfono inteligente de cerámica con una pantalla integral inédita, creado para la empresa Xiaomi. La dimensión sensorial se encuentra tanto en los objetos tecnológicos como en los grifos *Axor, Organic* —cuya forma se inspira en la naturaleza— y *Axor Starck V* (2012), que dejan ver los movimientos del agua a su paso, generando una experiencia háptica. La desmaterialización vuelve a hacerse presente en el trabajo creativo transversal sobre el champán, en el caso de Roederer, y sobre la cerveza de agricultura ecológica, *1664*, así como en los perfumes *Starck Paris collection Peau* (2014), una exploración de los éteres orientada hacia lo intangible y lo inmaterial.

Starck made an appeal for the protection of the values of work and know-how. In 2009, the *Zartan* chair was conceived using recycled materials and ethical bioplastics. In 2010, with the *Broom* chair, Starck revolutionized industrial production using waste recycled at source. The *V+* electric vehicle (2010), the *Starckbike* electrically assisted bicycle (2012) and the *Ipanema with Starck* sandals (2013), 100% recyclable and featuring 30% recycled plastic, were reflections of this same demand for sustainability. For the design studio TOG – AllCreatorsTOGether, Starck created the *Misa Joy* chair (2012), the seat composed of interchangeable elastomeric strips, where simplicity goes along with the possibility of customization in participative design. The conception of *Misa Joy* sought to resolve the paradox of mass production, in associating supreme quality and high technology with a craft approach, while also responding to each individual's needs. Starck's creations extend to hotels, restaurants and even ships, the most emblematic being the *A* yacht (born of the waves) (2004) and *Venus* (2008), the yacht of Steve Jobs, with a minimalist design, along with the Bénéteau sailing boats, with their organic contours.

Someone who defines himself as a "naive utopian" has never failed to reinvent uses that are nomadic and innovative, whether the Bluetooth-connected *Zik* (Parrot) headphones in 2010 (and its evolutions in *Zik 2.0* and *Zik 3*), or, more recently, intelligent everyday objects like the *Netatmo* thermostat (2011) and *Mimix* (2014), a ceramic smartphone with a unique, integral screen (*Xiaomi*). The sensorial dimension is found as well in objects with connected technology, like the taps *Axor, Organic* – their shapes inspired by nature – and *Axor Starck V* (2012), which allow us to see the movement of water, generating a haptic experience. Dematerialization is seen once more in the creative, transversal work done together with Roederer champagne and the production of beer from ecological agriculture (*1664*), as well as the perfume collection *Starck Paris Peau* (2014), an intangibly immaterial study in scents.

9. Véase Valérie Guillaume (dir.), *Écrits sur Starck*, París, Éditions du Centre Pompidou, 2003.

9. See Valérie Guillaume, ed., *Écrits sur Starck*, Paris: Éditions du Centre Pompidou, 2003.

Tras la exposición que el Centre Pompidou dedicó a Philippe Starck en 2003,[9] el Centre Pompidou Málaga presenta *Starck, dibujos secretos. 4.000 croquis desvelados*, una exposición que narra una obsesión fundacional, la de la creación. Como un vórtice o una «máquina energética», esta exposición sumerge a los visitantes en el corazón del proceso creativo de Starck a través de la inmersión en miles de dibujos, esbozos y estudios. Starck define como *solitario* un proceso de creación que parte de un papel de calco, un lápiz y una intuición. Al cubrir completamente las paredes con sus diseños, Starck transforma el espacio expositivo en un entorno cerebral, una especie de cueva ornamentada que nos devuelve a los gestos primordiales y a una dimensión ritual de la creación. Este *all-over* de diseños se muestra como un cuadro fuera de lo común, cuya teatralidad deja entrever, sin desvelarlo del todo, un «misterio» que no es otro que el de la creación. Starck extrae de los mecanismos inconscientes del sueño los principios de «desplazamiento» y «condensación» que transforman los objetos y los lugares. Lo real y el sueño comparten aquí una misma materia.

Cada creación de Starck es, a la vez, una fusión de posibilidades y la instauración de escenas joviales, misteriosas, intrigantes, construidas a base de incongruencias, de juegos mentales y de sorpresas fértiles. El título de esta exposición, también paradójico (dibujos escondidos y desvelados al mismo tiempo), podría remitir a lo «real escondido» de André Breton. La muestra se ha transformado así en palimpsesto de una creación tan secreta y enigmática como evidente y prolija. La exposición del Centre Pompidou Málaga, como una cámara de resonancia donde uno vuelve sin cesar al inconsciente de la creación, a esa «sombra misteriosa» que obsesiona a Starck, dilucida la trayectoria de los objetos a lo largo del proceso de creación, su necesidad de cobrar cuerpo, para revelar toda su «energía poética».

After the exhibition dedicated to Philippe Starck at the Centre Pompidou in 2003,[9] the Centre Pompidou Málaga now presents *Starck, Secret Drawings: 4,000 Sketches Unveiled*, a show that tells the story of a foundational obsession, the tale of creation. Like a vortex or "energetic machine", this exhibition plunges visitors into Starck's creative process, immersing them into thousands of drawings, sketches and studies. Starck defines his creative approach as solitary, starting with tracing paper, a pencil and intuition. By totally covering the walls with his drawings, Starck transfigures the exhibition space into a mental environment, like an ornate grotto transporting us back to primordial gestures and the ritual domain of creation. This "all-over" drawing is a sort of abnormal tableau, where theatricality enables us to perceive (though not all at once) a "mystery" that is none other than creation itself. Starck charges the unconscious mechanisms of dreams with the principles of "displacement" and "condensation", transforming objects and spaces. Here the real and the dream both share the same materiality.

Each Starck creation is at once a plethora of scenarios and the revivification of joyfully mysterious scenes, integrating scenarios built up of incongruences, mental games and fertile surprises. The title of this exhibition, in itself paradoxical – drawings that are concealed and revealed at the same time – could recall André Breton's "hidden reality". The exhibition is just as well transformed into a written palimpsest of creation as secret and enigmatic as it is evident and loquacious. Like an echo chamber where you are incessantly returned to the unconscious character of creation, in this "mysterious shadow" obsessing Starck, the exhibition at the Centre Pompidou Málaga sheds light on how objects progress in the creative process, their necessity still to come, so revealing their abounding "poetic energy".

15

Croquis

Sketches

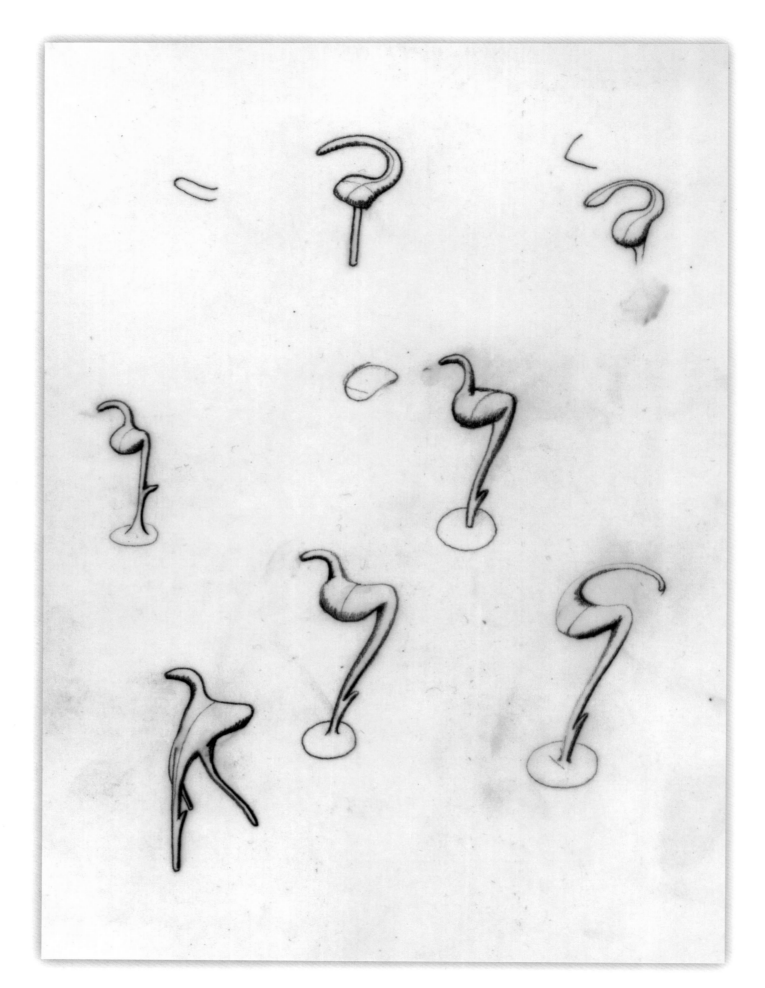

TOTO LA TOTO A TOTO.

NOUS AVONS LA CHANCE D'ETRE A UN DELAI
IDEAL D'UNE DATE SYMBOLIQUE QU'EST
LE PASSAGE AU 3° MILLENAIRE.
CET EVENEMENT SERA BRASSE PAR LES
MEDIAS ET POUR UNE FOIS NOUS POURRONS
NOUS EN REJOUIR ET SAISIR L'OPORTUNITE
OFFERTE
EN EFFET UNE FIN DE MILLENAIRE OBLIGE
A L'AUTOCRITIQUE ET AU CONSTAT. CELUI
CI NE VA PAS S'AVERER TRES BRILLANT
UNE NOUVELLE ERE IMPLIQUE DES PROPOSITIONS
ET UN PROJET, CELA EST PLUS PROMETTEUR.
NOTRE SOCIETE NE POURRA, SI ELLE VEUT
SURVIVRE, FAIRE L'ECONOMIE DE CETTE
METHODE.
                    ET SOUHAITABLE
IL PARAIT PROBABLE QUE ~~LES GRANDES LIGNES~~
~~SE SUIT~~ LE CONSTAT ACCUSE LA MACHINE
D'AVOIR REMPLACE L'HOMME ET QUE LE
PROJET SOIT DE CORRIGER UNE DEVIATION
DU PROJET ORIGINAL APPELLE ~~PRO~~ LE PROGRES

CARTE

STARCK

VOUS AVEZ VOTRE GOOD GOOD'S
NOUS L'AVONS ELABORE AVEC RIGUEUR ET AMOUR
MAIS L'ACHAT N'EST PAS VITAL
L'INTERESSANT EST DE LE LIRE ENTRE LES LIGNES

VOTRE AMI
PH.S.

ENVELOPPE STARCK

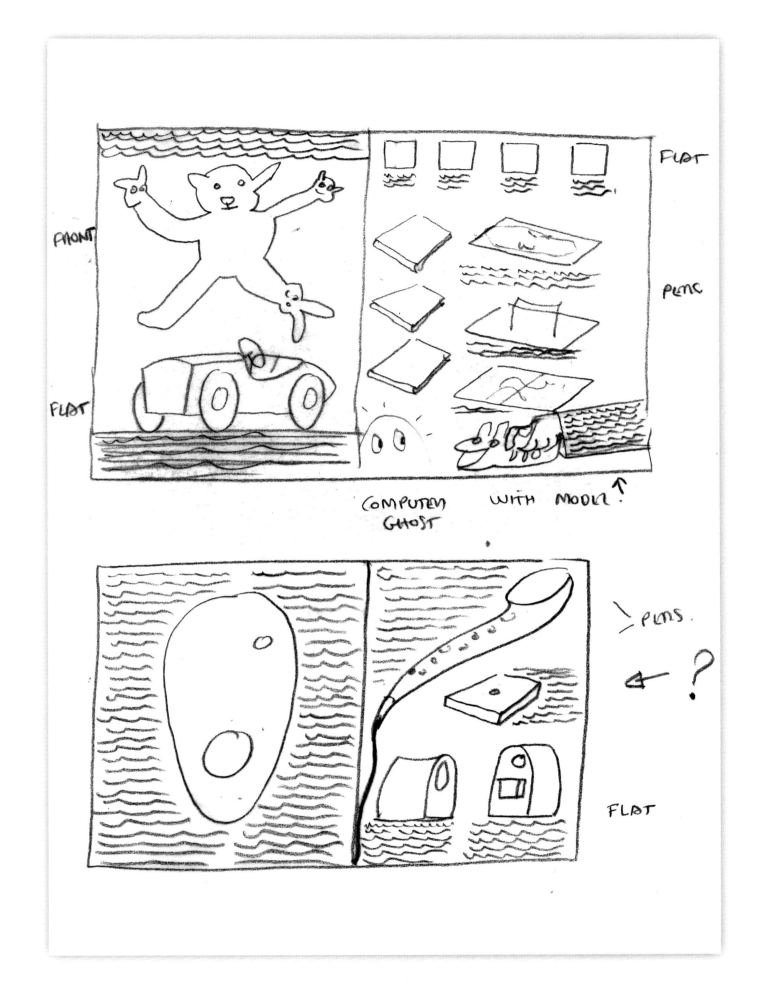

21

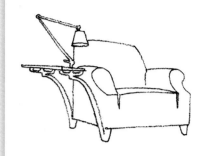
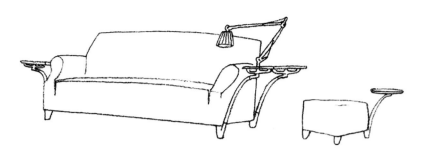

THE LAZY WORKING SOFA COLLECTION

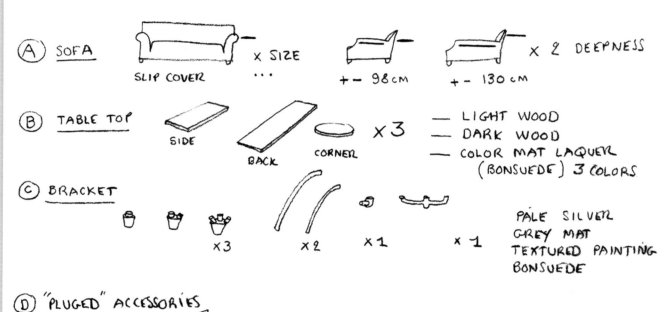

(A) SOFA

SLIP COVER   ...   X SIZE

+- 98 CM   +- 130 CM   X 2 DEEPNESS

(B) TABLE TOP

SIDE   BACK   CORNER   X 3

— LIGHT WOOD
— DARK WOOD
— COLOR MAT LAQUER
   (BONSUEDE) 3 COLORS

(C) BRACKET

X 3   X 2   X 1   X 1

PALE SILVER
GREY MAT
TEXTURED PAINTING
BONSUEDE

(D) "PLUGED" ACCESSORIES

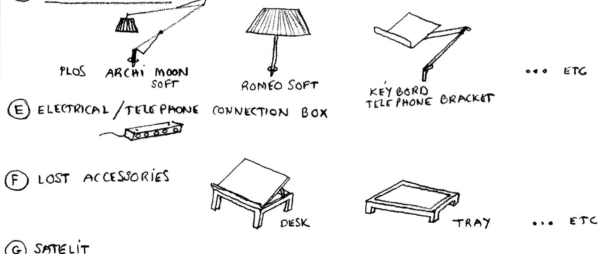

PLOS ARCHI MOON SOFT   ROMEO SOFT   KEYBORD TELEPHONE BRACKET   ... ETC

(E) ELECTRICAL / TELEPHONE CONNECTION BOX

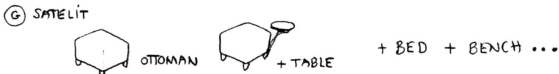

(F) LOST ACCESSORIES

DESK   TRAY   ... ETC

(G) SATELIT

OTTOMAN   + TABLE   + BED + BENCH ...

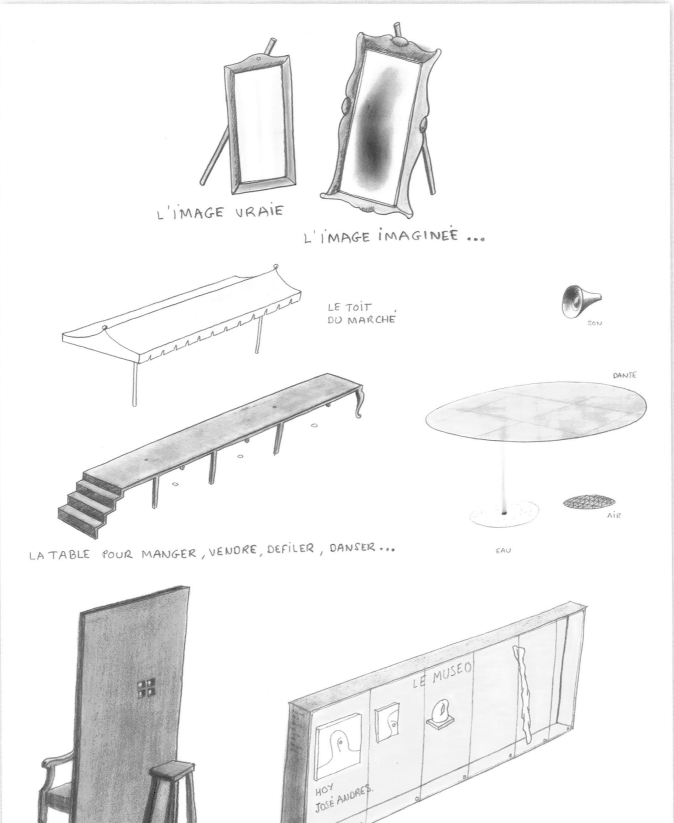

BON JOUR
LES AMIS DE ZARTAN ET DE JANE

JE NE VEUX SURTOUT PAS VOUS CONTRARIER, MAIS LA MATIÈRE PLASTIQUE "ECO", COULEUR ET TRANSLUCIDE EST FORMIDABLE UNE VRAI NOUVOTÉ, UNE VRAIE DIFFÉRENCE.
IL FAUT LA MONTRER. C'EST POUR CELA

QUE JE CROIS PROFONDEMENT A L'ACCOUDOIR EN PLASTIQUE. IL FAUT PLUS DE PLASTIQUE "ECO" QUE DE BOIS. OU SANS CA, IL FAUT TOUT FAIRE EN BOIS. LE MODÈLE, ZARTAN, C'EST LA MATIÈRE AVANT TOUT.
MAIS COMME L'INVESTISSEMENT EST FAIBLE ET QUE L'INTERFACE EST LA MÊME, ON PEUT FAIRE LES 2 (A) ET (B) VOIR PROTO.
OU (A') ET (B')

MERCI

CIAO

PH, S.

FLOS

D'ELIGHT

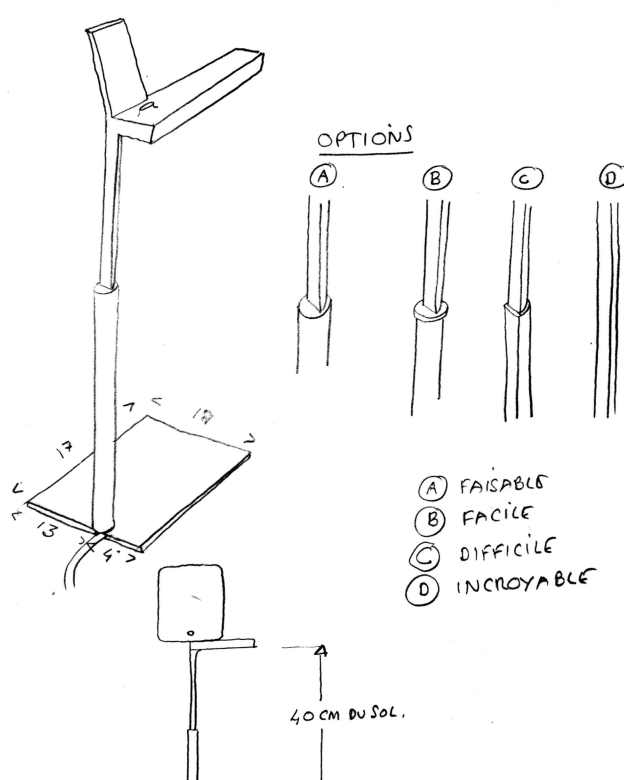

OPTIONS

Ⓐ   Ⓑ   Ⓒ   Ⓓ

17   < 7   ⊙

⟨ 13   ⟨ 4·7

Ⓐ FAISABLE
Ⓑ FACILE
Ⓒ DIFFICILE
Ⓓ INCROYABLE

40 CM DU SOL.

8 mm.

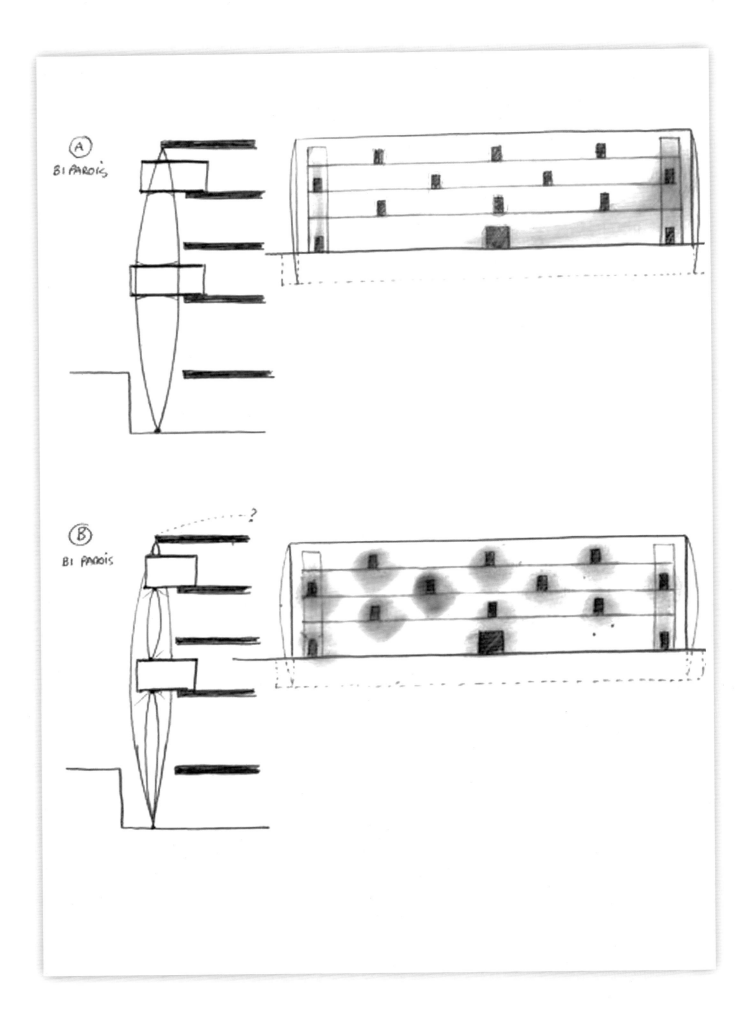

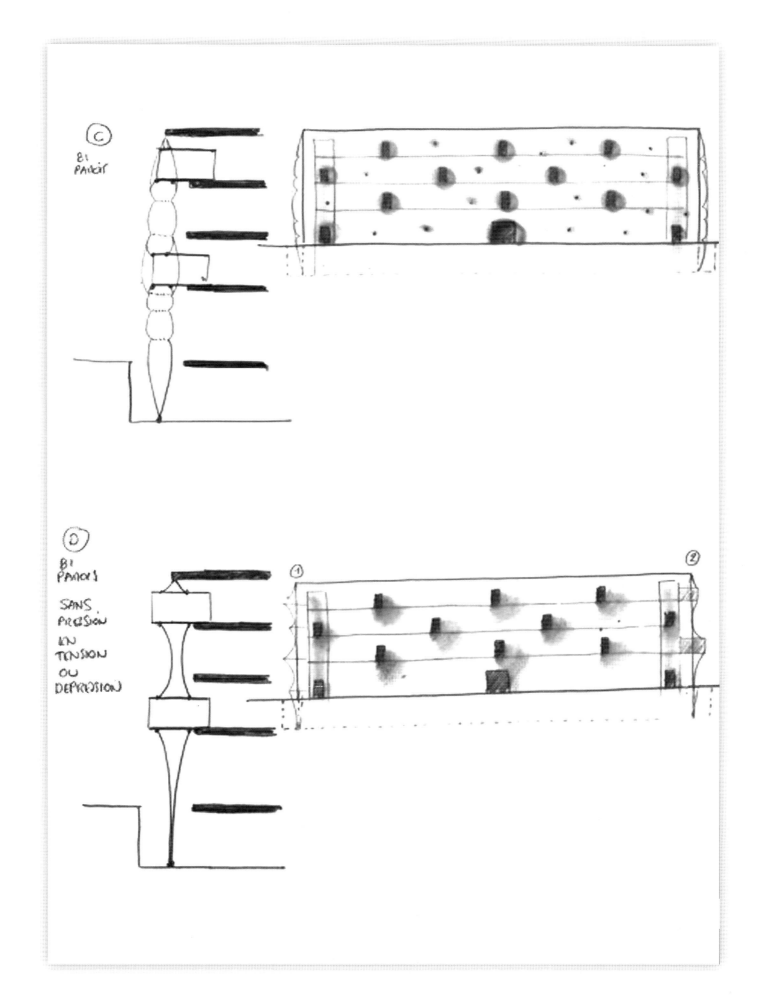

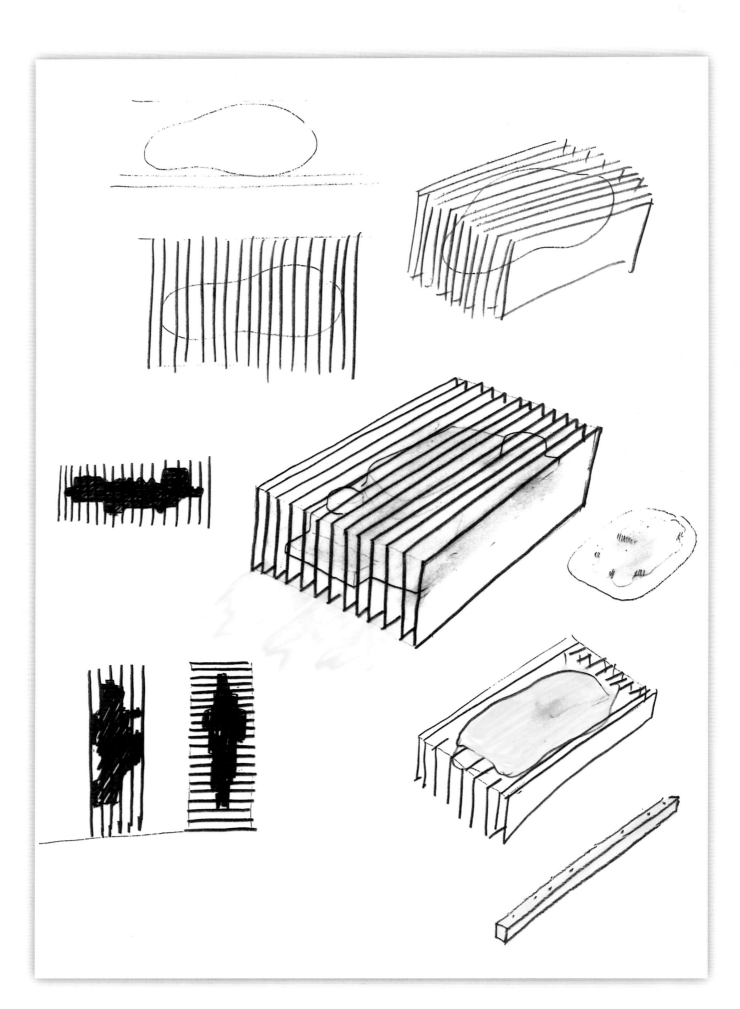

KARTELL
UNCLE

DEMANDER ESSAI
SUR UNE PIECE
PLUS GRANDE
DE FORME SOUPLE
(M' IMPOSSIBLE ?)
EN PLUS DES COULEURS
DEJA CHOISI A MILAN

MERCI

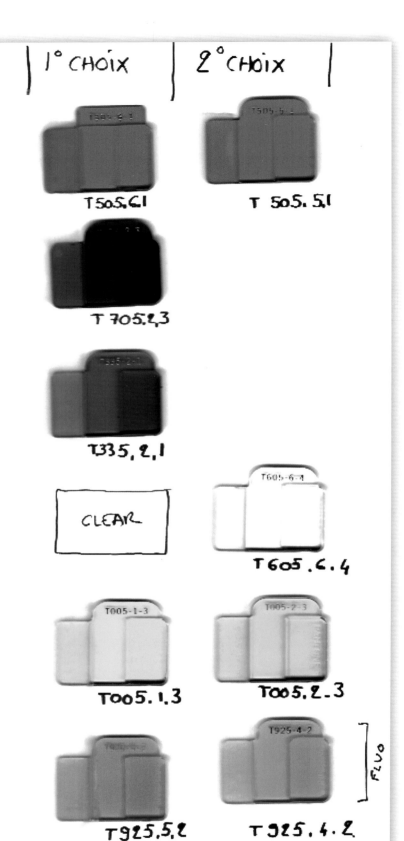

1° CHOIX   2° CHOIX

T 5o5.C.1   T 5o5.5.1

T 705.2.3

T 33 5.2.1

CLEAR   T 6o5.C.4

T oo 5.1.3   T oo 5.2.3

T 925.5.2   T 925.4.2

FLUO

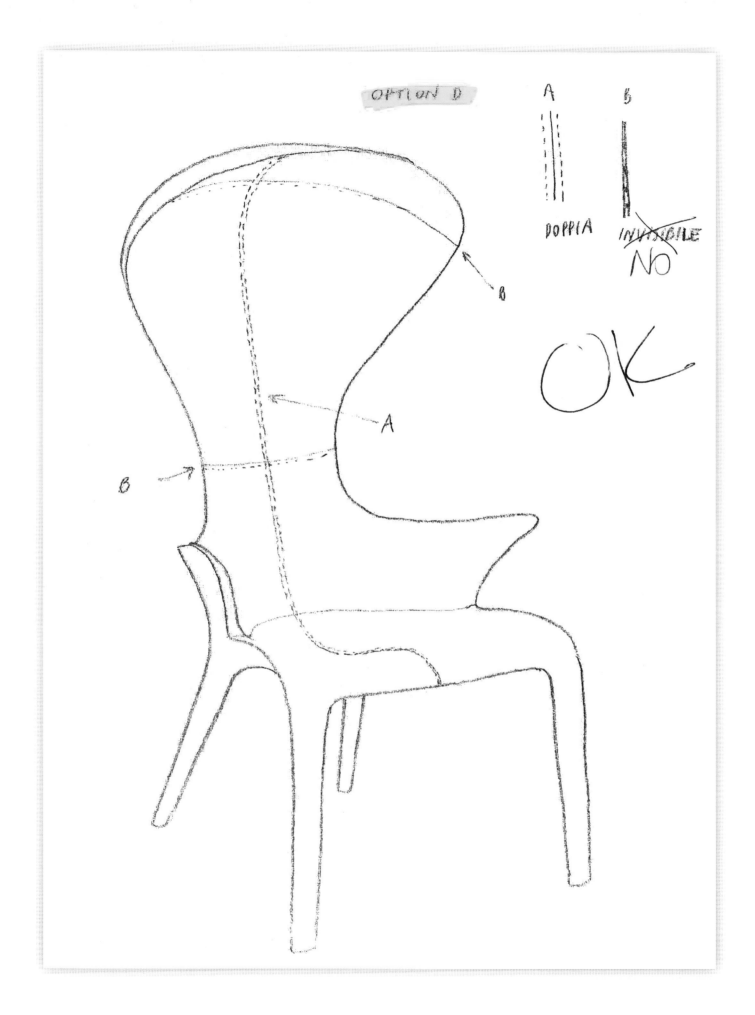

OPTION D

A

B

DOPPIA

INVISIBILE

NO

OK

A

B

B

ATTENTION DESSIN SANS ECHELLE

SE REFERER AUX DIMENSIONS INTOUCHÉES
POUR RETROUVER LES PROPORTIONS

(A) RALLONGER ET BAISSER LES ACCOUDOIRS

(B) EPAISSIRE DANS LES LIMITES DE
L'EMPILABILITÉ

(C) REMONTER ET RETENDRE DANS LES
LIMITES EMPILABILITÉ

(D) CREUSER ASSISE
DE 1CM

(E) AUGMENTER
"DIAMETRE" EN
HAUT, RENDRE
PLUS CONIQUE
POUR MEILLEUR
LIAISON OPTIQUE
ET MECANIQUE

DESSINER
PIEDS
CREUX
(?)

PLUS CREUX
DE 2 CM
SANS CHANGER
POSITION DU DOS.

(G) REDUIRE LA LARGEUR DES ACCOUDOIRS 1 CM

DESCENDRE

ADOUCIRE
LA PARTIE
HAUTE DE
LA LIAISON

1CM.

TOUTES LES
AUTRES DIMENSIONS
OU LIGNES
SONT INCHANGÉS

550

1CM.

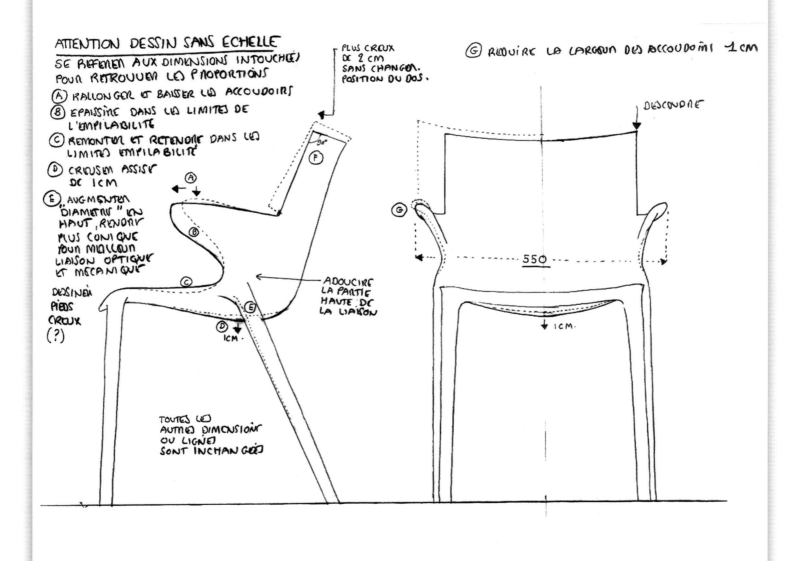

32

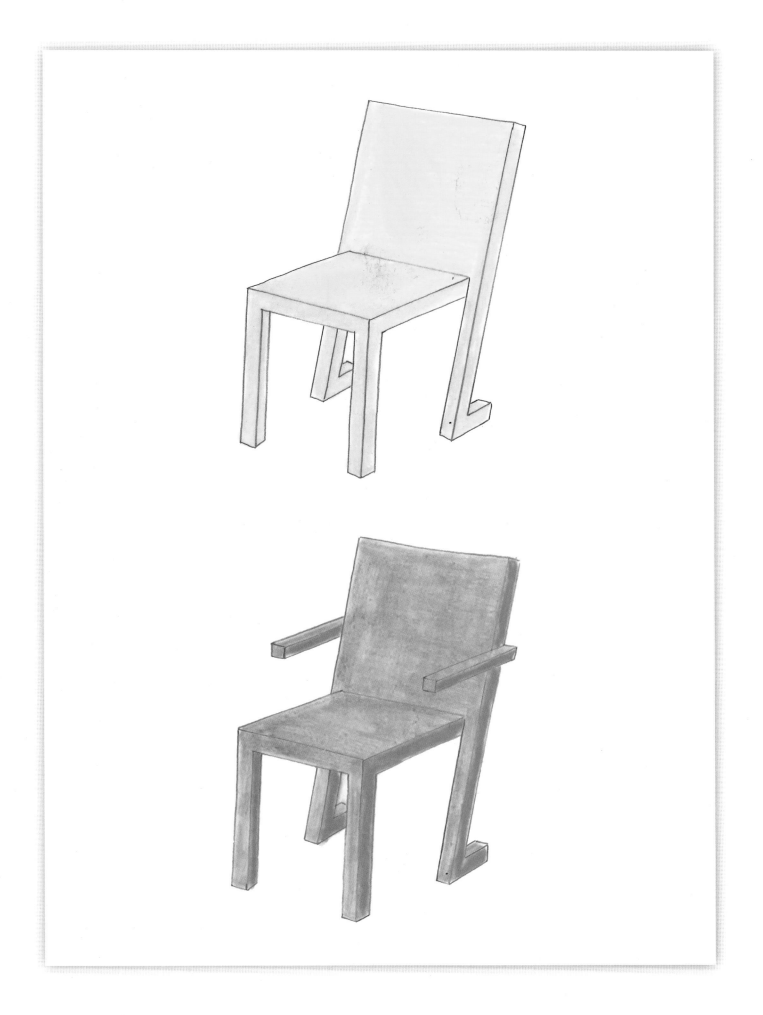

ULTIME
INTELLIGENT
SEXY
CHIC
SNOB
SUPER COMFORTABLE

S+M

COLLECTION	M	A	S	S	
USAGE	MUD	ASPHALT	SAND	SNOW	
PNEU	O	O	O	O (S+)	
VELO	CADRE POLI BROSSE VERNIS CUIVRE	CADRE POLI BROSSE VERNIS ANTHRACIT CHAUD	CADRE POLI BROSSE VERNIS NICKEL CHAUD	CADRE POLI BROSSE VERNIS VERT PALE GLACIER	- FOURCHE MONOBRAS ? (CANNONDALE) - PEDALES REPLIABLES ? (SABLE, SNOW) - JANTES ? ASSORTIES OU NOIR ?
	LOGO NOIR / BLANC / ORANGE FLUO SELLE GEL ROYAL COUVERT CUIR OU SUEDE NATUREL ? POIGNEES ANATOMIQUE CUIR NAT VERSION ECO IDEM MAIS PEINTURE METALLISE MAT TUBE FOURCHE CUIVRE FOURCH CUIVRE ? FOURCHE CUIVRE FOURCHE ARGENT ?				
CASQUE	METALLISATION BROSSE VERNIS COLORE BRILLANT OU MAT OU PEINTURE METALLISE MAT CUIVRE INT. CUIR NAT	ANTHRACITE CACHEMIRE ANTH.	NICKEL JAUNE SANS	VERT PALE GLACIER "LOUP" ARGENTE	- DESSINE RECHERCHE FABRICANT. - PREP. IMAGE SYNTHESE
GANTS (CAUSSE)	MOYEN CUIR NAT AVEC ET SANS DOUBLURE CACH. BRISE	MOYEN ANTHRACITE AVEC ET SANS DOUBLURE CACH.	COURT CUIR NAT	SEMI MOUFFLE CUIR NAT "LOUP"	A PROTOTYPER
LUNETTES VERRE PHOTOSENSIBLE	ALUMINIUM (CUIVRE ?)	PLAST. EPAIS GRIS ANTHRACIT. SEMI OPAQUE	BIO 2010 FINE TRANSPARENT CLEAR.	PLAST. EPAIS TRANSLUCIDE DEPOLI	A CHOISIR ET AMENAGER. COLLER STARCK
BLOUSON AVEC CAPUCHE	CUIR NAT OU NYLON GRIS	NYLON MAT EPAIS (LIMONTA) GRIS ANTH. DOUBLURE ?	COUPE VENT NYLON LEGER. TRAIT. PLASMA. GRIS PALE.	CUIR NAT DOUBLE "LOUP"	EN COURS DE PROTO
T.SHIRT SWEAT	T.SHIRT ET SWEAT A CAPUCHE MANCHE LONGUE GRIS CLAIR, GRIS FONCE LOGO N, B, ORANGE FLUO.				PROTO FAIT RECHERCHE FAB.
BACK PACK	CUIR NAT	NYLON ANTHRACITE	CUIR NAT OU NYLON GRIS PALE	"LOUP" ARGENTE	A DISCUTER
DIVERS	- PROTECTION CADRE EN FOURRURE POUR FROID - "HOUSSE" DE CADRE IDEM EN TISSU POUR FAIRE SAC DE CADRE - CACHE BLOC MOTEUR ALU NUMERIQUE. POLI COLORE OU NON.				

ZIK 2
ECOUTEUR
DROIT

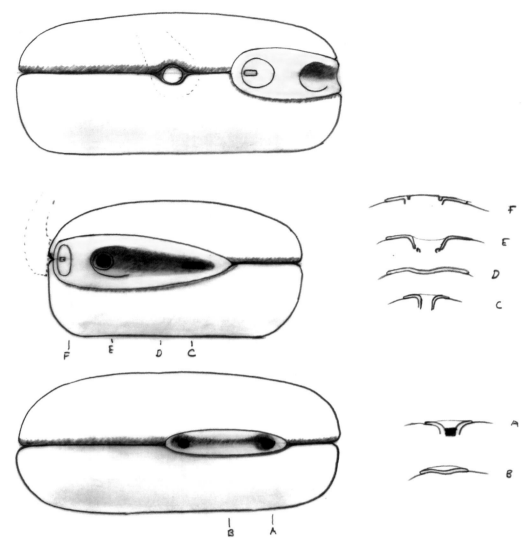

L'ASTUCE VIENDRAIT
D'UN PREFORMAGE DE
LA "PEAU" SUR UNE
MOUSSE MOULÉE

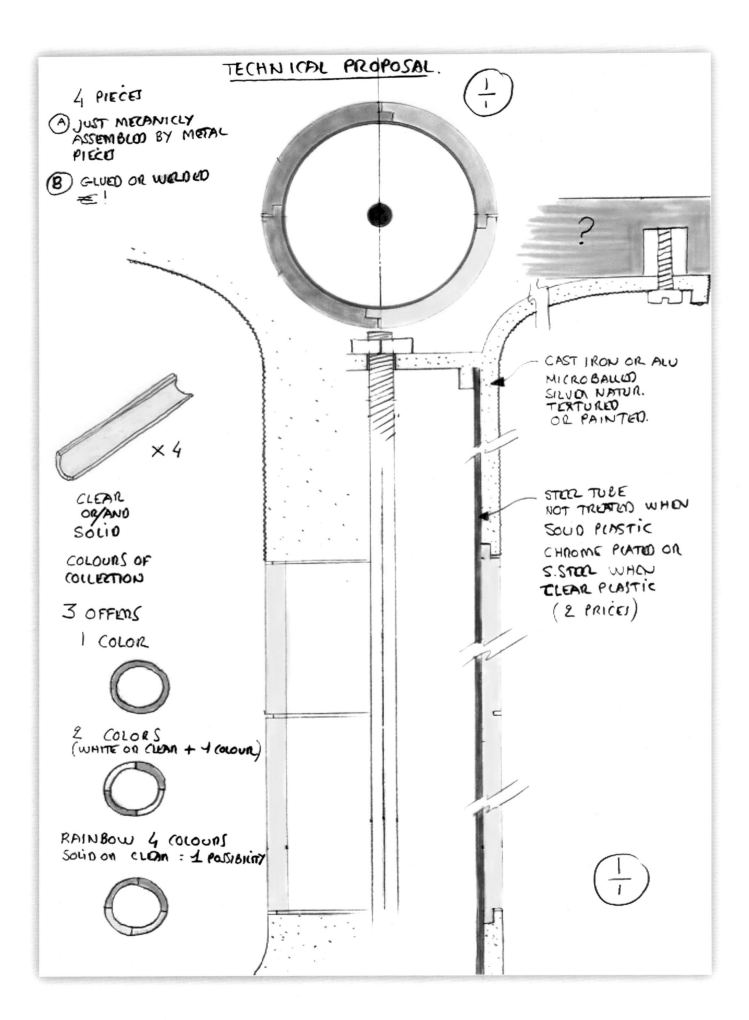

TECHNICAL PROPOSAL.

4 PIECES

(A) JUST MECANICLY ASSEMBLED BY METAL PIECES

(B) GLUED OR WELDED ≡ !

× 4

CLEAR OR/AND SOLID

COLOURS OF COLLECTION

3 OFFERS

1 COLOR

2 COLORS
(WHITE OR CLEAR + 1 COLOUR)

RAINBOW 4 COLOURS
SOLID OR CLEAR : 1 POSSIBILITY

CAST IRON OR ALU
MICROBALLED
SILVER NATUR.
TEXTURED
OR PAINTED.

STEEL TUBE
NOT TREATED WHEN
SOLID PLASTIC
CHROME PLATED OR
S.STEEL WHEN
CLEAR PLASTIC
(2 PRICES)

?

| TOG | AMBROISE NICOLAS |

"CAFÉ" TABLE
FOR MISAJOY AND EMASAO ...

___ TOP _ INDUSTRIAL FROM CATALOGUE WITH SPECIAL COLORS?

___ CAST IRON OR ALUMINIUM

___ ONE INJECTED PLASTIC PART X 4.

___ USE THE MAIN COLORS OF THE COLLECTION FOR INDUSTRIAL OR SHOP CUSTOMISATION.

___ THE TECHNIC IS JUST A PROPOSAL, THE TARGET PRICE IS VITAL

ORDER CHOICES :

(A) MONOCOULEUR.

   SOLID OR CLEAR.

(B) 2 COLORS STRIPED
ALWAYS WHITE + 1 COLOR.

   SOLID OR CLEAR.

(C) RAINBOW
4 FIXED COLORS
   SOLID OR CLEAR.

OPTION (B)

37

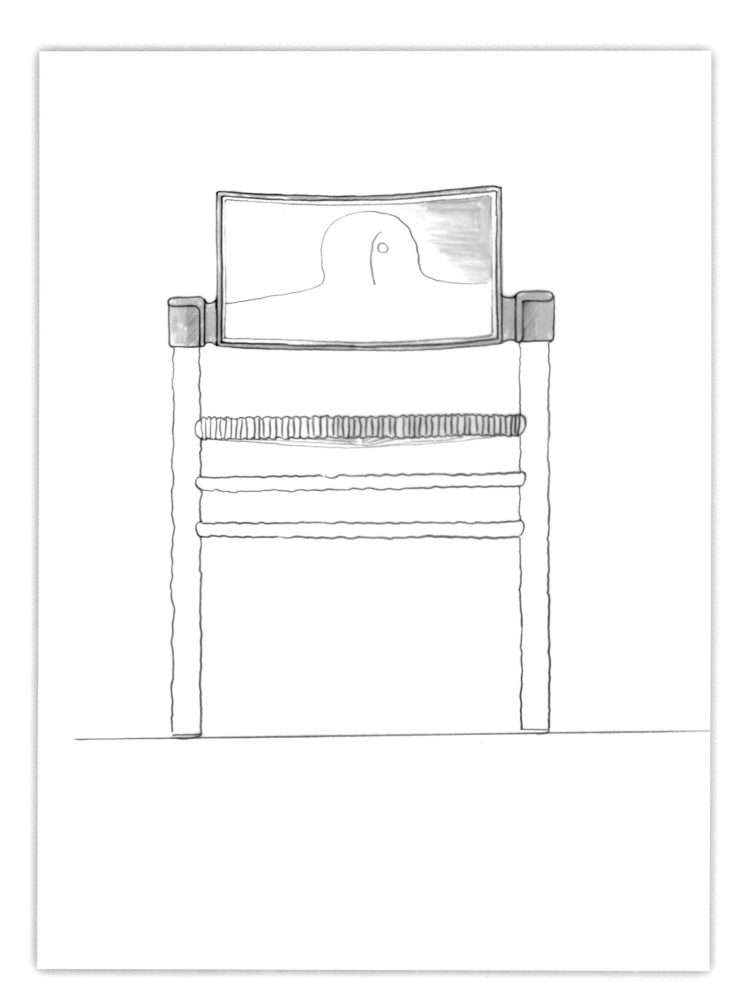

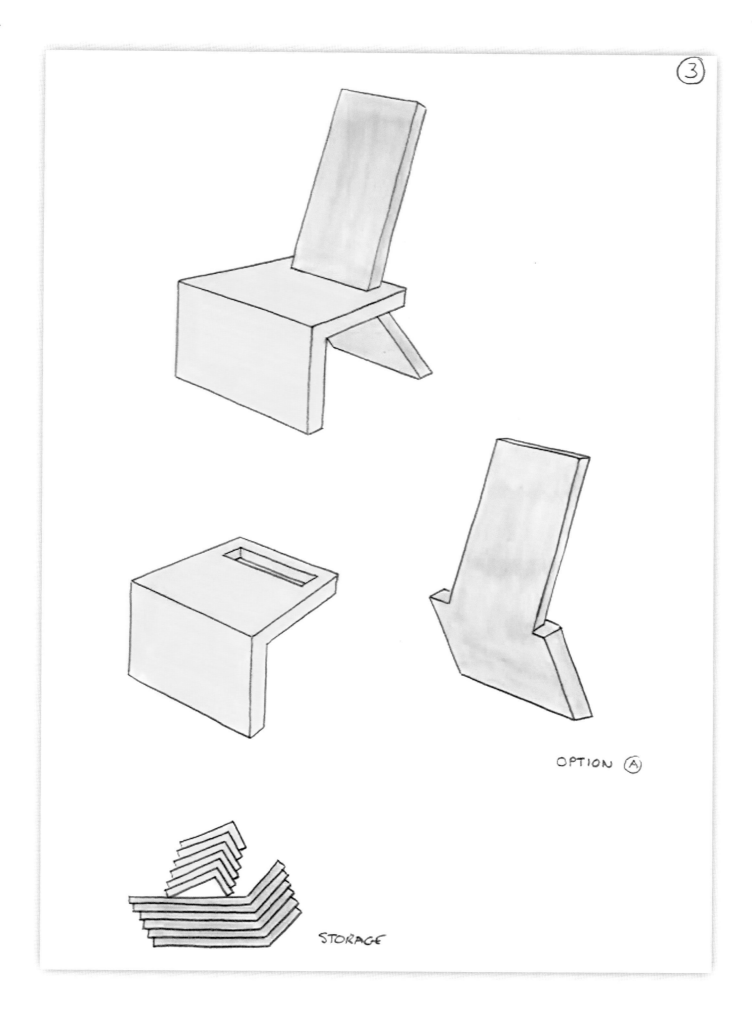

39

OPTION Ⓐ

STORAGE

~~ETHER~~ BON JOUR

COLLECTION EXHAUSTIVE
A PROPOS DE L'EXTREME ELEGANCE
DU MINIMUM
ETHER DOIT ETRE UNE MAGIE AVEC
UNE TECHNOLOGIE INVISIBLE
UNE CREATIVITE TECHNOLOGIQUE
AINSI QU'UN COMBAT ACHARNE CONTRE
LA MATIERE ET LA DIMENSION DOIT
PROVOQUER UNE STUPEFACTION, UNE
INCOMPREHENSION ENCHANTEE, NON
PAS POUR UNE INNOVATION FORMELLE
MAIS POUR UNE PHILOSOPHIE DE LA
DISPARITION POUSSEE A L'ULTIME

SI RIEN NE PEUT ETRE MOINS QU'ETHER
ETHER SERA TOUT POUR LONGTEMPS.

(ETHER : _L'AIR LE PLUS PUR ESPACES CELESTES
          _FLUIDE SUBTILE EMPLISSANT TOUT L'ESPACE   )
                                        DICTIONNAIR

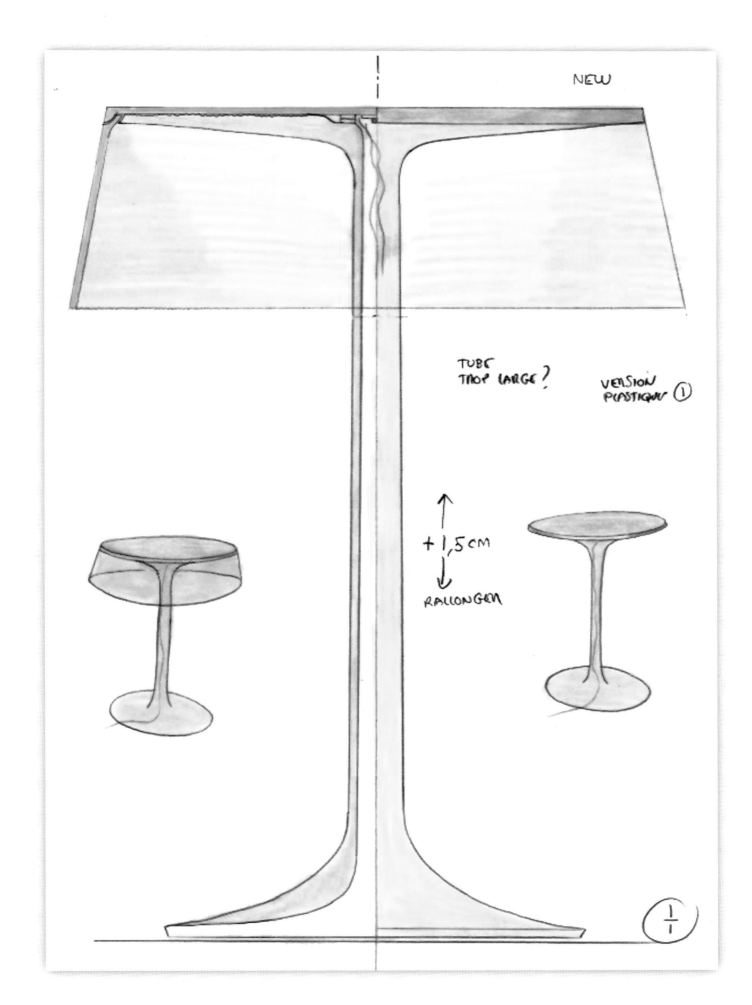

NEW

TUBE
TROP LARGE?

VERSION
PLASTIQUE ①

+ 1,5 CM

RALLONGER

41

①/①

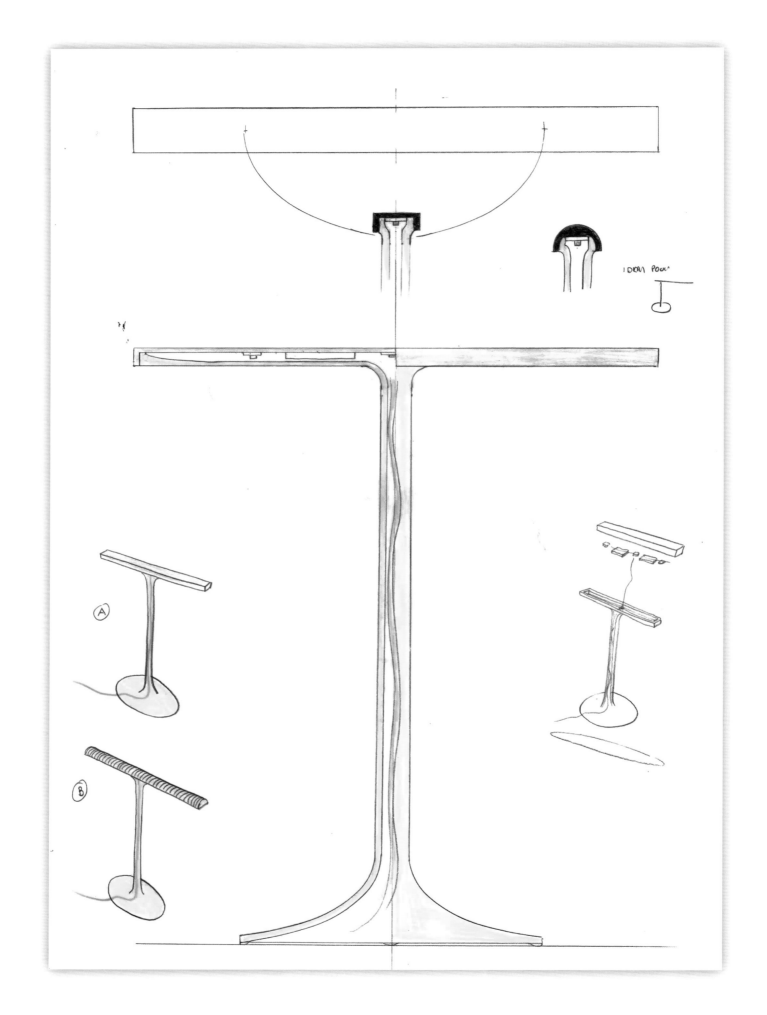

IDEA POUR

A

B

FAUX

VUE SUR LED. ?

APNEE

— U.V < EAU
          TUYAU
— COUDE ROTATIF
— ECRAN TRES LISIBLE
MAIS QUI S'ETEINT

QUOTIDIEN

— VISUALISATION . PRESSION
              — FUITE MASQUE
— REMPLISSON / LAVEUR REGULIER

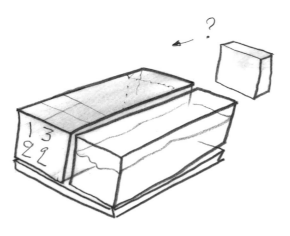

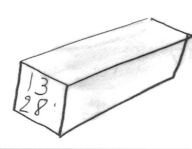

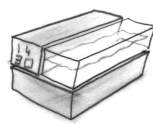

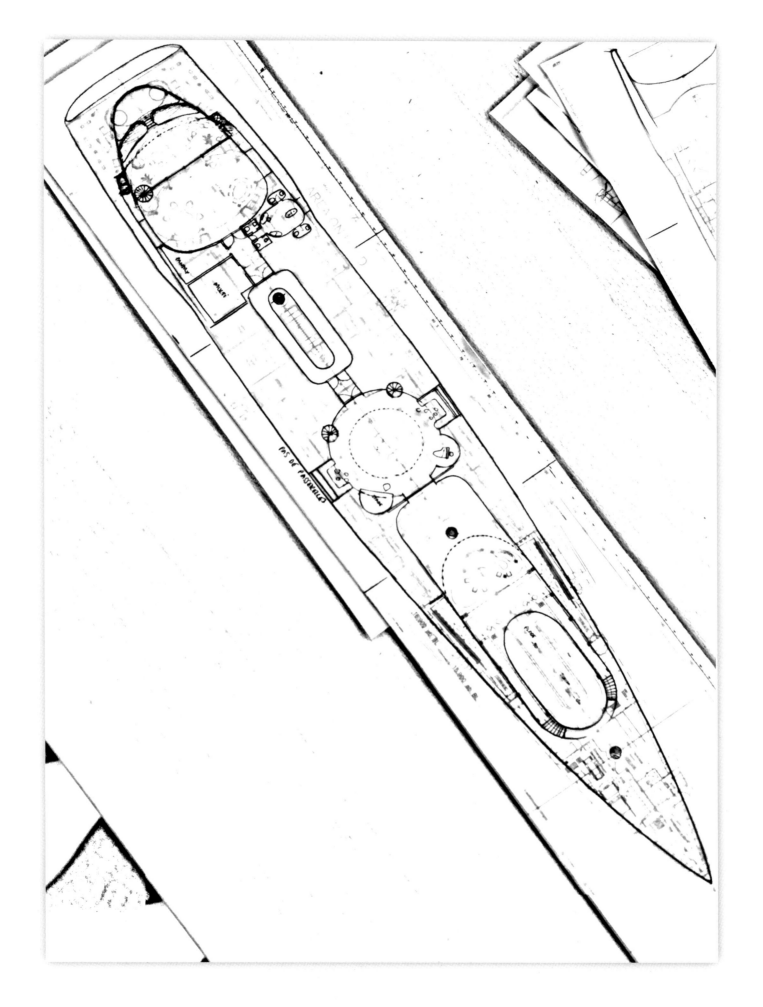

Obras de catálogo

Catalogue of Works

Exprimidor
Juicy Salif
Juicy Salif
citrus squeezer

Este exprimidor fabricado en aluminio fundido es uno de los primeros proyectos de Philippe Starck para Alessi. En 1987, Starck diseñó cuatro utensilios de cocina, que fueron producidos entre 1988 y 1990: un hervidor de agua (*Hot Bertaa*), un colador (*Max le Chinois*), un reloj (*Walter Wayle*) y este exprimidor (*Juicy Salif*). Para celebrar los veinticinco años del producto, se realizó una edición limitada de dos versiones inéditas del *Juicy Salif*, en bronce y en blanco.

El biomorfismo del *Juicy Salif*, así como su aspecto, a caballo entre lo humano, lo objetual y lo animal, llama la atención. «Hice un trabajo de topografía inversa», dirá Starck de él. En efecto, en la forma de trípode de este objeto funcional puede verse tanto el esqueleto de un calamar gigante como *La araña* de Louise Bourgeois, o incluso la máquina imaginada por el diseñador Edgar P. Jacobs en 1947 en su ilustración para la novela de ciencia ficción de H. G. Wells *La guerra de los mundos*.

Este utensilio de cocina, de un uso muy simple, desafía la regla según la cual un exprimidor debe ser un objeto tripartito, compuesto por una prensa, un filtro y un recipiente. El *Juicy Salif* dio paso así a una nueva gama de objetos funcionales que remiten más al principio simbólico del objeto que al simple objeto de uso.//M.V.

This citrus squeezer, made in cast aluminium, was one of the first projects Philippe Starck conceived for Alessi. In 1987, Starck designed four objects for the kitchen, produced between 1988 and 1990: a kettle (*Hot Bertaa*), a strainer (*Max le Chinois*), a clock (*Walter Wayle*) and this juice squeezer (*Juicy Salif*). Two original versions of *Juicy Salif* were also produced in bronze and white, in limited editions, celebrating the twenty-fifth anniversary of its first release.

Juicy Salif's biomorphic quality and allure lie between the human, object and animal realms. "I did a project with an inverted topography", said Starck. In fact, the tripoidal shape of this functional object, like a giant calamari skeleton, had already been suggested by Louise Bourgeois's *L'Araignée*, or even by the apparatus dreamt up by designer Edgar P. Jacobs in 1947, in his illustration for *The War of the Worlds*, the visionary novel by H. G. Wells.

This extraordinarily simple kitchen object defies the rule whereby a juice squeezer must be a three-part object made up of a press, a filter and a recipient. *Juicy Salif* would emerge as the starting point for a new line of functional objects privileging the symbolic principle of the object over and above mere objects of use.//M.V.

Exprimidor *Juicy Salif*	*Juicy Salif* **citrus squeezer**
1988	1988
Aluminio fundido moldeado	Cast aluminium
29 × 14 cm	29 × 14 cm
Fabricante: Alessi, Crusinallo, Italia	Producer: Alessi, Crusinallo, Italy
Donación Alessi, 1992	Gift of Alessi, 1992

Taburete *W.W.*

W.W. stool

Compuesto por tres pies orgánicos y un fino asiento con forma de radícula, el diseño del taburete *W.W.* tiene su origen en una conversación de Philippe Starck con el cineasta alemán Wim Wenders sobre su forma de trabajar. «Yo prefiero trabajar de pie, porque al sentarse uno pierde nervio. [...] Quiero una gran mesa vacía, y simplemente estar de pie», decía Wim Wenders.

Fascinado por el empuje vitalista del mundo vegetal, Starck imaginó un trípode para «sentarse de pie», cuyos pies esbeltos evocan verdes brotes, mientras que el objeto en su conjunto recuerda a una escultura vegetal. El taburete, como una muleta o una prótesis, es concebido como un elemento de reposo, un apoyo momentáneo. La sobriedad de las líneas y la reducción de la materia a su mínima expresión liberan el objeto de su masa.

En 1992, Vitra editó una pequeña cantidad de ejemplares de esta pieza en aluminio fundido moldeado a la arena y lacado con un tinte verde lechoso. Starck añadió una ramificación en la parte frontal de la estructura del prototipo original que sirve de reposapiés. La forma dinámica se expande en el espacio como un insecto gigante o una extensión del ser humano.//M.S.

Composed of three organic legs and a thin seat in the shape of a root structure to sit on, the *W.W.* stool was designed by Philippe Starck following a conversation with German filmmaker Wim Wenders about his way of working. "Well, for myself, I prefer to work standing up, because when you sit, you get sluggish... I prefer to work on a large, empty table, and I simply wish to be standing up", explained Wim Wenders.

Fascinated by the vitalist force of vegetable growth, Starck imagined a "sitting-standing" tripod, with the splayed legs evoking seedlings and the entire object suggestive of a botanical sculpture. The stool, like a set of crutches or a prosthesis, was conceived as a resting instrument, a momentary site of support. The sobriety of the lines and the reduction of the material to strict minimums relieve the object of its mass.

In 1992, this piece was produced in a limited quantity by Vitra in aluminium, using sand casting, and was lacquered in a lettuce-green stain. Starck added a branch to the front of the original structure of the prototype, as a kind of footrest. The dynamic shape seems to be expanding in space, like a giant insect or an extension of human form.//M.S.

Taburete *W.W.*
1988
Prototipo diseñado tras una
conversación con el cineasta
Wim Wenders
Haya natural, masilla de poliéster
97.5 × 58 × 53 cm
Fabricante: Vitra, Weil am Rhein,
Alemania
Donación del artista, 2005

***W.W.* stool**
1988
Prototype conceived following a
conversation with the filmmaker
Wim Wenders
Natural beechwood, polyester putty
97.5 × 58 × 53 cm
Producer: Vitra, Weil am Rhein,
Germany
Gift of the artist, 2005

Casa *Starck*

Starck House

En 1990, Philippe Starck puso en marcha el proyecto de una casa prefabricada, disponible a través del catálogo de 3 Suisses. El comprador interesado obtenía una caja de madera con las instrucciones para construir la casa, los planos completos, un libro de trabajo de construcción y dos cuadernos, uno en blanco y otro con el detalle de las fases de gestación del proyecto y el tipo de madera a utilizar, así como indicaciones en cuanto a la fontanería y la electricidad. El estuche incluía también una cinta VHS en la que podían verse las fases de montaje, un martillo de carpintero y una bandera para colocar en el armazón una vez terminada la casa.

En este proyecto de casa de 150 metros cuadrados solo se estipulan el plano (cuadrado y a escala 1:50), los materiales (madera, vidrio y zinc), el techo bajo e inclinado y el patio que la rodea; el resto queda en manos del propietario, que puede elegir cómo personalizar su casa.

La original casa *Starck* surge de la reflexión del diseñador acerca de la desigualdad en el acceso a la construcción. Este es también uno de los primeros proyectos de Starck suscritos a una dimensión sostenible. La aspiración de Starck a una arquitectura ecológica y democrática prosigue en 2012 gracias al proyecto P.A.T.H. (Prefabricated Accessible Technological Homes), un concepto de casas de madera prefabricadas desarrollado junto con la constructora eslovena Riko y cuyas propuestas de viviendas sostenibles incluyen la posibilidad de un balance energético positivo.//M.V.

In 1990, Philippe Starck launched a project for a kit home, accessible by catalogue through 3 Suisses. The interested purchaser received a wooden box with instructions to follow to build the home, with complete plans, the site binder, and two notebooks (one blank and the other explaining the stages of the project's development and the type of wood to use, as well as instructions on plumbing and electricity). The box also contained a VHS tape explaining the assembly steps, a carpenter's hammer and a flag to be placed onto the frame once the house was finished.

In this project for a 150-square-metre home, only the plan (square, printed at 1:50 scale), the materials (wood, glass and zinc), the lower and peaked roof and the surrounding terrace are preset. The rest is up to the owner, who can choose how the house will develop and end up.

This original project arose from Starck's reflection on inequality in construction. The *Starck House* was also one of the first Starck projects to establish criteria of durability. Starck's search for a democratic, ecological architecture would be revived in 2012 thanks to the project for *P.A.T.H.*, or *Prefabricated Accessible Technological Homes*, a concept for prefabricated wooden homes developed with the Slovene builder RIKO, where the solution of long-lasting living space is combined with the possibility of a positive energy-use balance.//M.V.

Casa *Starck*
1990
Instrucciones para construir una casa: planos, libro de trabajo de construcción, dos cuadernos, videocasete, martillo de carpintero y bandera de cima; presentación en caja de madera
10 × 82 × 63 cm
Fabricante: 3 Suisses, Croix, Francia
Donación de la Société des Amis du Musée national d'art moderne, 2006

Starck House
1990
Instructions to build a home: plans, site binder, 2 notebooks, K7 video, carpenter's hammer and flag; presented in a wooden box
10 × 82 × 63 cm
Producer: 3 Suisses, Croix, France
Gift of the Société des Amis du Musée national d'art moderne, 2006

Teléfono *Alo*

Alo telephone

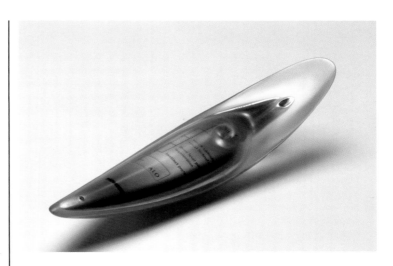

Diseñado en 1996 para la marca francesa Thomson, *Alo* es un teléfono de activación por voz con la forma de una crisálida de piel elástica y transparente. Starck ideó un proyecto pionero, un asistente personal inteligente, capaz de responder a peticiones vocalizadas. Moldeado en aluminio, el teléfono se inserta en una envoltura de polímero transparente capaz de vibrar y emitir calor durante la comunicación. Lejos de las tipologías tradicionalmente asociadas a este objeto, Starck replantea las relaciones entre el hombre y la máquina al apostar por la sensibilidad táctil y la democratización de la inteligencia artificial. *Alo* carece de pantalla, pero puede proyectar hologramas gracias a una cámara incorporada, capaz de leer mensajes y vídeos.

Philippe Starck imagina un futuro, quizá la era de la prótesis, iluminado por el *bionismo*, un concepto que «se basa en lo orgánico para crear tecnologías más adaptadas al ser humano». Tanto por su nombre minimalista, una interjección que refleja su función, como por la sobriedad de sus líneas orgánicas, que se convierten en una prolongación del individuo, *Alo* desaparece de nuestro campo perceptivo para fundirse con nuestro cuerpo y elevarse a una metasensorialidad.//M.S.

Conceived in 1996 for the French brand Thomson, *Alo* is a voice-recognition telephone in the shape of a chrysalis, with an elastic, transparent surface. Starck thought that this project could be a precursor of an intelligent personal assistant, able to respond to any request made orally. Cast in aluminium, it fits into a translucid polymer sheath, vibrating or turning off depending on the communication activity level. Freed from the traditional typology assigned to the object, Starck rethought the relationship between man and machine by focusing on its tactile sensitivity and the democratization of artificial intelligence. *Alo* is devoid of a screen, but is able to project holograms thanks to a built-in camera that can read messages and videos.

Philippe Starck here conceives a future that could belong to the prosthesis, clarified by the concept of "bionism", which "inspires itself in organic form to create technologies that are better adapted to human beings." With its pared-down name, an interjection denoting its function, as well as the sobriety of its organic lines, a prolongation of the individual, *Alo* is removed from our visual field so as to fuse with our body, becoming meta-sensorial.//M.S.

Silla *La Marie*

La Marie chair

«A largo plazo, el diseño alcanzará una de las líneas más fundamentales de nuestra evolución: la desmaterialización». La silla *La Marie*, de una «depuración matemática», se ve reducida así a la pura invisibilidad por efecto del policarbonato transparente. Bajo el lema «a menos materia, más inteligencia», Starck diseñó un objeto humilde, anónimo e intemporal. No obstante, *La Marie*, un asiento monobloque apilable de 7 kg de peso y hecho de plástico antirrayaduras, es de una extraordinaria modernidad por la innovadora técnica de moldeado utilizada en su fabricación.

Partiendo de la interpretación del arquetipo de la silla en nuestra memoria colectiva, Philippe Starck ideó un objeto de líneas estructurales simples y aéreas. Siempre desde una lógica minimalista y orientada hacia la democratización del diseño, redujo el coste de la silla, que fue presentada en 1999 en el catálogo de venta por correspondencia *Good Goods*, realizado por Starck para La Redoute. Según él mismo, *La Marie* viene a ser «el no-producto indispensable», que remite a la disolución del gesto del creador. Si forma parte de sus creaciones favoritas es porque pertenece a ese grupo de «objetos de segunda mirada, aquellos que si uno no quiere ver, no ve».//M.S.

"In the long term, design will have merged with one of the most fundamental paths of our evolution, that of dematerialization." *La Marie*, a chair of "mathematical refinement", is likewise reduced to pure invisibility in the choice of transparent polycarbonate. Guided by the slogan "less matter for greater intelligence", Starck conceived of a humble object, anonymous and timeless. *La Marie* – a seven-kilo, single-block, non-scratch, stackable chair – is enveloped in modernity thanks to its innovative casting technique, the basis for its manufacture.

Taking as his starting point the chair archetype in collective memory, Philippe Starck rethinks the object with aerially simple structural lines. Set firmly within a logic of minimums and pointing to the democratization of design, the cost of the chair was lowered, as seen in the mail-order catalogue *Good Goods*, which he designed for la Redoute. In his own words, *La Marie* was to be "the indispensable non-product", referring to the effacement of the creator's gesture. If it remains among his favourite creations, it is, Starck says, for its status among "objects for second looks: that is, if you don't want to see them, you won't see them".//M.S.

Silla *La Marie*
1996
Policarbonato transparente
86 × 39 × 55 cm
Fabricante: Kartell, Noviglio, Italia
Donación de Kartell, 2007

La Marie chair
1996
Transparent polycarbonate
86 × 39 × 55 cm
Producer: Kartell, Noviglio, Italy
Gift of Kartell, 2007

Butaca *Louis Ghost*

Louis Ghost armchair

La butaca *Louis Ghost*, fabricada por la marca milanesa Kartell en 2000, es uno de los objetos más emblemáticos de la producción de asientos de Philippe Starck. Esta pieza icónica, elaborada en policarbonato moldeado por inyección —un resistente material plástico transparente—, ahonda en el principio de desmaterialización e invisibilidad iniciado con la silla *La Marie* (1996). Starck añade aquí a ese principio la dimensión de la memoria colectiva, que combina con la alta tecnología en el momento de la fabricación. El diseño de esta silla supone una revisión del estilo Luis XVI, característico del siglo XVIII francés y que se corresponde con un retorno al clasicismo. El medallón del respaldo de la *Louis Ghost*, al igual que los delgados brazos en ángulo recto y las patas rectilíneas, es típicamente neoclásico. Para Starck, la butaca es, como si de un «fantasma» se tratara, «la sombra de una butaca de estilo».

Philippe Starck revisita este periodo de la historia del arte haciendo de esta silla ceremonial del siglo XVIII, ricamente ornamentada, un mueble ligero (5,4 kg), depurado, industrial, es decir, reproducible, destinado tanto a los espacios interiores como exteriores. Según Starck, «la *Louis Ghost* es fruto de nuestro subconsciente colectivo, no es más que el resultado natural de nuestro pasado, nuestro presente y nuestro futuro. También, por su tecnología, permite ofrecer un buen diseño, una buena tecnología, a buen precio. Es la continuidad del diseño democrático».//M.V.

The *Louis Ghost* armchair, designed for the Milan producer Kartell in 2000, is one of the flagship pieces within Philippe Starck's seating production. An iconic object made in injection-moulded polycarbonate – a resistant, transparent plastic material – it extends the principle of dematerialization and invisibility already ventured upon with the *La Marie* chair (1996). Here, however, Starck adds a layer of collective memory, combined with that of high technology, in its production. The conception of this chair looks back to the Louis XVI style, in eighteenth-century France, thus appearing to be a return to classicism. The medallion on the backrest of *Louis Ghost*, as well as the armrests with their right angles and the rectilinear underframe, are typical of this neoclassicism. For Starck, the armchair, referred to as a "ghost", is "the shadow of stylish seating".

Philippe Starck returns to this period in the history of art in making a chair suggestive of the richly adorned furniture of the eighteenth century, though lightweight (5.4 kg), refined and industrial, destined to be used both indoors and out. As Starck describes it, "the *Louis Ghost* was developed from our collective subconscious; it is nothing but the natural result of our past, our present and our future. Its technology enables us to offer good design, good technology, and at a good price. It is the continuation of democratic design."//M.V.

Butaca *Louis Ghost*
2000
Policarbonato transparente
96 × 54 × 64 cm
Fabricante: Kartell, Noviglio, Italia
Donación de Kartell, 2007

Louis Ghost armchair
2000
Transparent polycarbonate
96 × 54 × 64 cm
Producer: Kartell, Noviglio, Italy
Gift of Kartell, 2007

Silla *Oscar Bon*

Oscar Bon chair

Diseñado en 2005, el prototipo *Oscar Bon* es un asiento monobloque en fibra de carbono negra obtenida con un moldeado en caliente, lo cual representa todo un desafío técnico. Esta creación, en cuyo diseño colaboró la NASA, es única por su aspecto completamente futurista y su tecnología de vanguardia. La silueta envolvente y orgánica de su asiento se ajusta a los contornos del cuerpo, conciliando elegancia y ergonomía. Para su fabricación se eligió la fibra de carbono por sus propiedades: alta resistencia, flexibilidad y ligereza.

Fueron necesarios cuatro años de investigación y pruebas para que esta pieza excepcional, emblemática por el uso de las nuevas técnicas de moldeado e inyección, llegara a ser comercializada. Con un peso inferior a 2 kg, esta silla portátil ultraligera se ajusta a la perfección al modo de vida contemporáneo orientado hacia la movilidad. Disponible en negro o en plata, su asiento en forma de concha presenta una textura estriada que crea sutiles reflejos de luz. La silla se asienta sobre unos pies finos y delgados, que la hacen ligera y moderna pese a que, por sus líneas, parezca revisitar el espíritu de los años cincuenta.//M.S.

Conceived in 2005, the *Oscar Bon* prototype is a single-block seat in black carbon fibre, produced by heat moulding, which represented a veritable technical challenge. Imagined as a collaboration with NASA, this creation is unique for its resolutely futuristic appearance and high-grade technical nature. The all-encompassing, organic profile of the shell is fused with the curves of the body, combining elegance and ergonomics. The carbon fibre was chosen precisely for the virtues of its properties: maximum resistance, flexibility and lightness.

Emblematic for its use of new techniques in injection moulding, this exceptional piece would need four years of research and testing before coming onto the market. Weighing less than two kilograms, it is an ultra-light, portable chair, in perfect harmony with new practices of contemporary life in relation to mobility. Available in black or silver, the shell-shaped seat is criss-crossed with textured striations, setting off subtle plays of light. It rests on long, stretched out legs, giving it an airy, modern feel, its lines nevertheless suggestive of the spirit of the 1950s.//M.S.

Silla *Oscar Bon*
2002
Prototipo de la base
Fibra de carbono
60 × 41 × 43 cm
Fabricante: Driade, Caorso, Italia
Donación del artista, 2007

***Oscar Bon* chair**
2002
Prototype of base
Carbon fibre
60 × 41 × 43 cm
Producer: Driade, Caorso, Italy
Gift of the artist, 2007

Silla *Oscar Bon*
2002
Fibra de carbono
70 × 59 × 65 cm
Fabricante: Driade, Caorso, Italia
Donación de Driade, 2007

***Oscar Bon* chair**
2002
Carbon fibre
60 × 41 × 43 cm
Producer: Driade, Caorso, Italy
Gift of the artist, 2007

Colección *Gun*

Gun collection

Starck realizó en 2003 una serie de lámparas para el fabricante italiano Flos, que incluye tres modelos: *Bedside Gun*, *Lounge Gun* y *Table Gun*. La estructura del pie de cada una de estas lámparas está realizada en aluminio moldeado a presión y dispone de un revestimiento de polímero fundido chapado en oro mate de 18 quilates. Starck confiere un sentido especial a cada uno de los modelos y a sus elementos estructurales: «El oro de las armas representa la colusión del dinero y la guerra. *Table Gun* representa el Este; *Bedside Gun* es Europa, y *Lounge Gun*, el Oeste. La pantalla negra significa la muerte, y las cruces negras en el interior nos recuerdan a nuestros muertos».

Esta atípica serie se inscribe en la problemática del lenguaje comprensible desarrollada por Starck, es decir, la evocación mesurada o violenta de nuestra memoria colectiva. La imagen provocativa del pie de la lámpara en forma de arma es para el diseñador un «signo de los tiempos» que encarna esta pregunta: «¿Cómo mejorar un utensilio afinando el sentimiento surgido de esta memoria?». Este objeto, que evidencia su carácter cínico, ejemplifica también un compromiso moral, ya que el 20% de los beneficios de esta colección se destina a la asociación Frères des Hommes, que lucha por la erradicación de la pobreza en el mundo.//M.V.

Starck made a series of lamps for the Italian lighting brand Flos, in 2003. The series included three models, *Bedside Gun*, *Lounge Gun* and *Table Gun*. The structure of the base of each of these lamps was made in moulded aluminium under pressure, with a coating of overmoulded polymer of pressed, matt, 18-karat gold. Starck recalled the particular meaning of each of the models and their structural elementals: "Gold on weapons represents the collusion between money and war. *Table Gun* represents the East, *Bedside Gun* is Europe, and *Lounge Gun* is the West. The black lampshade represents death, while the crosses inside recall our own dead."

This unusual series finds meaning in the context of the problematic of understandable logic as developed by Starck, that is, the measured or violent evocation of our collective memory. The provocative image of the lamp base in the form of a weapon was, for the designer, a "sign of the times", embodying the question: "How might we enhance the object of use by refining the feeling arising from this memory?" These objects, which put their cynical foot forward, were accompanied by a moral commitment, as 20% of all sales were passed on to the association Frères des Hommes, dedicated to the eradication of world poverty.//M.V.

Lámpara de mesa *Table Gun*
2003
Pie metalizado en oro mate de 18 quilates galvanizado, pantalla de tela negra
93 × 28 cm; diámetro de pantalla: 51 cm
Fabricante: Flos, Bovezzo, Italia
Donación de Flos, 2007

***Table Gun* table lamp**
2003
Base in unpolished, 18 karat, matt, galvanized gold; lampshade in black fabric
93 × 28 cm; diameter of lampshade: 51 cm
Producer: Flos, Bovezzo, Italy
Gift of Flo s, 2007

Lámpara de mesa *Bedside Gun*
2003
Pie chapado en oro mate de 18 quilates, pantalla de papel negro
43 × 16 cm; diámetro de pantalla: 24 cm
Fabricante: Flos, Bovezzo, Italia
Donación de Flos, 2007

***Bedside Gun* table lamp**
2003
Base in 18 karat, matt gold; lampshade in black paper
43 × 16 cm; diameter of lampshade: 24 cm
Producer: Flos, Bovezzo, Italy
Gift of Flos, 2007

Lámpara de pie *Lounge Gun M16*
2003
Pie chapado en oro mate de 18 quilates, pantalla de papel negro
170 × 43 cm; diámetro de pantalla: 56 cm
Fabricante: Flos, Bovezzo, Italia
Donación de Flos, 2007

***Lounge Gun M16* floor lamp**
2003
Base in 18 karat, matt gold plate; lampshade in black paper
170 × 43 cm; diameter of lampshade: 56 cm
Producer: Flos, Bovezzo, Italy
Gift of Flos, 2007

Aceite de oliva
LA Organic
LA Organic
olive oil

En 2005, Starck se une al enólogo Michel Rolland para producir dos aceites de oliva con un espíritu cercano al del vino a partir de materias primas ecológicas. LA Organic, una marca andaluza de aceite de oliva virgen extra 100% ecológico, se convierte en el primer aceite de oliva ecológico elaborado por un enólogo. El diseño del bidón, decididamente tradicional, apela a la memoria colectiva y permite captar su contenido de un solo vistazo.

Starck elige una paleta de colores cuyos matices se articulan en torno a las tonalidades de la aceituna: amarillo para un aroma dulce y verde para un sabor más intenso. El envase de aluminio garantiza la hermeticidad y la impermeabilidad a la luz, y un barniz protector interno mantiene intactas las cualidades del producto.

«No soy una persona inteligente. Hago las cosas que se imponen por sí mismas. Todo fluye de forma natural. ¿El envase? Un bidón por una cuestión de impermeabilidad a la luz. ¿Los colores? Distintas tonalidades de verde oliva para recuperar el espíritu del contenido. ¿El nombre? LA, porque solo hay una», dice Starck, que desea también «hacer justicia a España», el mayor productor de aceite de oliva.//M.G.

In 2005, Starck teamed up with the oenologist Michel Rolland to create two kinds of olive oil, drawing from the spirit of winemaking and using primary materials that were also ecological. LA Organic is an Andalusian brand of 100% ecological extra virgin olive oil, created by an oenologist. The conception of the container is resolutely traditional, referring to collective memory and making it possible to read what is inside all at once.

Starck chose a colour palette where the nuances are articulated around olive tones: yellow for a softer taste, green for a stronger flavour. The aluminium container ensures it is airtight and fully blocks out light, while a protective lacquered internal layer guarantees that the product's features are kept intact.

"You know, I am not an intelligent being. I make choices that are really imposing themselves. Everything follows its own logic. The content? The container, for its total impermeability to light. The colours? Different olive greens to revive the spirit of the container. The name? LA is the name because it is right there, there is just one of them", Starck explains, who also wanted to "do justice to Spain," the world's leading producer of olive oil.//M.G.

Aceite de oliva	LA Organic
LA Organic	olive oil
2004	2004
Aluminio lacado	Lacquered aluminium
Contenido: 100 cl	Content: 100 cl
Fabricante: LA Organic,	Manufacturer: LA Organic,
LA Amarilla, Ronda, España	LA Amarilla, Ronda, Spain
Donación del artista, 2007	Gift of the artist, 2007

Butaca
Mister Impossible
Mister Impossible armchair

La butaca *Mister Impossible* nace de la idea aparentemente imposible de unir dos bases ovales en una única estructura. Pese a su evidente simplicidad y la búsqueda estricta de la máxima ligereza y confort, *Mister Impossible* surge tras un proceso de concepción complejo que combina el diseño orgánico y la tecnología de vanguardia con una reflexión sobre los materiales plásticos. La innovación de Starck consiste en la unión de dos óvalos hemisféricos de policarbonato, soldados entre sí con laser, y un discreto travesaño que se funde en el asiento, «suspendido», como en estado de ingravidez.

Para Philippe Starck, la elegancia moderna y sincera del objeto deriva de la «búsqueda de la esencia»: «Entiendo por esencia la idea del objeto despojado de toda cultura. Es una búsqueda del olvido», añade. La apuesta estética por el policarbonato transparente se refleja en la inmaterialidad de la silla, que desaparece de nuestra vista, y responde además a una conciencia ética, ya que se trata de un tipo de plástico no tóxico, resistente y estable ante los cambios climáticos.//M.S.

The *Mister Impossible* armchair was born from the apparently impossible idea of joining two oval shells into a single structure. Despite its apparent simplicity and its strict quest for maximum lightness and comfort, *Mister Impossible* arose from a complex process of conception, uniting organic design and cutting-edge technology with a reflection on plastic materials. Starck's most original idea was to fuse two hemispheric polycarbonate shells, connected by laser with a discreet underframe that merges with the chair, "in suspension", as if in zero gravity.

For Philippe Starck, the sincerely modern elegance of the object is the result of "research into essence": "By essence, I mean the idea of the object freed from all culture. I am speaking of research into forgetfulness," he would add. The aesthetic choice of transparent polycarbonate is expressed through the immateriality of the chair, which shies from our gaze, taking on an ethical conscience, tied in with a type of non-toxic plastic that is resistant and stable when exposed to climatic changes.//M.S.

Butaca *Mister Impossible*
2005
Prototipo
Policarbonato transparente
84 × 55 × 54 cm
Fabricante: Kartell, Noviglio, Italia
Donación de Kartell, 2007

***Mister Impossible* armchair**
2005
Prototype
Transparent polycarbonate
84 × 55 × 54 cm
Producer: Kartell, Noviglio, Italy
Gift of Kartell, 2007

Butaca *Pip-e*

Pip-e armchair

La serie de sillas y butacas *Pip-e* es fruto de una nueva colaboración entre Starck y Driade. Elaborada en polipropileno monobloque, la silla está disponible en varios colores (gris, naranja, blanco o amarillo). *Pip-e* se fabrica de modo industrial, mediante la presión de hierro fundido y acero galvanizado. El plástico ocupa un lugar importante en el vocabulario material de Starck y responde a su deseo de un diseño democrático. Es para él un material indispensable, ya que ofrece aún más posibilidades que los materiales naturales.

Pip-e se estructura en base a una sucesión de elementos horizontales de polipropileno que forman el respaldo y el asiento; la alternancia de vacíos y llenos contribuye a la desaparición de la materia, a la desmaterialización del objeto, tan apreciada por el diseñador. La coherencia entre la forma y la función de esta silla transmite un mensaje simple y sincero, producido por la reinvención de la forma ordinaria, lo que confiere una sensación de *déjà vu* y refleja la evidencia del trabajo de Starck.//M.V.

The series of *Pip-e* chairs and armchairs is the result of a new collaboration between Starck and Driade. Produced in single-block polypropylene, the chair comes in various tones (grey, orange, white or yellow). It is made following an industrial procedure, with cast-iron and galvanized steel. The plastic in Starck's material vocabulary responds to his will towards democratic design. As he sees it, this material is absolutely essential, as its possibilities are even richer than those of natural materials.

Pip-e is at the same time structured along a series of horizontal features in polypropylene, making up the backrest and the seat. The alternation of empty and full contributes to the disappearance of matter, to the dematerialization of the object, values that are dear to the designer. Coherence between form and function carries with it a simple, sincere message, produced by the reinvention of the ordinary shape, calling up a sensation of "déjà-vu", bearing witness to Starck's endeavour.//M.V.

Butaca *Pip-e*	
2008	***Pip*-e armchair**
Polipropileno	2008
83 × 44 × 52,2 cm; altura	Polypropylene
del asiento: 47 cm	83 × 44 × 52.2 cm; seat height: 47 cm
Fabricante: Driade, Caorso, Italia	Producer: Driade, Caorso, Italy
Donación de Driade, 2017	Gift of Driade, 2017

Lámpara *D'E-light*

D'E-light lamp

D'E-light es un concepto inédito de lámpara multifunción. Equipada con una placa para dispositivos iOS (puerto USB) situada en la parte superior de la pantalla, ofrece la posibilidad de recargar material Apple y Android al tiempo que ilumina. Esta lámpara, diseñada por Starck y fabricada por la empresa italiana Flos, funciona gracias a un teclado de ledes (diodos emisores de luz) situado en la pantalla rectangular de aluminio fundido. El teclado está equipado con un difusor de policarbonato, que permite una mejor distribución del flujo de luz, gracias al ajuste de la luminosidad en función de la fuente de luz natural. Acompañada de un sistema táctil que permite regular la intensidad de la luz, la *D'E-light* se sirve de la tecnología digital. Además de iluminar y recargar, su cabezal sirve de soporte para distintos aparatos electrónicos. Su elevada potencia y su diversidad de usos son inversamente proporcionales a su reducido tamaño.

La estructura minimalista de esta lámpara de mesa táctil, compuesta por un cabezal, un pie de aluminio extruido y una base de zamak, encaja a la perfección con la del dispositivo digital, también táctil y multifuncional.//M.V.

D'E-light is a unique concept for a multifunctional lamp with a card for iOS devices (USB port) found on top of the lampshade, offering the possibility of charging Apple and Android while carrying out its lighting function. This light, designed by Starck and produced by the Italian lighting company Flos, illuminates by means of a flat LED panel (using electroluminescent diodes) found within the rectangular head, atop an extruded aluminium stem. It has a polycarbonate diffuser, allowing an optimally distributed light flow while adjusting light intensity in relation to existing natural light. Accompanied by a soft-touch system making it possible to adapt light intensity, *D'E-light* takes full advantage of digital technology. In addition, besides illuminating and recharging, the head of the lamp acts as a support for various kinds of electronic devices. The increased power and range of services of this object is inversely proportional to its discreet size.

The minimal structure of this tactile table lamp, composed of a head, an extruded aluminium stem and a zamak base, fully corresponds to its status as a soft-touch, multifunctional, digital apparatus.//M.V.

Lámpara *D'E-light*
2009
Aluminio, fuente de luz led, puerto USB que permite recargar iPad, iPhone y iPod
31,7 × 12 cm; ancho del difusor: 21,6 cm
Fabricante: Flos, Bovezzo, Italia
Donación de Flos, 2017

***D'E-light* lamp**
2009
Aluminium, LED light source, USB port to recharge iPad, iPhone and iPod
31.7 × 12 cm; diffuser width: 21.6 cm
Producer: Flos, Bovezzo, Italy
Gift of Flos, 2017

Butaca *Lou Read*

Lou Read armchair

Fabricada por la marca italiana Driade en 2011, esta butaca de resina y fibra de vidrio con revestimiento de cuero de plena flor fijado a la estructura fue concebida originalmente para la renovación del palacio parisino Le Royal Monceau–Raffles Paris. El nombre de la butaca proviene del encuentro, en ese lugar, del diseñador y del artista Lou Reed, líder del grupo The Velvet Underground.

La línea orgánica de la butaca, junto con su estructura de fibra de carbono, le otorga cierta animalidad y un gran confort. La estructura de la *Lou Read* recuerda a la de algunos muebles modernistas, especialmente la primera serie de butacas de madera contrachapada de los arquitectos y diseñadores Charles y Ray Eames, realizadas hacia 1941-1945, de acuerdo con un método inédito de moldeado de delgadas chapas de madera en formas curvas.

Los reposabrazos antropomórficos de la *Lou Read*, que recuerdan a unos brazos abiertos, pueden relacionarse con la silueta de las butacas expresivas de Carlo Mollino (*Ardea Lounge Chair*, 1950) o con la de la *Organic Highback* (1940), fruto de la colaboración entre Eero Saarinen y Charles Eames. En 2016, en la línea de la butaca *Lou Read*, Philippe Starck realizó *Lou Eat* y *Lou Think*.//M.V.

Produced by the Italian furniture company Driade in 2011, this resin and glass-fibre armchair, covered in full-grain leather attached to the structure, was originally conceived for the renovation of Paris hotel, Le Royal Monceau – Raffles Paris. The chair's name was inspired by the designer meeting the musician Lou Reed, singer with the Velvet Underground, in the hotel.

The armchair's organic lines, relating to its carbon-fibre skeleton, give it a certain animal quality, but it is also decidedly comfortable. The structure of *Lou Read* recalls that of other modernist furniture designs, especially the first series of wood-veneer armchairs by the architect-designers Charles and Ray Eames, made from 1941 to 1945, the result of an original procedure moulding thin veneer sheets into curved shapes.

Lou Read's anthropomorphic armrests, resembling open arms, could recall the profile of the expressive armchairs of Carlo Mollino (*Ardea Lounge Chair*, 1950) or the collaborative effort of Eero Saarinen and Charles Eames (*Organic Highback*, 1940). In 2016, in the line of *Lou Read*, Philippe Starck created *Lou Eat* and *Lou Think*.//M.V.

Butaca *Lou Read*
2009
Estructura de poliuretano Baydur, soporte de acero con revestimiento de cuero natural
120 × 70 × 72 cm; altura del asiento: 42 cm
Fabricante: Driade, Caorso, Italia
Donación de Driade, 2017

***Lou Read* armchair**
2009
Baydur polyurethane structure, steel base upholstered in full-grain leather
120 × 70 × 72 cm; seat height: 42 cm
Producer: Driade, Caorso, Italy
Gift of Driade, 2017

Silla *Zartan*

Zartan chair

Philippe Starck defiende la idea visionaria de que el decrecimiento positivo en favor de la transición energética podría influir en las profundas transformaciones de nuestro mundo contemporáneo. Con la serie *Zartan* —anagrama de Tarzán—, compuesta por las primeras sillas rotomoldeadas completamente recicladas, Starck pone la innovación al servicio de un diseño democrático y ético. La *Zartan Eco* se distingue por su asiento de lino, yute o cáñamo, mientras que el del modelo *Raw* es de fibras de madera procedentes de la lignina. Pensada para el exterior, la *Zartan Basic* está elaborada en polipropileno reforzado con fibra de vidrio.

Junto con la firma italiana Magis, especializada en la producción de mobiliario de plástico moldeado, Starck ha desarrollado una técnica experimental basada en «bioplásticos éticos» ensamblados mediante un pegamento al agua y sin remaches. Sometido a alta presión, este material mixto se comporta como el plástico fundido, lo que facilita su inyección en un molde mediante una cánula. La carcasa envolvente del asiento, moldeada por compresión, reposa sobre cuatro esbeltas patas moldeadas por inyección en polipropileno de origen vegetal, una alternativa no tóxica a los plásticos derivados del petróleo.//M.S.

As a visionary, Philippe Starck is convinced that positive disbelief turned towards energetic transition can enhance the profound mutations going on in the contemporary world. He has put innovation at the service of democratic, ethical design in devising the series *Zartan* (an anagram of Tarzan), the first series of entirely recycled chairs made by rotomoulding. The *Zartan Eco* stands out for its seat in linen, jute or hemp, while the *Raw* model is made from wood fibre derived from lignin. Meant for the outdoors, the *Zartan Basic* is made in polypropylene reinforced by glass fibre.

Working with the Italian firm Magis, specialized in the production of moulded plastic furniture, Starck developed an experimental process based on "ethical bioplastics", which was assembled using water-based adhesives and without screws. Under high-pressure conditions, the composite material behaves like melted plastic, permitting it to be injected using a nozzle inserted into a cast. The enveloping shell of the seat, cast by compression, sits on four slender injection-moulded legs of plant-based polypropylene, with the aim of creating a non-toxic alternative to plastics derived from petroleum.//M.S.

Silla *Zartan*
2009
Fibra de madera, polipropileno reciclado
82 × 56 × 53 cm; altura del asiento: 44 cm
Fabricante: Magis, Torre di Mosto, Italia
Donación de Magis, 2017

Zartan chair
2009
Fibrewood, recycled polypropylene
82 × 56 × 53 cm; seat height: 44 cm
Producer: Magis, Torre di Mosto, Italy
Gift of Magis, 2017

Grifos monomando
Axor Starck Organic y *Axor Starck V*

Axor Starck Organic and *Axor Starck V* faucets

Con una visión a la par biónica y ecológica, Starck diseña una serie de grifos de formas elementales y escultóricas inspiradas en un lenguaje minimalista que magnifica la fluidez del agua.

La explotación inteligente del agua, de acuerdo con la idea del respeto por la naturaleza, está en la base de este diseño de mezclador monomando cromado, dotado de noventa microdifusores que generan una sensación de abundancia, pese a que el dispositivo reduce a la mitad el flujo de agua respecto a un grifo convencional. La temperatura está predefinida y controlada de modo intuitivo, con independencia del volumen de agua demandado. La experiencia sensorial resultante reactiva la dimensión ritual y vitalista del agua, que se proyecta por pulverización.

En 2012, con el *Starck V*, el diseñador persiste en esta búsqueda al desmaterializar el grifo para visibilizar así el fenómeno natural del vórtice del agua en movimiento. La forma orgánica y purista del caño, elaborado en vidrio cristalino, es toda una proeza técnica. Estético e innovador, el *Starck V* se difumina para reforzar la observación y la experiencia sensible del agua. Este grifo es el «mínimo absoluto, totalmente transparente. Es un milagro de la naturaleza que nace ante nuestros ojos».//M.S.

Using a bionic, ecological approach, Starck designed a series of flow limiters in elementary, sculptural shapes, where the minimalist language magnifies the water flow.

Driven by a concern to be respectful towards nature, the intelligent use of water is expressed through the conception of a chrome limiter, with 90 microjets to give a sense of abundance, as the device reduces the flow coming through a standard faucet by half. The temperature is preset and controlled intuitively, separately from the desired volume of flow, spurting out pulverized. Here, the sensorial experience of the water affirms its vital, ritualistic role.

In 2012, with *Axor Starck V*, Starck continued his research into dematerializing the tap, seeking to visualize the natural phenomenon of the dynamic water vortex. The organically purist shape of the glass pouring spout is a technical accomplishment. Visually attractive and innovative, *Starck V* lowered its own profile in accenting the observation and experience of pouring water. This tap is "absolutely minimal, totally transparent. It is a miracle of nature, come to life right in front of us."//M.S.

Grifo monomando
Axor Starck Organic
2010
Acabado metálico cromado
31 × 19 cm; diámetro: 7 cm; caudal: 3,5-5 ml
Fabricante: Axor, Alemania
Donación de Axor, 2017

Grifo monomando
Axor Starck V
2012
Combinación de cristal y metal
25,1 × 12,5 cm; diámetro: 5 cm; caudal: 4 l/min
Fabricante: Axor, Alemania
Donación de Axor, 2017

Axor Starck Organic
faucet
2010
Chrome metal finish
31 × 19 cm; diameter: 7 cm; flow limiter: 3.5 ml. to 5 ml
Producer: Axor, Germany
Gift of Axor, 2017

Axor Starck V
faucet
2012
Metal and glass combination
25,1 × 12.5 cm; diameter: 5 cm; flow limiter: 4 l/min
Producer: Axor, Germany
Gift of Axor, 2017

Coche eléctrico *V+*

V+ Electric car

V+, el único coche diseñado por Philippe Starck que ha llegado a materializarse, fue fabricado en 2010 por la empresa francesa Volteis a petición del propio Starck.

Al igual que el *X4*, el coche *V+* está equipado con dos motores eléctricos de 4 kWh, su autonomía es idéntica y alcanza una velocidad máxima de 60 km/h. En 1996 Starck había explorado ya las vías de movilidad con *Toto*, un coche de cuatro plazas que no fue más allá de la fase de proyecto.

Comercializado desde junio de 2012, el *V+* está fabricado a base de tubos de aluminio; los asientos y el salpicadero han sido tejidos en ratán sobre un marco de acero inoxidable.

Para Starck, se trata de «un vehículo sencillo. Casi de un juguete. Con cuatro ruedas. Un volante. Y electricidad. Un vehículo pensado para transportarnos. A nosotros y a nuestras cosas. Casi nada. Para que tengamos más con menos. Más humanidad. Más respeto. Más opciones para demostrar que nos preocupamos por nuestro medio ambiente».//M.V.

V+ is the only automobile designed by Philippe Starck that has not stopped at the project stage: it was produced in 2012 by the French electric car manufacturer Volteis. The manufacturer built the vehicle following Philippe Starck's proposals.

V+ was derived from the model *X4*, launched by Volteis in 2009: an electric car featuring a tarp as a roof and designed without doors; autonomy was 60 kilometres. Like the *X4*, the *V+* car was equipped with two 4 kWh electric motors, with an identical autonomy and a maximum speed of 60 kph. In 1996 Starck had already explored the realm of mobility with *Toto*, a four-person car which never got past the concept stage.

Available for purchase starting in June 2012, the *V+* was fabricated with aluminium tubing while the seats and dashboard were woven from rattan, set over a stainless-steel base.

For Starck, it was "a totally simple vehicle. Almost kid's play. With four wheels. A steering wheel. And electricity. A vehicle for transportation. To transport us, and to transport our business. Almost nothing. For anyone who gets more from less. With greater humanity. More respect. And more choice when it comes to showing that we care about our environment."//M.V.

65

Coche eléctrico *V+*
2010
Aluminio, acero inoxidable, plomo, tela, mimbre sintético, batería de litio, focales lenticulares, 8 kw, 11 hp, 2 motores de 4 kWh
172 × 178 × 267 cm
Fabricante: Volteis, Davézieux, Francia
Colección Philippe Starck

***V+* electric car**
2010
Aluminium, stainless steel, lead, fabric, synthetic wicker, lithium battery, lenticular optical system, 8 kWh capacity, 11 hp, two 4-watt motors
172 × 178 × 267 cm
Manufacturer: Volteis, Davézieux, France
Philippe Starck Collection

Silla *Broom*

Broom chair

Diseñada según el lema «menos estilo, menos diseño, menos materiales y menos energía», la silla monobloque y apilable *Broom* ofrece una funcionalidad, un confort y una resistencia óptimos, así como un diseño ético y comprometido. En 2010, Starck revoluciona el diseño ecológico reestructurando la producción industrial mediante el reciclaje de desechos en origen. Utilizando materiales abandonados en aserraderos y plantas de fabricación de plástico, se obtuvo un compuesto reciclado, constituido en un 75% de desechos de polipropileno y en un 15% de serrín de fibras de madera y reforzado con un 10% de fibra de vidrio.

Creada a partir de un material innovador, la serie de sillas *Broom* encarna una visión estética y ecológica del objeto en cuanto a la reducción de residuos, el gasto energético y las emisiones de CO_2. El nombre de la silla, *Broom* (escoba), evoca la imagen de «un tipo que coge una humilde escoba y empieza a limpiar el taller y, con el polvo, crea una magia nueva». Para Starck, barrer y recoger lo que ha quedado reducido a la «nada» son actos poéticos de los que puede surgir un objeto-arquetipo indisociable de los distintos *ciclos de vida* que lo atraviesan. La ambigua materialidad de la silla *Broom* es deudora del pasado de los desechos, mientras que su intemporalidad formal y su robustez son sinónimos de futuro.//M.S.

Conceived with "less style, less design, less material and less energy," the single-block, stackable *Broom* chair is functional, comfortable and highly resistant, as well as expressing committed, ethical values. In 2010, Starck revolutionized the concept of the ecological by restructuring industrial production to recycle waste at source. Thanks to the collection of material thrown out in sawmills and industrial plastic factories, he obtained a recycled composite, composed of 75% polypropylene waste and 15% wood-fibre chips and powder, reinforced by 10% glass fibre.

Arising as it does in the context of innovation, the *Broom* series of chairs embodies an aesthetically ecological approach to the object, reducing waste, energy expenditures and CO_2 emissions. The name *Broom* calls to mind an image, that of "a person who picks up a modest broom and begins to clean up the studio, and with specks of dust is able to make magic." For Starck, sweeping and gathering what has been reduced to "nothing" is the poetic act at the beginning of the object-archetype, inseparable from the various *life cycles* running through it. The ambiguous material nature of the *Broom* chair pays tribute to the history of remnants, while its formal timelessness and robust body are synonymous of the future.//M.S.

Silla *Broom*
2010
Silla fabricada a partir de elementos de desecho industrial reciclados:
75% de polipropileno reciclado,
15% de serrín de madera reciclada,
10% de fibra de vidrio
48 × 50 × 83 cm; altura del asiento: 43 cm
Fabricante: Emeco, Hanover, Pensilvania, Estados Unidos
Donación de Emeco, 2017

***Broom* chair**
2010
Chair made from recycled industrial debris
75% recycled polypropylene,
15% recycled wood powder,
10% glass fibre
48 × 50 × 83 cm; seat height: 43 cm
Producer: Emeco, Hanover (PA), USA
Gift of Emeco, 2017

Disco duro
Blade Runner
Blade Runner external hard drive

En 2009, Starck diseñó para LaCie, una marca francesa de periféricos informáticos fundada por Philippe Spruch, dos discos duros externos, *Starck Desktop Hard Drive* y *Starck Mobile Hard Drive*. Estas unidades de disco duro, con una cobertura de aluminio, están equipadas con una superficie sensible al tacto. Ya en 1992, Starck había diseñado para D2, la primera empresa de Philippe Spruch, el disco duro externo *Apollo*, fabricado en aluminio.

En 2013, Starck volvió a colaborar con la marca creando un nuevo disco duro: *LaCie Blade Runner*. Este dispositivo de cuatro terabytes, producido en una edición limitada de 9.999 ejemplares, es único en su forma. El armazón del dispositivo consiste en un núcleo de metal antropomórfico y una carcasa compuesta de una serie de tiras de aluminio que actúan como radiador. El adaptador externo se encuentra fuera de la máquina, en la parte inferior, de modo que los cables de alimentación se sitúan discretamente entre las aletas y no perturban la uniformidad estética y funcional del dispositivo.//M.V.

In 2009, working for LaCie, a French manufacturer of computer peripherals created by Philippe Spruch, Starck conceived two external hard drives, *Starck Desktop Hard Drive* and *Starck Mobile Hard Drive*. These hard drives, with an aluminium casing, feature a touch sensitive, reactive tactile surface. In 1992 Starck had already designed the external hard drive *Apollo* for D2 (Philippe Spruch's first company), also made in aluminium.

In 2010, this collaboration with Starck was renewed with the creation of a new hard drive: the *Blade Runner*. This four-terabyte peripheral, produced in a limited edition of 9,999 units, has a completely original shape. The body of the device is an anthropomorphic metallic core, with a hard, metallic exterior made up of aluminium strips wrapped around the outside, serving as a radiator. The external adaptor is found on the outside of the device, on its lower side, so that the cables move discreetly between the fins and do not alter the visual and functional homogeneity of the device.//M.V.

Disco duro *Blade Runner*
2011
Exterior de aluminio
14,1 × 19,3 × 7,4 cm
Fabricante: LaCie, París, Francia
Colección Philippe Starck

Blade Runner **external hard drive**
2011
Aluminium casing
14.1 × 19.3 × 7.4 cm
Producer: LaCie, Paris, France
Philippe Starck Collection

Butaca *Uncle Jim*

Uncle Jim armchair

En 2011, Philippe Starck realizó para la firma italiana Kartell la colección *Aunts and Uncles*, una serie de muebles que incluye un sofá (*Uncle Jack*), una butaca (*Uncle Jim*), una silla (*Uncle Jo*), una otomana (*Uncle Otto*), una mesa de comedor (*Aunt Jamy*) y una consola (*Aunt Maggy*). Cada una de estas piezas fue diseñada en policarbonato transparente y monobloque gracias a un proceso de moldeado por inyección de plástico, un método que permite obtener muebles ligeros y sólidos.

El sofá *Uncle Jack* ostenta un récord en términos de moldeado por inyección, debido a su tamaño de más de dos metros de largo. El diseño de la forma del molde es fruto de cuatro años de investigación. En cuanto a la butaca *Uncle Jim*, su respaldo ancho y largo, su asiento curvado y sus brazos hacen de él un mueble cálido a la vez que minimalista.

El título de la colección remite a las fuentes de inspiración utilizadas por Starck a la hora de diseñar la serie: el recuerdo de sus tíos y tías realizando sus tareas domésticas o simplemente descansando, sentados en amplias y confortables butacas, leyendo o contando historias, o bien sentados alrededor de grandes mesas familiares.//M.V.

In 2011 Philippe Starck made the collection "Aunts and Uncles" for the Italian design company Kartell, a furniture set including a couch (*Uncle Jack*), an armchair (*Uncle Jim*), a chair (*Uncle Jo*), an ottoman (*Uncle Otto*), a dining table (*Aunt Jamy*) and a console (*Aunt Maggy*). Each of these pieces was designed in transparent single-block polycarbonate, thanks to the injected plastic moulding procedure, ideal for making furniture that is light and solid at the same time.

The *Uncle Jack* couch broke a record in terms of injection moulding, in that the piece is ten metres long. The conception of the mould shape was the consequence of four years of research. As for the *Uncle Jim* armchair, its high, wide backrest, curved seat and armrests give us a warm yet simplified piece of furniture.

The title of this collection recalls Starck's sources of inspiration, conceived from the memory of his uncles and aunts, whether taking a breather from their domestic chores or simply unwinding, seated in large, comfortable armchairs, reading, telling stories, or just as well sitting down around large, dining room tables.//M.V.

Butaca *Uncle Jim*
2011
Policarbonato
72 × 68 x 103 cm; altura del asiento: 43 cm
Fabricante: Kartell, Noviglio, Italia
Donación de Kartell, 2017

***Uncle Jim* armchair**
2011
Polycarbonate
72 × 68 x 103 cm; seat height: 43 cm
Producer: Kartell, Noviglio, Italy
Gift of Kartell, 2017

Silla *Misa Joy*

Misa Joy chair

TOG-AllCreatorsTOGether es una comunidad creativa abierta que apuesta por el futuro del diseño personalizable en la era de la democratización de la impresión 3D y de los Fab Lab. La producción de mobiliario ha adquirido una nueva dimensión a raíz de la creación de la marca de colaboración italo-brasileña en 2014. Para Philippe Starck, TOG es un estado de ánimo político, que reúne los mundos «de la alta tecnología industrial, la producción en masa y la artesanía». Guiado por una conciencia ética, Starck busca soluciones innovadoras frente al consumismo y la crisis ecológica. Así, *Misa Joy* es un objeto «interactivo y participativo» que el usuario puede hacer suyo.

Como la icónica *Sandows Chair* de René Herbst, esta silla tiene un respaldo de tiras de elastómero desmontables e intercambiables. Su estructura, que queda totalmente al descubierto, se fabrica en una gama de seis colores y viene acompañada de accesorios presentados en doce tonos. El asiento, simple y básico, está diseñado en policarbonato moldeado por inyección, el único método de alta calidad apto para la producción en masa y a bajo coste. *Misa Joy* es un objeto democrático y duradero, que destaca por su carácter lúdico y personalizable.//M.S.

TOG – AllCreatorsTOGether is a creative community that believes in the future of customizable design, while encouraging the democratization of 3D printing and Fab Labs. Furniture production has taken on a new dimension since the creation of the collaborative Italo-Brazilian brand in 2014. For Philippe Starck, TOG is a political spiritual state, uniting the worlds of "high industrial technology, mass production and craft practices". Guided by an ethical conscience, Starck is on a quest for innovative solutions in the face of consumerism and the ecological crisis. *Misa Joy* is thus an "interactive and participative" object the user is encouraged to appropriate.

Recalling the emblematic *Sandows Chair* by René Herbst, this chair has a backrest conceived in moveable, interchangeable elastomer strips. The line is produced in a set of six colours, accompanied by accessories played out in twelve tones. The seat is sober and elementary, and is made using injection moulding polycarbonate, itself of very high quality, making it possible to produce industrially at low cost. *Misa Joy* is a durable, democratic object, seducing us with its fun-loving, personable character.//M.S.

Silla *Misa Joy*

2012
Silla apilable translúcida
Respaldo de cadena de elastómeros desmontable, asiento de policarbonato transparente
83 × 43 × 56 cm
Fabricante: TOG, Milán, Italia
Colección Philippe Starck

***Misa Joy* chair**

2012
Transparent stackable chair
Elastomeric wire backrest, transparent polycarbonate seat
83 × 43 × 56 cm
Producer: TOG, Milan, Italy
Philippe Starck Collection

M.A.S.S. (Snow).
Starckbike with Moustache

M.A.S.S. (Snow).
Starckbike with Moustache

Como usuario incondicional de las dos ruedas, Philippe Starck considera la bicicleta una de las pocas producciones del intelecto humano comprometida «con la desmaterialización, síntoma de nuestra civilización». Además de *Pibal*, una bicicleta urbana de una ergonomía revolucionaria diseñada para la ciudad de Burdeos en 2012, la colección *M.A.S.S.* cuenta con cuatro bicicletas eléctricas, llamadas *Mud*, *Asphalt*, *Sand* y *Snow* en referencia a las especificaciones técnicas que las caracterizan.

Snow es al mismo tiempo una BTT eléctrica y un objeto de recreo destinado al placer de conducir por paisajes nevados y montañosos. Formada por un cuadro de aluminio de la más alta calidad y de tubos de espesor variable, esta bicicleta queda al desnudo. Su horquilla monobrazo de aluminio extruido permite una evacuación óptima de la nieve, mientras que sus ruedas, gruesas y adherentes, ponen de manifiesto su capacidad de adaptarse a los terrenos más hostiles. Cuenta, además, con acabados estéticos y funcionales: un forro sintético que protege la batería de las temperaturas extremas, así como los elementos de cuero de los puños del manillar y de la silla, hacen de esta bicicleta un objeto elegante y confortable en el que la alta tecnología y la alternativa ecológica van de la mano de la movilidad.//M.S.

A dedicated user of two-wheeled vehicles, Philippe Starck considers the bicycle to be one of the rare productions of committed human intelligence, "along the path of dematerialization, symptom of our civilization." After *Pibal*, in 2012, an urban bike conceived for the City of Bordeaux with revolutionary ergonomics, the *M.A.S.S.* collection is made up of four electrically assisted bicycles (EABs), called *Mud*, *Asphalt*, *Sand* and *Snow*, referencing the technical specificities each is designed for.

Snow is both an electrically assisted mountain bike and a leisure vehicle, dedicated to the pleasure of cycling through snowy, mountain landscapes. Composed of a high-quality aluminium frame and variable-width tyres, this bike has been laid bare. The fork and handlebars, in extruded aluminium, allow for optimal movement through snow, as the wide, gripping tyres confirm its capacity to adapt to the most hostile of terrains. Attractively functional finishing is featured: the synthetic, fur cover protecting the battery from extreme temperatures, as well as other leather features on the handlebar grips and the saddle, turns this bicycle into a comfortably elegant object, where advanced, alternative, environmentally sound technique finds an ally in mobility.//M.S.

M.A.S.S. (Snow).
Starckbike with Moustache
2012
Bastidor de aluminio de alta calidad, tubos extruidos hidroformados de espesor variable, ruedas de carbono, sistema VTT eléctrico, horquilla RockShox, Bluto monobrazo, e-bike
Tamaños: S/41 (1,55-1,70 m); M/47 (1,68-1,85 m); L/53 (1,83-1,95 m) aprox.
Fabricante: Moustache Bikes, Golbey, Francia
Donación de Moustache Bikes, 2017

M.A.S.S. (Snow).
Starckbike with Moustache
2012
High-quality aluminium frame, extruded hydroformed tubes in variable thickness, carbon wheels, electric VTT system, RockShox Bluto fork, EAB
Size S/41 (1.55 to 1.70 m); M/47 (1.68 to 1.85 m); L/53 (1.83 to 1.95 m), approximately
Manufacturer: Moustache Bikes, Golbey, France
Gift of Moustache Bikes, 2017

Lámpara *Bon Jour*

Bon Jour lamp

En 2013, Philippe Starck diseñó *Bon Jour*, una serie de lámparas de tipo evolutivo y personalizable para la firma italiana Flos. En la línea de sus propuestas anteriores (lámpara *Miss Sissi*, 1991), Starck recurrió a la riqueza del tópico y al juego mental. En ese sentido, el objeto se presenta de tal modo «que cada cual se imagina inconscientemente una lámpara»: una pantalla cónica, un pie y una base.

La elegancia intemporal y etérea de la colección *Bon Jour* se basa en la voluntad de mejorar tecnológica y estéticamente el objeto. Su base desnuda y alargada, casi inmaterial, rematada con una pantalla en forma de cono truncado, es personalizable, gracias a una gran variedad de accesorios y acabados intercambiables que permiten adaptar la lámpara al gusto de cada usuario.

Este modelo ofrece dos versiones: una lámpara de mesa y una lámpara portátil autónoma recargable por cable microUSB, en formato reducido. Su luz difusa es producto de una tecnología innovadora, la Edge Lighting Led, que permite ajustar la intensidad lumínica y mejorar la difusión térmica, una garantía de durabilidad.//M.S.

In 2013, Philippe Starck designed *Bon Jour*, a series of lamps with a progressive, customizable design made by the Italian firm Flos. In a line of continuity with previous experiences (such as *Miss Sissi*, 1991), it draws on the richness of common places and mental games. As evident here, the object is to achieve "what anyone might unconsciously imagine to be a lamp": a conical lamp shade, an upright, a base.

The timeless, ethereal elegance of the *Bon Jour* collection emerges from the will to improve the object technologically and aesthetically. The bare, elongated base, almost immaterial, is capped by a conical, truncated lampshade, customizable thanks to a large variety of accessories and interchangeable finishing options, responding to each individual set of tastes.

The model is available in two versions: as a table lamp or in miniature form as a portable, autonomous lamp, rechargeable with a small USB cable. The soft light coming from this lamp is obtained by use of innovative Edge Lighting LEDs, allowing the intensity to be adjusted while improving heat distribution, a true measure of durability.//M.S.

Lámpara *Bon Jour*
2013
Led, cromo, plástico, inyección color, cable eléctrico, bombilla tipo EDGE LIGHTING 2700 K, 13 W
Grande: 41 × 28,3 cm; diámetro de base: 21,2 cm. Pequeña: 27 × 9,01 cm; diámetro de base: 10,3 cm
Fabricante: Flos, Bovezzo, Italia
Donación de Flos, 2017

Bon Jour lamp
2013
LED lighting, chrome, plastic, injected colour, electric cable, Edge Lighting 2700K, 13 W
Large: 41 × 28.3 cm; base diameter, 21.2 cm. Small: 27 × 9.01 cm; base diameter, 10.3 cm.
Producer: Flos, Bovezzo, Italy
Gift of Flos, 2017

Sandalias
Ipanema with Starck
Ipanema with Starck sandals

En 2013, Starck comenzó a desarrollar un concepto de sandalias para la marca brasileña Ipanema. La primera colección, que vio la luz en 2015, consta de un conjunto de cuatro modelos con tiras y suelas de plástico, disponibles en doce colores (entre ellos, verde, naranja y rosa), que forman un total de cuarenta y ocho combinaciones posibles. Las sandalias se elaboran en fábricas brasileñas éticas y ecorresponsables, a partir de un 30% de material plástico reciclado por inyección. Son 100% reciclables, lo que hace de ellas un producto ecológico, además de accesible a todos los públicos, que combina la ligereza con un diseño minimalista y orgánico.

«La colección *Ipanema with Starck* explora el territorio de la elegancia, de la inteligencia y de lo mínimo. Cuando la elegancia está al alcance de todos por unos cuantos dólares o euros, ya no se trata de magia, sino de un milagro moderno», afirma Philippe Starck. En este sentido, le parece coherente imaginar que los pies que nos sostienen a lo largo de toda una vida tengan una «influencia directa en el bienestar del cuerpo y de la cabeza». Starck ha concedido, de hecho, una gran importancia a la fabricación del material y al diseño de la sandalia, buscando la máxima comodidad, sensualidad y armonía en relación a la anatomía del pie.//M.V.

In 2013, Starck began to develop a sandal concept for the Brazilian brand Ipanema, with the line launched in 2015. The sandals feature a set of four models featuring plastic straps and soles, available in twelve colour combinations derived from green, orange and pink, making forty-eight possible variations. They are produced in Brazilian factories dedicated to ethical, ecologically responsible production, and are made from 30% recycled plastic material by injection moulding; they are fully recyclable themselves, making them an environmentally sound product accessible to everyone, combining lightness with a minimalist, organic design.

"The Ipanema with Starck collection explores the domain of elegance as grounded in intelligence and minimum expression. When elegance is accessible for a few dollars or euros, it is no longer magic at work, it is a modern miracle," explains Philippe Starck. In this regard, it seems that, for the creator, it was a question of imagining the feet holding us up throughout our lives, "directly influencing the wellbeing of both body and mind". Thus Starck put great emphasis on the importance of how the material was made and the sandal's design, as he sought comfort, sensuality and a harmonious relation with the foot's anatomy.//M.V.

Sandalias *Ipanema with Starck*
2013
Plástico y plástico reciclado,
edición en doce colores
Todas las tallas
Fabricante: Ipanema,
Río de Janeiro, Brasil
Colección Philippe Starck

Ipanema with Starck sandals
2013
Plastic and recycled plastic,
edition in 12 colours
All sizes
Producer: Ipanema,
Rio de Janeiro, Brazil
Philippe Starck Collection

Auriculares *Zik 3*

Zik 3 headset

Philippe Starck diseñó estos dispositivos acústicos y portátiles haciendo uso de las tecnologías más avanzadas y de un acercamiento sensible al sonido. La búsqueda de una experiencia sensorial inédita está en la base del proyecto *Zik* de Parrot, que encarna por sí mismo las aspiraciones al movimiento y a la movilidad, así como el deseo de una ergonomía intuitiva.

Considerados como un auténtico milagro tecnológico, los *Zik 3* son unos auriculares portátiles de diseño minimalista equipados con un potente procesador digital, que garantiza una reproducción musical armoniosa. Como sus predecesores (*Zik* y *Zik 2.0*), constan de un arco metálico de aluminio anodizado en cuyos extremos se sostienen dos cascos ovalados negros y confortables de cuero sintético graneado o texturizado.

Concebidos como una extensión de nuestro cuerpo, los *Zik 3* presentan un sistema de reducción adaptable del ruido que garantiza un confort de escucha adaptado al tumultuoso estilo de vida urbano. El *Street Mode* permite escuchar música y recibir llamadas en modo manos libres, gracias a su tecnología Voz HD. Los *Zik 3* son compatibles con los relojes inteligentes y las estaciones de carga por inducción (Qi). Un panel de control táctil intuitivo situado en el auricular derecho permite controlar el volumen, los temas musicales o las llamadas.//M.S.

Philippe Starck conceives objects combining portability and acoustics by relying on highly advanced technologies and a sensitive approach to sound. Research into a fresh sensorial experience is at the heart of the *Zik* project, by Parrot, the expression of a will to movement and mobility, desire for intuitive ergonomics.

Considered a veritable technological miracle, *Zik 3* is a portable headset with a minimalist design, equipped with a digital processor that ensures harmonious musical reproduction. Like its predecessors (*Zik* and *Zik 2.0*), it is composed of an anodized aluminium arch, with two comfortable, black, oval earphones in synthetic leather, full-grain or textured, at both ends.

Conceived as an extension of our body, *Zik 3* has an adaptable noise adjuster for more comfortable listening amid tumultuous city life. The "Street Mode" makes it possible to listen to music and receive handsfree calls thanks to Voix HD technology. *Zik 3* is compatible with smartwatches and inductive charging pads (Qi). An intuitive tactile control panel on the right ear allows you to adjust the volume, the musical track or calls.//M.S.

Auriculares *Zik 3*
2013
Cuero mate graneado pespunteado, acabado cromado
20,2 × 17,5 × 3,93 cm
Fabricante: Parrot, París, Francia
Donación de Parrot, 2017

***Zik 3* headset**
2013
Matt leather, grained or overstitched, chrome finishing
20.2 × 17.5 × 3.93 cm
Producer: Parrot, Paris, France
Gift of Parrot, 2017

Champagne
Brut Nature 2009

Champagne
Brut Nature 2009

En septiembre de 2014, Philippe Starck y Louis Roederer presentaron su añada *Brut Nature 2009*, fruto de numerosos años de una colaboración inédita y transversal entre un creador y una bodega de champán bicentenaria. El resultado es un champán sin azúcares añadidos, producido en el corazón de las colinas arcilloso-calcáreas de Cumières, Hautvillers y Vertus, en Champaña, en la explotación vitícola de Louis Roederer.

Al diálogo iniciado por Frédéric Rouzaud, presidente y director general de la casa Louis Roederer, le siguió la creación de una excelente añada *Brut Nature 2009*.

El diseño de los estuches y las etiquetas de las botellas también es obra de Starck, quien quiso plasmar el carácter de este vino y el de aquellos que lo han producido: «sincero, espontáneo, sin artificios».

En 1998, y junto con el productor Jean-Pierre Fleury, Starck había experimentado ya con la producción de bebidas creando el continente, aunque no el contenido, de la botella de un champán *brut* elaborado con uva ecológica, embotellado por la bodega de Jean Pierre Fleury y seleccionado para OAO, una marca de comida ecológica creada por Starck.//M.V.

In September 2014, Philippe Starck and Louis Roederer presented their *Brut Nature 2009* cuvée, the result of years of a unique, crossover collaboration between a creator and a bicentenary champagne house. What we get is a champagne with no added sugar, produced in the heart of the chalky-clay slopes of Cumières, Hautvillers and Vertus, on the Louis Roederer estate in Champagne.

The dialogue, initiated by Frédéric Rouzaud, president and general manager of the house of Louis Roederer, led to the creation of a vintage *2009 Brut Nature* cuvée.

The boxed sets and the labels, also created by Philippe Starck, are true to the image of this wine house and what it produces: "sincere, spontaneous, without artifice".

In 1998, Starck had already experimented with the production of beverages for the producer Jean-Pierre Fleury, designing the container (and not what was in it): a bottle for a brut champagne made from ecologically produced grapes, developed on the estate of Jean-Pierre Fleury and selected by OAO, an ecological food brand created by Starck.//M.V.

Champagne	*Champagne*
Brut Nature 2009	*Brut Nature 2009*
Roederer y Starck	Roederer x Starck
Botella de champán	Bottle of Roederer
brut Roederer	champagne, brut
2014	2014
Cristal, cartón	Glass, cardboard
75 ml	75 ml
Fabricante: Roederer,	Producer: Roederer,
Reims, Francia	Reims, France
Colección Philippe Starck	Philippe Starck Collection

Perfumes
Starck Paris

Starck Paris perfumes

En 2014, Philippe Starck crea la marca Starck Paris y presenta la colección *Peau*, compuesta por tres fragancias elaboradas en colaboración con tres grandes maestros perfumistas, a modo de poemas olfativos conceptuales de los que Starck sería «el guía espiritual». Creado junto con Dominique Ropion, *Peau de soie* es un perfume cuya feminidad se despliega alrededor de un corazón masculino, poniendo de manifiesto la diferencia entre la superficie y el núcleo, en el cual se expresa la realidad misteriosa de la mujer. *Peau de pierre*, concebido junto con Daphné Bugey, es un perfume masculino que revela en su interior la parte femenina del hombre. *Peau d'ailleurs*, creado junto con Annick Ménardo, es indefinible e inaprensible, una evasión hacia el territorio infinito de la desmaterialización, hacia una «tierra incógnita».

Feliz de desprenderse de la materia, Starck se había negado en un principio a diseñar el frasco. Finalmente optó por un diseño mínimo: rectángulos de vidrio minimalistas. Así como las fragancias se complementan entre sí y resuenan en armonía, los frascos se extienden visualmente para crear, al colocar los perfumes uno junto al otro, una escultura etérea, una forma orgánica y multicolor suspendida dentro de un continente desmaterializado. «Trabajar lo intangible, explorar la abstracción, hacer visible lo invisible, hacer vibrar el aire, colorear la vida, crear conexiones *mágicas, sumergirse en la poesía*; estos son los retos que me lanzo a *mí* mismo a través del perfume», afirma Starck.//M.S.

In 2014, Philippe Starck created the brand Starck Paris and presented the *Peau* collection, made up of three fragrances elaborated in collaboration with three great master perfumers: fragrances conceived as conceptual olfactory poems, where Starck would be "the conscientious director". Made in collaboration with Dominique Ropion, *Peau de soie* is a perfume where femininity is unveiled near the heart of a man, in a two-sided dialogue between surface and centre, where the mysterious reality of woman finds expression. *Peau de pierre*, conceived with Daphné Bugey, is a perfume for men, which essentially reveals the feminine side of man. *Peau d'ailleurs*, designed with Annick Ménardo, is undefinable and inconceivable, taking flight towards the infinite territory of dematerialization, towards a Terra Incognita.

Pleased to abandon strict materiality, at first Starck refused to design the bottles. Finally, he chose a minimalist solution, with simple glass rectangles. As the fragrances are complementary, resonating harmoniously, the bottles play this out visually, with the aim of creating an ethereal sculpture when the perfumes are placed side by side: a colourfully organic shape in suspension within a dematerialized flask. "Work on the intangible, explore abstraction, make the invisible visible, get the air to vibrate, colour life itself, conjure up magical lines, immerse oneself in poetry: these are the challenges I made for myself with these perfumes," states Starck.//M.S.

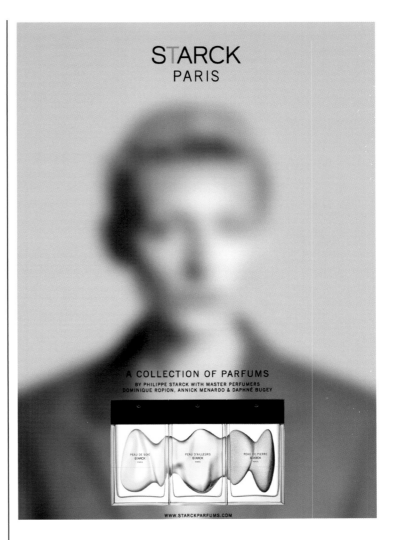

Perfumes *Starck Paris*
2014
Vidrio, materia orgánica,
perfume (alcohol)
Tres frascos de 90 ml
Fabricante: Starck Paris,
París, Francia
Colección Peau
Colección Philippe Starck

Starck Paris **perfumes**
2014
Glass, organic material,
perfume (alcohol)
Three 90 ml flasks
Producer: Starck Paris,
Paris, France
Peau Collection
Philippe Starck Collection

Exposición
Exhibition

Starck, dibujos secretos
4.000 croquis desvelados

Starck, Secrets Drawings
4,000 Unveiled Sketches

Centre Pompidou Málaga
10 de mayo de 2017 – 1 de octubre de 2017
10 May 2017 – 1 October 2017

Marie-Ange Brayer
Comisaria, conservadora jefe de la Colección Diseño, Mnam-Cci / Curator, Chief Curator of Architecture, Mnam-Cci

Veronica Ortega Lo Cascio
Comisaria adjunta / Assistant Curator

Claire Both
Responsable de colecciones / Collections Manager

Mélissa Etave
Registro de obras / Register

Barthélémy Seillan
Registro de exposición / Exhibition Space Manager

Marc Mameaux
Electromecánico / Electrical Engineer

Isabelle Prieur
Restauracion / Art Conservation

Alain Bova
Bruno Supervil
Embalaje / Packing

GAP Design
Montaje de los diseños / Assembly Company

Matthias Planche
Registro de la reserva / Registrar

El Taller
Juan Alberto Garcia de Cubas y/and **Juan Enrique Alvarez**
Arquitectura y escenografía / Architecture and Scenography

José Luis Suárez-Barcena
Juan Miguel Crespillo López
Enrique Guerra Navarro
Montaje / Assembly

Catálogo
Catalogue

Marie-Ange Brayer
Dirección de la publicación / Editor

Veronica Ortega Lo Cascio
Coordinación editorial / Editorial Co-ordination

Amarante Szidon
Coordinación editorial / Editorial Co-ordination

Marion Guibert
Mathilde Vallé
Marie Siguier
Textos / Notes

Perrine Renaud
Documentación iconográfica / Image Research

Georges Meguerditchian
Philippe Migeat
Bertrand Prévost
Hervé Véronèse
Fotógrafos / Photographers

Éditions du Centre Pompidou

Nicolas Roche
Director / Director

Claire de Cointet
Jefa del Servicio Editorial / Head of Publishing

Françoise Marquet
Responsable del Servicio Editorial / Editorial Manager

Élise Albenque
Jefa del Servicio Comercial / Head of Sales

Matthias Battestini
Responsable de ingresos y contratos / Receipts and
Contracts Manager

Queremos expresar nuestro sincero agradecimiento a
We would like to express our sincere gratitude to:

Philippe Starck y / and **Jasmine Starck**
Mahaut Champetier de Ribes
Mimouna Khaldi
Marlène Carincotte

Queremos agradecer particularamente a
We want to thank specially:

Alessi
Driade
Emeco
Flos
Hansgrohe
Kartell
Magis
Moustache Bikes
Robinson Ferreux Maeght
Starck Paris
Soundwalk

También damos las gracias a
We also want to thank:

Elsa Insergueix
Olivia Schmitt
Service des Collections / Documentalistas
Christine Devos
Juliette Dignat

Turner
Edición y producción / Edition and production

Comando-G
Diseño gráfico / Graphic design

la correccional
Traducción / Translation

Créditos fotográficos / Photographic credits
© Centre Pompidou, MNAM-CCI / Dist. RMN-GP;
photo Bertrand Prevost: p. 54
© Centre Pompidou, MNAM-CCI / Dist. RMN-GP;
photo Georges Meguerditchian: pp. 51 (derecha / right),
52, 53, 55, 56
© Starck Network: pp. 18-44, 51 (izquierda / left), 57-75

ISBN: 978-84-16714-55-1
DL: M-22122-2017

Mindset
Mathematics
Visualizing and Investigating
Big Ideas

Jo Boaler

Jen Munson

Cathy Williams

JB JOSSEY-BASS™
A Wiley Brand

Published by Jossey-Bass
A Wiley Brand
535 Mission Street, 14th Floor, San Francisco, CA 94105-3253—www.josseybass.com

Jossey-Bass books and products are available through most bookstores. To contact Jossey-Bass directly call our Customer Care Department within the U.S. at 800-956-7739, outside the U.S. at 317-572-3986, or fax 317-572-4002.

Wiley publishes in a variety of print and electronic formats and by print-on-demand. Some material included with standard print versions of this book may not be included in e-books or in print-on-demand. If this book refers to media such as a CD or DVD that is not included in the version you purchased, you may download this material at http://booksupport.wiley.com. For more information about Wiley products, visit www.wiley.com.

The Visualize, Play, and Investigate icons are used under license from Shutterstock.com and the following arists: Blan-k, Marish, and SuzanaM.

Library of Congress Cataloging-in-Publication Data

Names: Boaler, Jo, 1964– author. | Munson, Jen, 1977– author. | Williams,
     Cathy, 1962– author.
Title: Mindset mathematics : visualizing and investigating big ideas, grade 6
     / Jo Boaler, Jen Munson, Cathy Williams.
Description: First edition. | San Francisco : Jossey-Bass, [2019] | Includes
     index.
Identifiers: LCCN 2018040498 (print) | LCCN 2018049961 (ebook) | ISBN
     9781119358770 (Adobe PDF) | ISBN 9781119358671 (ePub) | ISBN 9781119358831
     (pbk.)
Subjects: LCSH: Games in mathematics education. | Mathematics–Study and
     teaching (Elementary)–Activity programs. | Sixth grade (Education)
Classification: LCC QA20.G35 (ebook) | LCC QA20.G35 B6296 2019 (print) | DDC
     372.7/044–dc23
LC record available at https://lccn.loc.gov/2018040498

Cover design by Wiley
Cover image: © Marish/Shutterstock-Eye; © Kritchanut/iStockphoto-Background
Printed in the United States of America

FIRST EDITION

PB Printing   V10006485_112818

Contents

To all those teachers pursuing a mathematical mindset journey with us.

Introduction

I still remember the moment when Youcubed, the Stanford center I direct, was conceived. I was at the Denver NCSM and NCTM conferences in 2013, and I had arranged to meet Cathy Williams, the director of mathematics for Vista Unified School District. Cathy and I had been working together for the past year improving mathematics teaching in her district. We had witnessed amazing changes taking place, and a filmmaker had documented some of the work. I had recently released my online teacher course, called How to Learn Math, and been overwhelmed by requests from tens of thousands of teachers to provide them with more of the same ideas. Cathy and I decided to create a website and use it to continue sharing the ideas we had used in her district and that I had shared in my online class. Soon after we started sharing ideas on the Youcubed website, we were invited to become a Stanford University center, and Cathy became the codirector of the center with me.

In the months that followed, with the help of one of my undergraduates, Montse Cordero, our first version of youcubed.org was launched. By January 2015, we had managed to raise some money and hire engineers, and we launched a revised version of the site that is close to the site you may know today. We were very excited that in the first month of that relaunch, we had five thousand visits to the site. At the time of writing this, we are now getting three million visits to the site each month. Teachers are excited to learn about the new research and to take the tools, videos, and activities that translate research ideas into practice and use them in their teaching.

1

Low-Floor, High-Ceiling Tasks

One of the most popular articles on our website is called "Fluency without Fear." I wrote this with Cathy when I heard from many teachers that they were being made to use timed tests in the elementary grades. At the same time, new brain science was emerging showing that when people feel stressed—as students do when facing a timed test—part of their brain, the working memory, is restricted. The working memory is exactly the area of the brain that comes into play when students need to calculate with math facts, and this is the exact area that is impeded when students are stressed. We have evidence now that suggests strongly that timed math tests in the early grades are responsible for the early onset of math anxiety for many students. I teach an undergraduate class at Stanford, and many of the undergraduates are math traumatized. When I ask them what happened to cause this, almost all of them will recall, with startling clarity, the time in elementary school when they were given timed tests. We are really pleased that "Fluency without Fear" has now been used across the United States to pull timed tests out of school districts. It has been downloaded many thousands of times and used in state and national hearings.

One of the reasons for the amazing success of the paper is that it does not just share the brain science on the damage of timed tests but also offers an alternative to timed tests: activities that teach math facts conceptually and through activities that students and teachers enjoy. One of the activities—a game called How Close to 100—became so popular that thousands of teachers tweeted photos of their students playing the game. There was so much attention on Twitter and other media that Stanford noticed and decided to write a news story on the damage of speed to mathematics learning. This was picked up by news outlets across the United States, including *US News & World Report,* which is part of the reason the white paper has now had so many downloads and so much impact. Teachers themselves caused this mini revolution by spreading news of the activities and research.

How Close to 100 is just one of many tasks we have on youcubed.org that are extremely popular with teachers and students. All our tasks have the feature of being "low floor and high ceiling," which I consider to be an extremely important quality for engaging all students in a class. If you are teaching only one student, then a mathematics task can be fairly narrow in terms of its content and difficulty. But whenever you have a group of students, there will be differences in their needs, and they will be challenged by different ideas. A low-floor, high-ceiling task is one in which everyone can engage, no matter what his or her prior understanding or knowledge, but also one that is open enough to extend to high levels, so that all students can be deeply challenged. In the last two years, we have launched an introductory week of mathematics lessons on our site that are open, visual, and low floor, high ceiling. These have been extremely popular with teachers; they have had approximately four million downloads and are used in 20% of schools across the United States.

In our extensive work with teachers around the United States, we are continually asked for more tasks that are like those on our website. Most textbook publishers seem to ignore or be unaware of research on mathematics learning, and most textbook questions are narrow and insufficiently engaging for students. It is imperative that the new knowledge of the ways our brains learn mathematics is incorporated into the lessons students are given in classrooms. It is for this reason that we chose to write a series of books that are organized around a principle of active student engagement, that reflect the latest brain science on learning, and that include activities that are low floor and high ceiling.

Youcubed Summer Camp

We recently brought 81 students onto the Stanford campus for a Youcubed summer math camp, to teach them in the ways that are encouraged in this book. We used open, creative, and visual math tasks. After only 18 lessons with us, the students improved their test score performance by an average of 50%, the equivalent of 1.6 years of school. More important, they changed their relationship with mathematics and started believing in their own potential. They did this, in part, because we talked to them about the brain science showing that

- There is no such thing as a math person—anyone can learn mathematics to high levels.
- Mistakes, struggle, and challenge are critical for brain growth.
- Speed is unimportant in mathematics.
- Mathematics is a visual and beautiful subject, and our brains want to think visually about mathematics.

All of these messages were key to the students' changed mathematics relationship, but just as critical were the tasks we worked on in class. The tasks and the messages about the brain were perfect complements to each other, as we told students they could learn anything, and we showed them a mathematics that was open, creative, and engaging. This approach helped them see that they could learn mathematics and actually do so. This book shares the kinds of tasks that we used in our summer camp, that make up our week of inspirational mathematics (WIM) lessons, and that we post on our site.

Before I outline and introduce the different sections of the book and the ways we are choosing to engage students, I will share some important ideas about how students learn mathematics.

Memorization versus Conceptual Engagement

Many students get the wrong idea about mathematics—exactly the wrong idea. Through years of mathematics classes, many students come to believe that their role in mathematics learning is to memorize methods and facts, and that mathematics success comes from memorization. I say this is exactly the wrong idea because there is actually very little to remember in mathematics. The subject is made up of a few big, linked ideas, and students who are successful in mathematics are those who see the subject as a set of ideas that they need to think deeply about. The Program for International Student Assessment (PISA) tests are international assessments of mathematics, reading, and science that are given every three years. In 2012, PISA not only assessed mathematics achievement but also collected data on students' approach to mathematics. I worked with the PISA team in Paris at the Organisation for Economic Co-operation and Development (OECD) to analyze students' mathematics approaches and their relationship to achievement. One clear result emerged from this analysis. Students approached mathematics in three distinct ways. One group approached mathematics by attempting to memorize the methods they had met; another group took a "relational" approach, relating new concepts to those they already knew; and a third group took a self-monitoring approach, thinking about what they knew and needed to know.

In every country, the memorizers were the lowest-achieving students, and countries with high numbers of memorizers were all lower achieving. In no country were memorizers in the highest-achieving group, and in some high- achieving countries such as Japan, students who combined self-monitoring and relational strategies outscored memorizing students by more than a year's worth of schooling. More detail on this finding is given in this *Scientific American* Mind article that I coauthored with a PISA analyst: https://www.scientificamerican.com/article/ why-math-education-in-the-u-s-doesn-t-add-up/.

Mathematics is a conceptual subject, and it is important for students to be thinking slowly, deeply, and conceptually about mathematical ideas, not racing through methods that they try to memorize. One reason that students need to think conceptually has to do with the ways the brain processes mathematics. When we learn new mathematical ideas, they take up a large space in our brain as the brain works out where they fit and what they connect with. But with time, as we move on with our understanding, the knowledge becomes compressed in the brain, taking up a very small space. For first graders, the idea of addition takes up a large space in their brains as they think about how it works and what it means, but for adults the idea of addition is compressed, and it takes up a small space. When adults are asked to add 2 and 3, for example, they can quickly and easily extract the compressed knowledge. William Thurston (1990), a mathematician who won the Field's Medal—the highest honor in mathematics—explains compression like this:

> Mathematics is amazingly compressible: you may struggle a long time, step by step, to work through the same process or idea from several approaches. But once you really understand it and have the mental perspective to see it as a whole, there is often a tremendous mental compression. You can file it away, recall it quickly and completely when you need it, and use it as just one step in some other mental process. The insight that goes with this compression is one of the real joys of mathematics.

You will probably agree with me that not many students think of mathematics as a "real joy," and part of the reason is that they are not compressing mathematical ideas in their brain. This is because the brain only compresses concepts, not methods. So if students are thinking that mathematics is a set of methods to memorize, they are on the wrong pathway, and it is critical that we change that. It is very important that students think deeply and conceptually about ideas. We provide the activities in this book that will allow students to think deeply and conceptually, and an essential role of the teacher is to give the students time to do so.

Mathematical Thinking, Reasoning, and Convincing

When we worked with our Youcubed camp students, we gave each of them journals to record their mathematical thinking. I am a big fan of journaling—for myself and my students. For mathematics students, it helps show them that mathematics is a subject for which we should record ideas and pictures. We can use journaling to encourage students to keep organized records, which is another important part of mathematics, and help them understand that mathematical thinking can be a long and slow process. Journals also give students free space—where they can be creative, share ideas, and feel ownership of their work. We did not write in the students' journals, as we wanted them to think of the journals as their space, not something that teachers wrote on. We gave students feedback on sticky notes that we stuck onto their work. The images in Figure I.1 show some of the mathematical records the camp students kept in their journals.

Another resource I always share with learners is the act of color coding—that is, students using colors to highlight different ideas. For example, when working on an algebraic task, they may show the x in the same color in an expression, in a graph, and in a picture, as shown in Figure I.2. When adding numbers, color coding may help show the addends (Figure I.3).

Color coding highlights connections, which are a really critical part of mathematics.

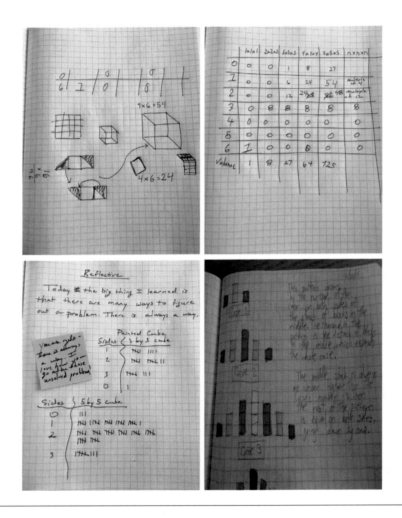

Figure I.1

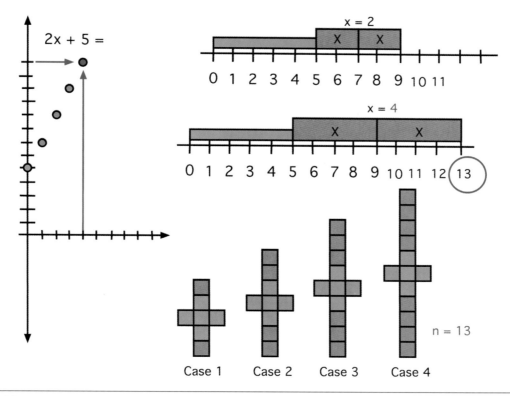

Figure I.2

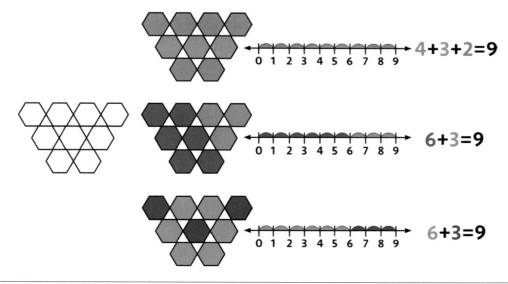

Figure I.3

Another important part of mathematics is the act of reasoning—explaining why methods are chosen and how steps are linked, and using logic to connect ideas. Reasoning is at the heart of mathematics. Scientists prove ideas by finding more cases that fit a theory, or countercases that contradict a theory, but mathematicians prove their work by reasoning. If students are not reasoning, then they are not really doing mathematics. In the activities of these books, we suggest a framework that encourages students to be convincing when they reason. We tell them that there are three levels of being convincing. The first, or easiest, level is to convince yourself of something. A higher level is to convince a friend. And the highest level of all is to convince a skeptic. We also share with students that they should be skeptics with one another, asking one another why methods were chosen and how they work. We have found this framework to be very powerful with students; they enjoy being skeptics, pushing each other to deeper levels of reasoning, and it encourages students to reason clearly, which is important for their learning.

We start each book in our series with an activity that invites students to reason about mathematics and be convincing. I first met an activity like this when reading Mark Driscoll's teaching ideas in his book *Fostering Algebraic Thinking*. I thought it was a perfect activity for introducing the skeptics framework that I had learned from a wonderful teacher, Cathy Humphreys. She had learned about and adapted the framework from two of my inspirational teachers from England: mathematician John Mason and mathematics educator Leone Burton. As well as encouraging students to be convincing, in a number of activities we ask students to prove an idea. Some people think of proof as a formal set of steps that they learned in geometry class. But the act of proving is really about connecting ideas, and as students enter the learning journey of proving, it is worthwhile celebrating their steps toward formal proof. Mathematician Paul Lockhart (2012) rejects the idea that proving is about following a set of formal steps, instead proposing that proving is "abstract art, pure and simple. And art is always a struggle. There is no systematic way of creating beautiful and meaningful paintings or sculptures, and there is also no method for producing beautiful and meaningful mathematical arguments" (p. 8). Instead of suggesting that students follow formal steps, we invite them to think deeply about mathematical concepts and make connections. Students will be given many ways to be creative when they prove and justify, and for reasons I discuss later, we always encourage and celebrate visual as well as numerical and algebraic justifications. Ideally, students will create visual, numerical, and algebraic representations and connect their ideas through color coding and through verbal explanations. Students are excited to experience mathematics in these ways, and they benefit from the opportunity to bring their individual ideas and creativity to the problem-solving and learning space. As students develop in their mathematical understanding, we can encourage them to extend and generalize their ideas through reasoning, justifying, and proving. This process deepens their understanding and helps them compress their learning.

Big Ideas

The books in the Mindset Mathematics Series are all organized around mathematical "big ideas." Mathematics is not a set of methods; it is a set of connected ideas that need to be understood. When students understand the big ideas in mathematics, the methods and rules fall into place. One of the reasons any set of curriculum standards is flawed is that standards take the beautiful subject of mathematics and its many connections, and divide it into small pieces that make the connections disappear. Instead of starting with the small pieces, we have started with the big ideas and important connections, and have listed the relevant Common Core curriculum standards within the activities. Our activities invite students to engage in the mathematical acts that are listed in the imperative Common Core practice standards, and they also teach many of the Common Core content standards, which emerge from the rich activities. Student activity pages are noted with a ⬡ and teacher activity pages are noted with a ▭.

Although we have chapters for each big idea, as though they are separate from each other, they are all intrinsically linked. Figure I.4 shows some of the connections between the ideas, and you may be able to see others. It is very

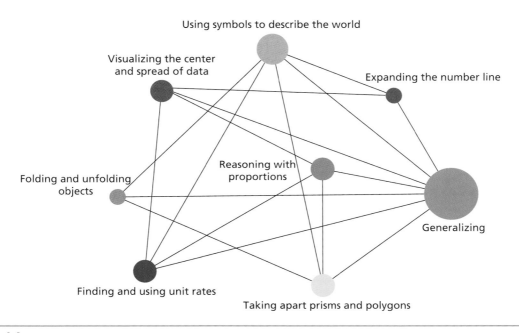

Figure I.4

important to share with students that mathematics is a subject of connections and to highlight the connections as students work. You may want to print the color visual of the different connections for students to see as they work. To see the maps of big ideas for all of the grades K through 8, find our paper "What Is Mathematical Beauty?" at youcubed.org.

Structure of the Book

Visualize. Play. Investigate. These three words provide the structure for each book in the series. They also pave the way for open student thinking, for powerful brain connections, for engagement, and for deep understanding. How do they do that? And why is this book so different from other mathematics curriculum books?

Visualize

For the past few years, I have been working with a neuroscience group at Stanford, under the direction of Vinod Menon, which specializes in mathematics learning. We have been working together to think about the ways that findings from brain science can be used to help learners of mathematics. One of the exciting discoveries that has been emerging over the last few years is the importance of visualizing for the brain and our learning of mathematics. Brain scientists now know that when we work on mathematics, even when we perform a bare number calculation, five areas of the brain are involved, as shown in Figure I.5.

Two of the five brain pathways—the dorsal and ventral pathways—are visual. The dorsal visual pathway is the main brain region for representing quantity. This may seem surprising, as so many of us have sat through hundreds of hours of mathematics classes working with numbers, while barely ever engaging visually with mathematics. Now brain scientists know that our brains "see" fingers when we calculate, and knowing fingers well—what they call finger perception—is critical for the development of an understanding of number. If you would like to read more about the importance of finger work in mathematics, look at the visual mathematics section of youcubed.org. Number lines are really helpful, as they provide the brain with a visual representation of number order. In one study, a mere four 15-minute sessions of students playing with a number line completely eradicated the differences between students from low-income and middle-income backgrounds coming into school (Siegler & Ramani, 2008).

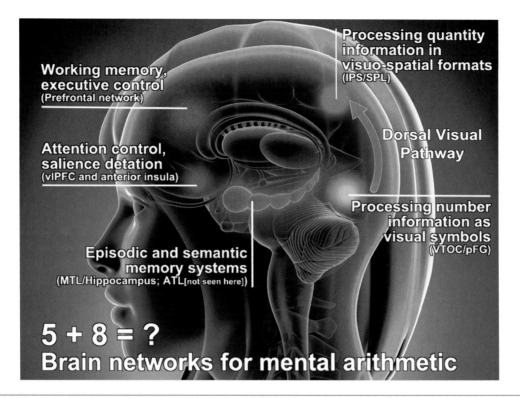

Figure I.5

Our brain wants to think visually about mathematics, yet few curriculum materials engage students in visual thinking. Some mathematics books show pictures, but they rarely ever invite students to do their own visualizing and drawing. The neuroscientists' research shows the importance not only of visual thinking but also of students' connecting different areas of their brains as they work on mathematics. The scientists now know that as children learn and develop, they increase the connections between different parts of the brain, and they particularly develop connections between symbolic and visual representations of numbers. Increased mathematics achievement comes about when students are developing those connections. For so long, our emphasis in mathematics education has been on symbolic representations of numbers, with students developing one area of the brain that is concerned with symbolic number representation. A more productive and engaging approach is to develop all areas of the brain that are involved in mathematical thinking, and visual connections are critical to this development.

In addition to the brain development that occurs when students think visually, we have found that visual activities are really engaging for students. Even students who think they are "not visual learners" (an incorrect idea) become fascinated and

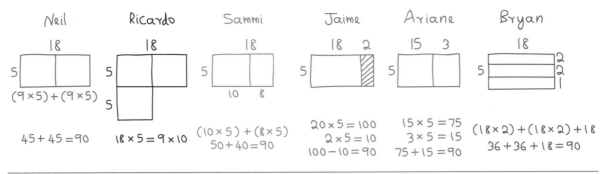

Figure I.6

think deeply about mathematics that is shown visually—such as the visual representations of the calculation 18 × 5 shown in Figure I.6.

In our Youcubed teaching of summer school to sixth- and seventh-grade students and in our trialing of Youcubed's WIM materials, we have found that students are inspired by the creativity that is possible when mathematics is visual. When we were trialing the materials in a local middle school one day, a parent stopped me and asked what we had been doing. She said that her daughter had always said she hated and couldn't do math, but after working on our tasks, she came home saying she could see a future for herself in mathematics. We had been working on the number visuals that we use throughout these teaching materials, shown in Figure I.7.

The parent reported that when her daughter had seen the creativity possible in mathematics, everything had changed for her. I strongly believe that we can give these insights and inspirations to many more learners with the sort of creative, open mathematics tasks that fill this book.

We have also found that when we present visual activities to students, the status differences that often get in the way of good mathematics teaching disappear. I was visiting a first-grade classroom recently, and the teacher had set up four different stations around the room. In all of them, the students were working on arithmetic. In one, the teacher engaged students in a mini number talk; in another, a teaching assistant worked on an activity with coins; in the third, the students played a board game; and in the fourth, they worked on a number worksheet. In each of the first three stations, the students collaborated and worked really well, but as soon as students went to the worksheet station, conversations changed, and in every group I heard statements like "This is easy," "I've finished," "I can't do this," and "Haven't you finished yet?" These status comments are unfortunate and off-putting for many students. I now try to present mathematical tasks without numbers as often as

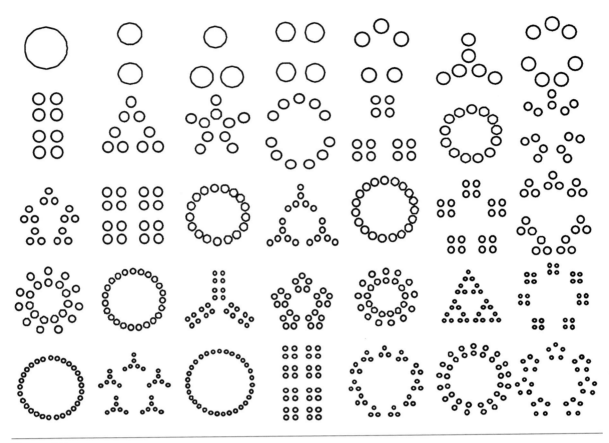

Figure I.7

possible, or I take out the calculation part of a task, as it is the numerical and calculational aspects that often cause students to feel less sure of themselves. This doesn't mean that students cannot have a wonderful and productive relationship with numbers, as we hope to promote in this book, but sometimes the key mathematical idea can be arrived at without any numbers at all.

Almost all the tasks in our book invite students to think visually about mathematics and to connect visual and numerical representations. This encourages important brain connections as well as deep student engagement.

Play

The key to reducing status differences in mathematics classrooms, in my view, comes from *opening* mathematics. When we teach students that we can see or approach any mathematical idea in different ways, they start to respect the different thinking of all students. Opening mathematics involves inviting students to see ideas differently, explore with ideas, and ask their own questions. Students can gain access to the same mathematical ideas and methods through creativity and exploration that they can by being taught methods that they practice. As well as reducing or removing status differences, open mathematics is more engaging for students. This is why we are inviting students, through these mathematics materials, to play with mathematics. Albert Einstein famously once said that "play is the highest form of research." This is because play is an opportunity for ideas to be used and developed in the service of something enjoyable. In the Play activities of our materials, students are invited to work with an important idea in a free space where they can enjoy the freedom of mathematical play. This does not mean that the activities do not teach essential mathematical content and practices—they do, as they invite students to work with the ideas. We have designed the Play activities to downplay competition and instead invite students to work with each other, building understanding together.

Investigate ?

Our Investigate activities add something very important: they give students opportunities to take ideas to the sky. They also have a playful element, but the difference is that they pose questions that students can explore and take to very high levels. As I mentioned earlier, all of our tasks are designed to be as low floor and high ceiling as possible, as these provide the best conditions for engaging all students, whatever their prior knowledge. Any student can access them, and students can take the ideas to high levels. We should always be open to being surprised by what our learners can do, and always provide all students with opportunities to take work to high levels and to be challenged.

A crucial finding from neuroscience is the importance of students struggling and making mistakes—these are the times when brains grow the most. In one of my meetings with a leading neuroscientist, he stated it very clearly: if students are not struggling, they are not learning. We want to put students into situations where they feel that work is hard, but within their reach. Do not worry if students ask questions that you don't know the answer to; that is a good thing. One of the damaging ideas that teachers and students share in education is that teachers of mathematics know everything. This gives students the idea that mathematics people are those who know a lot and never make mistakes, which is an incorrect and harmful message. It is good to say to your students, "That is a great question that we can all think about" or "I have never thought about that idea; let's investigate it together." It is even good to make mistakes in front of students, as it shows them that mistakes are an important part of mathematical work. As they investigate, they should be going to places you have never thought about—taking ideas in new directions and exploring uncharted territory. Model for students what it means to be a curious mathematics learner, always open to learning new ideas and being challenged yourself.

* * *

We have designed activities to take at least a class period, but some of them could go longer, especially if students ask deep questions or start an investigation into a cool idea. If you can be flexible about students' time on activities, that is ideal, or you may wish to suggest that students continue activities at home. In our teaching of these activities, we have found that students are so excited by the ideas that they take them home to their families and continue working on them, which is wonderful. At all times, celebrate deep thinking over speed, as that is the nature of real mathematical thought. Ask students to come up with creative representations of their ideas; celebrate their drawing, modeling, and any form of creativity. Invite your students into a journey of mathematical curiosity and take that journey with them, walking by their side as they experience the wonder of open, mindset mathematics.

References

Lockhart, P. (2012). *Measurement*. Cambridge, MA: Harvard University Press.

Siegler, R. S., & Ramani, G. B. (2008). Playing linear numerical board games promotes low income children's numerical development. *Developmental Science, 11*(5), 655–661. doi:10.1111/j.1467-7687.2008.00714.x

Thurston, W. (1990). Mathematical education. *Notices of the American Mathematical Society, 37*(7), 844–850.

Note on Materials

In middle schools, we often find that there is little use of manipulatives and that few may be available in the building for teachers to choose. But we believe, and extensive research supports, that all math learners benefit from mathematics that is visual, concrete, and modeled in multiple representations. Students need to physically create, draw, and construct mathematics to build deep understanding of what concepts represent and mean. Students need to interact with mathematics, manipulating representations to pose and investigate questions. Apps and digital games are another option, and we have found them to be valuable because they can be organized and manipulated with an unending supply. However, we want to emphasize that they should not be a replacement for the tactile experience of working with physical manipulatives. We support making different tools available for students to use as they see fit for the representation, and, following the activity, we encourage you to ask students to reflect on what the tools allowed them to see mathematically.

In our books for middle grades, you will find the same emphasis on visual mathematics and using manipulatives as in our elementary books, because these representations of mathematics are critical for all learners. If manipulatives are in short supply in your building, we encourage you to advocate for their purchase for the long-term benefit of your students. In the near term, you may be able to borrow the manipulatives we use in this book from your district's elementary schools.

Manipulatives and Materials Used in This Book

- **Snap cubes.** Snap or multilink cubes enable students to construct three-dimensional solids using cubic units. These are particularly useful in exploring volume and the connections between two- and three-dimensional space, but they can also be used for patterning, representing mathematical situations, and measurement.

- **Centimeter cubes.** Centimeter cubes enable students to explore volume while being precise about that volume using conventional units of measure. However, these are challenging for fine motor control because they don't attach to one another, which is why we like to use both these centimeter cubes and snap cubes as we explore volume.

- **Pattern blocks.** Pattern blocks give students opportunities to create tiling patterns, which in this book we use to explore rates, ratios, proportion, and representation with symbols. Pattern blocks are also useful for exploring angles and how they fit together and can be decomposed.

- **Cuisenaire rods.** While Cuisenaire rods are frequently used in elementary schools to decompose whole numbers and fractions, they also contain relationships that can be used to explore algebraic and symbolic thinking concretely. We prefer the rods that are not scored with individual units, allowing them to be assigned any value, not just whole numbers from 1 to 10, which supports algebraic thinking and flexibility.

- **Square tiles.** Square tiles are a flexible manipulative that can be used to literally represent square units for conceptualizing area and covering surfaces. They can also be used to represent patterns visually that are too often only represented symbolically, making them a useful algebraic manipulative.

- **Geometric solids.** Geometric solids allow students to touch, rotate, and sometimes decompose three-dimensional figures of different types. We use these in an optional extension, but we think they are a valuable addition to middle school mathematics classrooms.

- **Dice.** Dice are used for game play and generating data randomly. Here we reference typical six-sided dice, but we encourage you to explore the world of dice with different numbers of sides and values. Changing dice can change what ideas students have opportunities to explore.

- **Meter sticks, yardsticks, rulers, and/or measuring tape.** We use a variety of linear measurement tools to explore mathematical connections between measurement, data, and rates of change.

- **Stopwatches or timers.** Time is yet another dimension of measurement that students can explore in relation to questions of measurement, data, and rate of change. Students need experiences with both analog and digital measures of time, and continued use of analog clocks will support later work with circles and angles. We do not support using stopwatches and timers to record students' speed on math calculations.

- **Colors.** Color-coding work is a powerful tool to support decomposition, patterning, and connecting representations. We often ask that students have access to colors; we leave it up to you whether they are markers, colored pencils, or colored pens.

- **Adding machine tape.** Adding machine tape is an unsung hero of manipulatives. Students can create their own measurement tools, decompose linear spaces into units or fractions, construct number lines, fold and investigate symmetry, and connect all these ideas together. Further, adding machine tape can be made any length, written on, diagrammed, and color-coded. It is so inexpensive that students can make lots of mistakes and feel safe.

- **Patty paper.** Patty paper is like adding machine tape in that it is flexible and inexpensive, and supports mistakes. Patty paper is a thin, translucent paper used in the food industry to separate food items. Its advantages in mathematics are that it is square paper that can be folded, cut, written on, and seen through for tracing or comparing. Origami paper has many of these qualities, but it is typically more expensive, and it is not translucent.

- **Calculators.** Calculators are used as a resource in the book to enable students to focus on the bigger mathematical ideas, rather than spending their time performing calculations. Calculators are a tool that students need to know how to use, and they should increase students' access to big mathematical ideas.

- **Office supplies, such as paperclips, tape, glue sticks, and masking tape.** We use these across the book to construct charts, serve as markers in games or activities, mark spaces, display thinking, or piece together work.

Activities for Building Norms

Encouraging Good Group Work

We always use this activity before students work on math together, as it helps improve group interactions. Teachers who have tried this activity have been pleased by students' thoughtful responses and found the students' thoughts and words helpful in creating a positive and supportive environment. The first thing to do is to ask students, in groups, to reflect on things they don't like people to say or do in a group when they are working on math together. Students come up with quite a few important ideas, such as not liking people to give away the answer, to rush through the work, or to ignore other people's ideas. When students have had enough time in groups brainstorming, collect the ideas. We usually do this by making a What We Don't Like list or poster and asking each group to contribute one idea, moving around the room until a few good ideas have been shared (usually about 10). Then we do the same for the What We Do Like list or poster. It can be good to present the final posters to the class as the agreed-on classroom norms that you and they can reflect back on over the year. If any student shares a negative comment, such as "I don't like waiting for slow people," do not put it on the poster; instead use it as a chance to discuss the issue. This rarely happens, and students are usually very thoughtful and respectful in the ideas they share.

Activity	Time	Description/Prompt	Materials
Launch	5 min	Explain to students that working in groups is an important part of what mathematicians do. Mathematicians discuss their ideas and work together to solve challenging problems. It's important to work together, and we need to discuss what helps us work well together.	
Explore	10 min	Assign a group facilitator to make sure that all students get to share their thoughts on points 1 and 2. Groups should record every group member's ideas and then decide which they will share during the whole-class discussion. In your groups . . . 1. Reflect on the things you do not like people to say or do when you are working on math together in a group. 2. Reflect on the things you do like people to say or do when you are working on math together in a group.	• Paper • Pencil or pen
Discuss	10 min	Ask each group to share their findings. Condense their responses and make a poster so that the student ideas are visible and you can refer to them during the class.	Two to four pieces of large poster paper to collect the students' ideas

Paper Folding: Learning to Reason, Convince, and Be Skeptical

> Connection to CCSS
> 6.G.3
> 6.G.4

One of the most important topics in mathematics is reasoning. Whereas scientists prove or disprove ideas by finding cases, mathematicians prove their ideas by reasoning—making logical connections between ideas. This activity gives students an opportunity to learn to reason well by having to convince others who are being skeptical.

Before beginning the activity, explain to students that their role is to be convincing. The easiest person to convince is yourself. A higher level of being convincing is to convince a friend, and the highest level of all is to convince a skeptic. In this activity, the students learn to reason to the extent that they can convince a skeptic. Students should work in pairs and take turns to be the one convincing and the one being a skeptic.

Give each student a square piece of paper. If you already have 8.5 × 11 paper, you can ask them to make the square first.

The first challenge is for one of the students to fold the paper to make a right triangle that does not include any of the edges of the paper. They should convince their partner that it is a right triangle, using what she knows about right triangle to be convincing. The skeptic partner should ask lots of skeptical questions, such as "How do you know that this angle is 90 degress?" and not accept that they are because it looks like they are.

The partners should then switch roles, and the other student folds the paper into an equilateral triangle that does not include any of the edges of the paper. Their partner should be skeptical and push for high levels of reasoning.

The partners should then switch again, and the challenge is to fold the paper to make an isosceles triangle, again not using the edges of the paper.

The fourth challenge is to make a scalene triangle triangle. For each challenge, partners must reason and be skeptical.

When the task is complete, facilitate a whole-class discussion in which students discuss the following questions:

- Which was the most challenging task? Why?
- What was hard about reasoning and being convincing?
- What was hard about being a skeptic?

Activity	Time	Description/Prompt	Materials
Launch	5 min	Tell students that their role for the day is to be convincing and to be a skeptic. Ask students to fold a piece of paper into a rectangle that is not a square. Choose a student and model being a skeptic.	
Explore	10 min	Show students the task and explain that in each round, they are to solve the folding problem. In pairs, students alternate folding and reasoning and being the skeptic. After students convince themselves they have solved each problem, they switch roles and fold the next challenge. Give students square paper or ask them to start by making a square. The convincing challenges are as follows: 1. Fold your paper into a right triangle that does not include any edges of the paper. 2. Fold your paper into an equilateral triangle that does not include any edges of the paper. 3. Fold your paper into an isosceles triangle that does not include any edges of the paper. 4. Fold your paper into a scalene triangle that does not include any edges of the paper.	• One piece of 8.5" × 11" paper per student • Paper Folding worksheet for each student
Discuss	10 min	Discuss the activity as a class. Make sure to discuss the roles of convincer and skeptic.	

Paper Folding: Learning to Reason, Convince, and Be a Skeptic

1. Fold your paper into a right triangle that does not include any edges of the paper. Convince a skeptic that it is a right triangle.
    Reflection:

    Switch roles

2. Fold your paper into an equilateral triangle that does not include any edges of the paper. Convince a skeptic that it is an equilateral triangle.
    Reflection:

    Switch roles

3. Fold your paper into an isosceles triangle that does not include any edges of the paper. Convince a skeptic that it is an isosceles triangle.
    Reflection:

    Switch roles

4. Fold your paper into a scalene triangle that does not include any edges of the paper. Convince a skeptic that it is a scalene triangle.
    Reflection:

Taking Apart Prisms and Polygons

The mathematical concepts at the heart of this big idea are area and volume. Although these ideas call for students to learn through objects, holding them in their hands and exploring with them, many students are asked only to memorize formulas and so do not develop an understanding of area, volume, or the differences between them. In our Youcubed summer camp, we gave the students an activity with sugar cubes; they were invited to build different sized larger cubes with the sugar cubes. When we interviewed the students a year after they attended the camp, one of the boys told us that he now thinks about the sugar cubes every time he learns about volume, as they gave him a physical representation of a $1 \times 1 \times 1$ cube. His experience holding the cubes and building with them contributed to a deep understanding of volume that was powerful and enduring for him. In our Investigate activity, we invite the students to build with very similar cubes—snap cubes. In all of the activities, students are asked to build with two- and three-dimensional shapes.

In the Visualize activity, we ask students to find different ways to take apart two-dimensional complex shapes as they work to find area. We have used shapes that require students to reason about how to determine the area when its boundary doesn't fit exactly on a square grid. As students reason through determining the area, they also need to break the shape into other shapes they are familiar with, such as triangles and rectangles. This type of thinking is foundational for later work in geometry and calculus.

In the Play activity, we ask students to determine the area of a complex piece of artwork that is made from different polygons. We like to connect mathematics and art in our books, as it is important for students to see that mathematics can be beautiful, creative, and applied to all sorts of different real-world situations. Because of the uneven border of the shape, students will need to come up with different creative ways to find the area. This lesson also provides students opportunities to discuss estimation. In studies of mathematics in the world, estimation has been found to be one of the most used concepts and one that is undertaught in schools. We are sure your students will enjoy making their own piece of mathematical art.

In the Investigate activity, students build off the Visualize activity as they imagine complex two dimensional shapes as the bases of buildings. Students are asked to use multilink cubes to construct the buildings, giving them an important opportunity to understand volume. In this activity, we also provide an opportunity for students to work with rational numbers. Students in sixth grade are learning to expand their number system, yet questions in traditional textbooks often ask the students only to work with whole numbers. We have provided problems that use rational numbers, fractions, to support students' growth in understanding of both volume and rational numbers. Students are asked to visualize fractions of multilink cubes as they work to determine volume and connect the idea of volume to the idea of area for the shapes that they worked with in the Visualize activity. Students often have trouble understanding the difference between area and volume because they have not had enough experience spending time connecting their numbers with visual two- and three-dimensional models. We hope that this set of activities will provide time for fun and challenge together, and that students will get an enjoyable opportunity to struggle and to use their creativity in finding different ways to see and solve problems.

Jo Boaler

How Big Is the Footprint?

Snapshot

Students develop methods for finding the area of irregular polygons by exploring ways to decompose two-dimensional figures and reason about partial square units.

Connection to CCSS
6.G.1

Agenda

Activity	Time	Description/Prompt	Materials
Launch	5–10 min	Show students the Quadrilateral in Question sheet on the document camera and ask, How might we find the area of this shape?	Quadrilateral in Question sheet, to display
Explore	30+ min	Small groups develop methods for finding the area of the quadrilateral. For each method, groups create a visual proof to share with the class.	• Quadrilateral in Question sheets, multiple copies per group • Optional: colors
Discuss	20+ min	Groups present their solutions to the area of the quadrilateral, and the class discusses how they decomposed the shape and accounted for the partial squares. Come to consensus about methods that make sense.	
Explore	30+ min	Small groups choose from the Polygon 1–4 sheets to find the area of another shape, drawing on the previous discussion. Groups develop visual proofs of their solutions to share.	• Polygon 1–4 sheets, for groups to choose from • Optional: colors
Discuss	20+ min	Shape by shape, groups present their solutions and discuss what methods make sense. Discuss what the various methods have in common and how you might select a strategy for finding the area of a shape.	

To the Teacher

Two ideas are central to this lesson, one conceptual and one mindset. At the heart of the conceptual work students are doing in this activity is making sense out of partial square units. A colleague of ours conducted a study in a sixth-grade classroom in which students engaged in an area task similar to this one (Ruef, 2016). Students developed many ways of addressing the partial units created by the angled side. Some students ignored them, believing that only whole units counted. In this method, students focus on stacks of square units, as shown in the figure here. While this does not lead to a fully accurate count of the area of the figure, it anticipates the way calculus approximates the area under a curve. If students in your class invent this way of thinking about area, it is worth naming that they have an idea that they will use in calculus to deal with the challenge of curves.

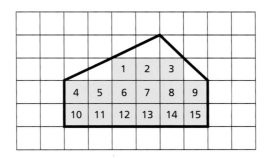

Some students count only whole squares when finding the
area of an irregular shape.

Other students in Ruef's study developed various ways to create whole units out of the partial units, including ways that use the space *not* covered by the shape. For instance, some students visualized the partial units as half of larger rectangles, as in the methods shown in the next images. Both of these methods are accurate and have connections to thinking about slope, fractions, and decomposition of two-dimensional figures.

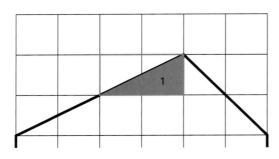

Some students make a rectangle and halve the area.

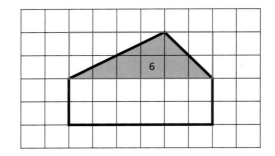

Some students make a large rectangle to cover the top of the larger shape that is a triangle and then halve the area.

The second central idea in this lesson is students' authority over the mathematics. This activity will challenge students to develop methods that they are uncertain about, or even, as in Ruef's study, to attempt incomplete or conflicting methods. It is crucial that students be the ones to determine whether a method makes sense, accounts for the full area, and is accurate. Ruef found that when placing the authority with students to make sense and come to consensus in this seemingly simple task, students took as long as three days to explore, debate, gather evidence, discuss, and come to agreement, and even then, they wanted their teacher to confirm that they were correct. The teacher resisted being positioned as the mathematical authority in the room, which made students responsible for deciding when *they* were convinced. We encourage you to take from this example the fortitude to resist students' requests that you decide who is correct and what makes sense. This is a prime activity in which to establish your students, at the beginning of the year, as the only ones who can decide whether and how a mathematical argument makes sense.

Activity

Launch

Launch the activity by showing the class the Quadrilateral in Question sheet in the document camera. Ask, How might you find the area of this shape? What do you notice that could help you? Give students a chance to turn and talk to a partner about these questions. Allow students to share some of their observations with the class. Pose the task for the day.

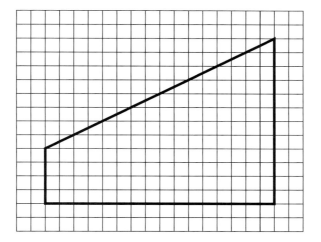

Quadrilateral in Question

Explore

Students work in small groups using the Quadrilateral in Question sheet to find its area. Ask students to find as many different ways as they can to make sense out of the area. You may want to provide groups with multiple copies of the Quadrilateral in Question sheet to represent each of their methods. Ask students to make a proof of their solutions on the sheet to share with the class to convince others that their solutions make sense. A proof can include drawings, numbers, arrows, calculations, and any other features that make reasoning clear and convincing, and colors can help students communicate about different parts of their solutions.

Discuss

Begin the discussion by asking each group to present their different solutions. If possible, try to make these solutions visible side by side so that the class can compare the solutions and methods. If there is disagreement about the area, discuss what led to these different results. Ask, Which methods do we think make the most sense? Why? It is likely that differences in method and solution will center on how students dealt with partial squares. Focus the class discussion on the following questions:

- How did you decompose the shape to find its area?
- How did you account for the partial squares?
- How do you know that you have accurately counted the area?
- How do the different methods prove each other? What do they have in common? What differences do you see?

Be sure the class can come to agreement about the area of this shape and methods that accurately count the partial squares. This is a crucial opportunity to promote argumentation, justification, and student authority over mathematics. Allow students to continue to work on developing consensus even if that requires sending groups back to work on making sense of the different methods, and reconvening the discussion afterward.

Explore

Ask students in their small groups to choose a shape from the Polygon sheet set. Provide copies of all the Polygon sheets. For each shape they choose, ask students to explore the following questions:

- What is the area of the shape? How do you know?
- How can you use what you learned in the first shape to help you find the area of other shapes?

Ask groups to develop visual proofs for each shape they work with. Again, you may want to provide groups with colors to support communicating about the different parts of their solutions.

Discuss

Begin the discussion by asking groups to share the areas they found for the different shapes, talking about each shape in turn. Come to consensus about the area and draw connections between the methods and reasoning students used for different shapes.

Discuss the following questions:

- What methods make the most sense for finding the area of irregular polygons?
- How can we decide what method to use for a given shape?

Come up with some class conjectures about the best methods to use based on your results from today.

Look-Fors

- **How are students making sense out of the partial square units?** This is the central mathematical concept of the lesson and one that students will likely struggle with. Encourage students to use color or to diagram the shape to make visible the ways they are counting. Ask students how they are dealing with the partial squares and ask them to describe their reasoning. If students argue that the partial squares do not count, push them to articulate why. If they are counting the partial square, push them to describe how they are doing so and how they know they have counted accurately. As you interact with students as they develop methods, be sure that all students are ready to share their reasoning with the class so that you can have a fruitful discussion about the contradictions in their methods.

- **How are students decomposing the shapes to find area?** Some students may decompose based on whole and partial squares, while others may decompose using larger polygons. For instance, some students may see this shape as a rectangle with a triangle on top. This is a useful way of thinking about nonrectangular polygons, as all can be decomposed into triangles and rectangles, so the methods students develop here thinking in terms of triangles and rectangles can be used generally. When these students share their thinking with the class, be sure to provide time for all students to see the polygon as the composition of other shapes.

- **How are students making sense of conflicting solutions?** Students may or may not be concerned by having multiple solutions presented simultaneously. This is a task with only one correct answer, though there are many ways to reason about that answer. Groups will undoubtedly have different methods and some different answers about a shape's area. Be sure to draw their attention to these by asking, Can this shape have different areas, or only one area? Why? If the class can agree that a shape can have only one area, then they need to consider which of the potential areas makes sense, and it is only based on sense making that a method can be deemed correct. You may want to examine some methods side by side to determine why they lead to different (or even the same) answer. Support the class in narrowing the field of solutions by deciding which they can agree do not make sense and why. If students still have multiple answers, they may need additional time to work on each method before returning to discuss them again.

- **How are students using what they learned from the first shape to help them find the areas of other polygons?** The first shape is intended to provide opportunities to reason about partial squares and the decomposition of two-dimensional figures. Both of these ideas are supportive of finding the areas of the polygons in the second round of exploration. If students get stuck, you may want to ask them to refer back to the class's previous discussion and the set of methods they agreed made sense. You might ask, How could you adapt these methods to use with this polygon? Why would those methods make sense? How is this shape like the Quadrilateral in Question? How could that help you think about methods that could make sense? In the closing discussion, ask the class to make connections between the methods used across shapes, to support them in seeing generalizable methods for finding the area of polygons.

Reflect

What do you think are the best methods for finding the area of polygons? Why?

Reference

Ruef, J. (2016). *Building powerful voices: Co-constructing public sensemaking* (Doctoral dissertation). Stanford, CA: Stanford University.

Quadrilateral in Question

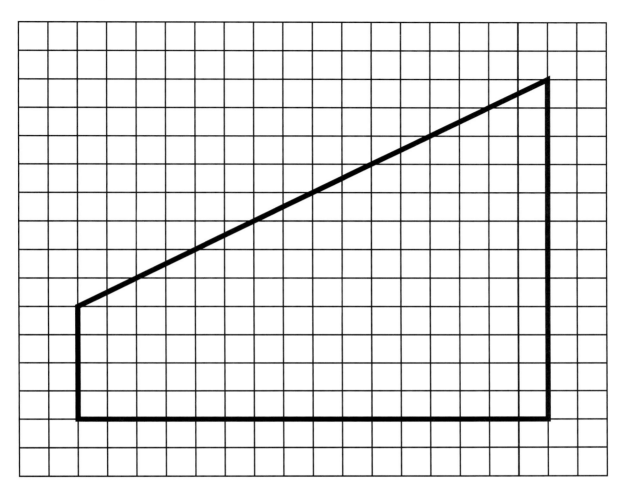

 **Polygon 1**

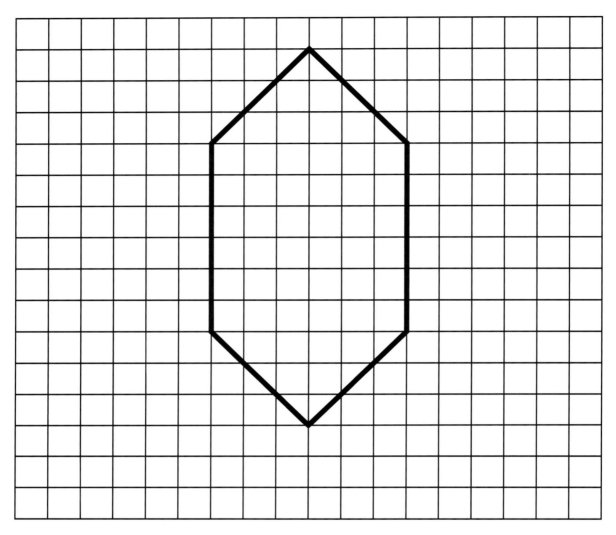

Polygon 2

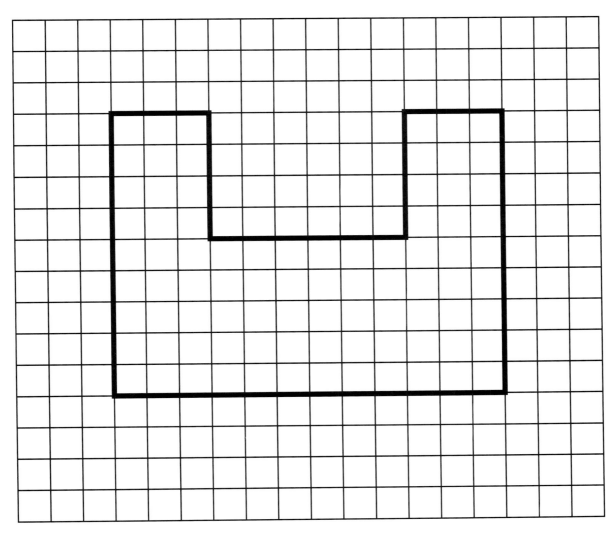

Polygon 3

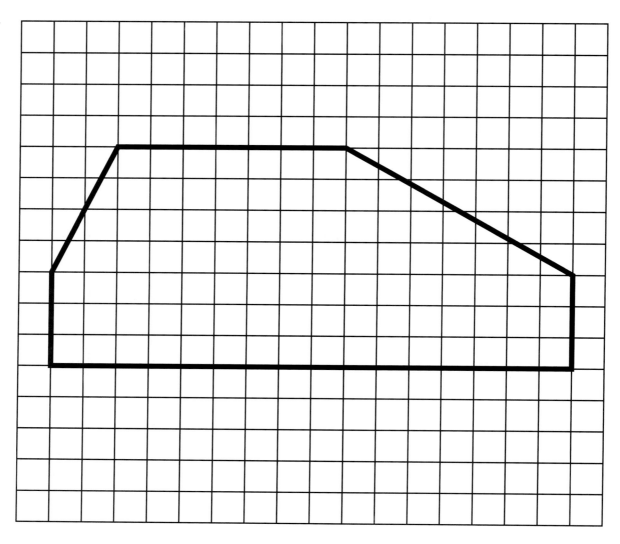

Polygon 4

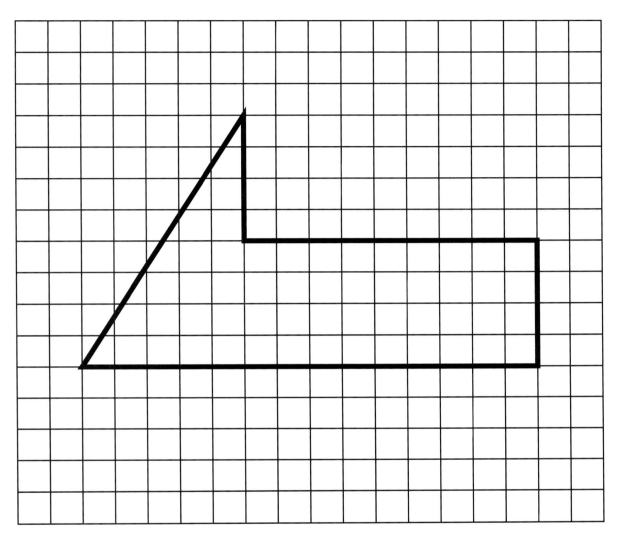

Shards of a Shape

Snapshot

Students play with different ways to decompose a complex polygon to find its area.

Connection to CCSS
6.G.1

Agenda

Activity	Time	Description/Prompt	Materials
Launch	5–10 min	Show students the Shards of a Shape sheet and ask them what they notice. Focus attention on the way the figure is decomposed into simpler polygons. Ask students how they might decompose the same figure to find its area.	Shards of a Shape sheet, to display
Play	25–30 min	Students work in partnerships or small groups to figure out how to decompose the figure to find its area. Students make a poster to show visual proof of the ways they are finding the area of the different parts of the figure.	• Shards of a Shape Outline sheet, multiple copies per group • Posters, one per group • Make available: colors, rulers or other straightedges, and tape
Discuss	20+ min	Conduct a gallery walk of students' posters and compare the ways groups have decomposed the image. Invite students to share their strategies for finding area. Ask, What are the most useful ways we have come up with?	

Activity	Time	Description/Prompt	Materials
Explore	20–30 min	Groups continue to work on finding the complete area of the figure using the most useful strategies shared in the discussion.	Make available: Copies of Shards of a Shape Outline sheet, colors, rulers or other straightedges, and tape
Discuss	15+ min	The class discusses the area of the figure and comes to consensus on what area makes sense given the evidence provided by different groups.	

To the Teacher

This activity represents a leap in complexity from the shapes students explored in the Visualize activity. We encourage you to focus the first part of the lesson purely on decomposing the figure. Give students the space to play with and explore different ways they might decompose the figure to find its area. At this stage, finding the area itself is not the goal. Rather students should focus on thinking about how to partition the figure into shapes that they might be able to use to find the area of the whole. There are an infinite number of ways to do this, and some decompositions are more useful, efficient, and elegant than others. Students may need many copies of the figure as they iterate to find ways to decompose that they think will be useful.

As students move to finding the area of the decomposed parts and the whole figure, they will need strategies for finding the area of such complex pieces. You may want to provide patty paper for students to use to trace, rotate, and flip as they work, if that helps them think through their decomposition.

Finally, we have not provided the answer to this task, precisely because it is critical that students be in charge of determining what area makes sense for this figure. You may find yourself in the position that you yourself do not know who or what is correct. Embrace this ambiguity and entrust students with the authority to use evidence to determine what makes sense.

Activity

Launch

Launch the activity by showing the class the Shards of a Shape sheet on a document camera. Ask, What do you notice about this shape? Give students a chance to turn and talk to a partner about what they notice. Ask students to share some of their observations with the class. Students may notice how the different polygons fit together to make a larger shape, or, conversely, they may see the larger shape as being cut into simpler polygons. Draw students' attention to the way the figure is decomposed into triangles and quadrilaterals. Students may notice that this decomposition makes you see things (like pyramids, mountains, or textures) that you wouldn't see otherwise.

Shards of a Shape

Tell students that today they are going to be playing with finding the area of this complex polygon. Point out that while this image shows a really interesting decomposition, it's not as useful for finding area as the ways students were decomposing shapes in the Visualize activity. Pose the question, How would you decompose this shape to find its area?

Play

Working with partners or in small groups, students use the Shards of a Shape Outline sheet, in which just the outline of the figure is shown on dot paper. Invite students to try the following and consider these questions:

- Study the image. What do you notice? What strategies could you use to decompose?
- Try more than one way to decompose the figure into smaller shapes that could help you find the figure's area. Which way to decompose the shape looks like it will be the most useful?

- Find the area of the shape. Color-code the different parts of your decomposed shape to help others see how you found the area. Put your shape on a poster so that you have more room to show how you are finding the area of the figure. Make proofs of your solution.

It is unlikely that all groups will finish finding the area of the entire figure before you call the class together to discuss their work in progress. Simply ask students to show on their chart as much of their thinking as it currently stands before posting it for the discussion. They will have the chance to return to it afterward.

Discuss

Display all the posters of students' decomposed figures. Do a gallery walk and ask students to think about the following questions as they look at the class's work in progress:

- What do the different ways of decomposing have in common? Why do you think we used this shared strategy?
- How are our strategies different? Which ideas are most interesting and why?

After students have had a chance to examine one another's work, discuss the following as a class:

- What differences and similarities did you notice about the ways we decomposed the figure?
- (Zoom in on specific parts of the image that students tackled differently.) Why did the groups decompose this portion of the figure differently? Which ways do you think will be the most useful for finding area? Why?
- What strategies did groups use for finding the area of different parts of the figure? (Invite students to explain some of the different ways they tackled area, with particular attention to partial units.)
- What are the most useful ways to decompose and find area we have come up with? Why? What questions do we still have?

Explore

Students return to working on finding the area of the Shards of a Shape figure. Invite students to continue using the poster they have started or to get a fresh copy of the Shards of a Shape Outline sheet to start over. Students should be free to use any of the strategies shared in the previous discussion, combining or adapting them as they see fit to find an area they feel confident in. Groups should be prepared with visual proof of their area to share with and convince the class.

Discuss

Post all of the groups' work for the class to see. Invite groups to share the area they found for the figure. Ask, What is the area? How do we know? The goal of this discussion is to come to agreement on the area. Students will undoubtedly have different areas. As you discuss what students have found, ask the class to examine these differing areas to figure out why they are different and what they believe is the most accurate answer. This debate is crucial for students to make sense of the task and use evidence to convince one another. Identifying errors and convincing others of what led to those errors are critical skills of argumentation.

Look-Fors

- **How are students decomposing the figure?** There are an infinite number of ways to decompose this polygon. Some ways will lead to more challenges when attempting to find area, while others will reduce the complexity of finding area. Pay attention to how students are using the vertices and sides of the figure, and whether students are decomposing into shapes that have right angles. Using right triangles will make finding area much more manageable than using the triangles shown in the original Shards of a Shape image. If students are struggling to come up with a decomposition strategy, focus their attention on just part of the image. You might ask them to point to a part of the image that looks most familiar, or where they can see a shape hidden inside. Then ask, How could you find the area of this part? What shape do you see? Ask students to mark it on their outline and show evidence of the area, before repeating this process building outward from the part they just figured out.

- **What strategies are students using to find area? How are they dealing with partial units?** Draw on the strategies that students developed in the Visualize activity and notice as you look at students' work which of these strategies students are using. Are there any strategies students are ignoring? Are students attending to partial units with meaning? You may want to make explicit connections between this shape and the work from the Visualize activity by pointing out the posters students made on that day. You might ask, How are you counting the partial squares? Which strategy from the other day are you using here? How do you know you've counted the area accurately? Push students to make connections and justify.

- **Are students accounting for the entire shape?** In decomposing such a complex shape, it is possible students will simply miss some of the parts. This is particularly likely if students work from several different starting points, say by lopping a triangle off on one side, then pulling a rectangle out of the middle, then moving to another triangle on the far side. Encourage students to look at the entire figure and color-code the different parts to help them keep track of all the shapes they have created through decomposition. Students may want to start over with a new sheet if they get too tangled up in the many shapes they have created. You may also want to encourage students to explore whether cutting the figure into more or fewer shapes makes finding the area (and keeping track) easier.

- **Are students using evidence to determine what makes sense?** In the discussion of the area of the figure, it is critical that agreement on the area is based on evidence rather than on whose voice has the most power or authority in the classroom. Discussions like these can sometime hinge not on *what* is being said but on *who* is saying it. Use this opportunity to enforce the norm that arguments must be supported with evidence from mathematics, not just loud, confident voices. You might ask the class, Are you convinced? Why or why not? Is there another possible answer? Why? Which parts of the area can we agree on? Why are the other parts difficult for us to agree on? What do we need to figure out? How will we do that? Use these kinds of facilitation questions to hold the class to a high standard of evidence, even if it means the discussion must continue on another day.

Reflect

What strategy for decomposing to find area did you find most useful? Why?

Shards of a Shape

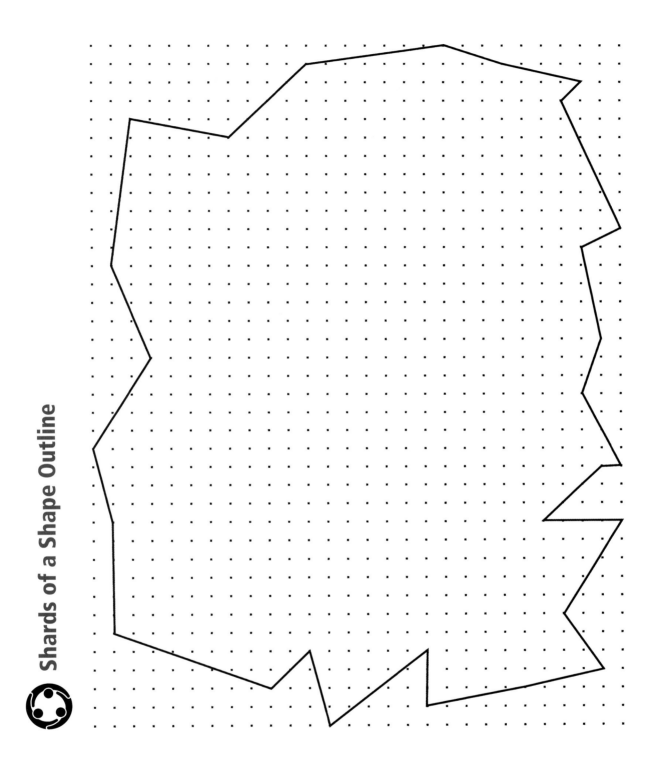

Mindset Mathematics, Grade 6, copyright © 2019 by Jo Boaler, Jen Munson, Cathy Williams. Reproduced by permission of John Wiley & Sons, Inc.

Shards of a Shape Outline

Rising from the Footprint

Snapshot

Students explore finding the volume of solids that are not rectangular by constructing buildings on shapes explored in the Visualize activity.

Connection to CCSS
6.G.2

Agenda

Activity	Time	Description/Prompt	Materials
Launch	5–10 min	Show students the Shanghai Skyline image and draw attention to the different shapes and heights of the buildings. Show the U-Shaped Building Footprint sheet and ask students to imagine that this is the footprint of a building $6\frac{1}{2}$ units tall. Ask, What will it look like? How might you find its volume?	• Shanghai Skyline, to display • U-Shaped Building Footprint sheet, to display
Explore	20–30 min	Students work in partnerships or small groups to develop methods for finding the volume of the U-shaped building, and others that are not rectangular solids.	• U-Shaped Building Footprint sheet, one per partnership • Make available: snap cubes and copies of the Building Footprint A–D sheets
Discuss	15–20 min	Discuss the different methods students have developed to find the volume of the U-shaped building and come to consensus on its volume.	

Activity	Time	Description/Prompt	Materials
Explore	30+ min	Students return to work in their groups to find the volumes of other buildings, posting their solutions clustered by building. Then groups of students curate each building's solutions and determine what can be shared and discussed about the solutions for that building.	• Building Footprint A–D sheets, one per partnership for students to choose from • Snap cubes • Display space for solutions for each building
Discuss	15–20 min	Each curating group shares something about the solutions for their building, and the class discusses any questions these groups pose. Tell students these figures are all prisms. Ask, How do you find the volume of a prism?	

To the Teacher

In this activity, we build on the foundation laid in the Visualize activity. In that work, students decomposed figures to find their area, and in this activity, we use similar shapes as footprints for buildings that rise from them. We have provided these similar figures here on grid paper, this time using square units that are the same size as most snap cubes so that students can build up, layer by layer, if they wish. The footprints with partial units pose a challenge, and students will need to figure out how they might build and find the volume using whole cubes when the footprints are not made of whole units. For buildings with a whole number of units in the footprint, we have made the heights fractional, pushing students to think about the volume with half cubes.

In each of these cases, we think that using whole snap cubes is a valuable experience for constructing volume and provides a concrete model for discussing what is happening with partial units either in the base or the height. The challenge will necessitate students to visualize how what they can construct is different from the figure being described in the activity.

Activity

Launch

Launch the activity by showing the Shanghai Skyline image (see next page). Point out that the buildings in any city or town come in different shapes and heights. You might ask students what shapes they see in this skyline or what differences they notice among the buildings. Then show the class the U-Shaped Building Footprint sheet and remind students that they explored the area of a shape similar to this in the Visualize activity.

Shanghai Skyline

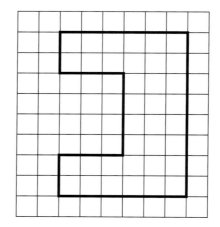

U-Shaped Building Footprint

Ask students to imagine that this is the footprint of a building in a city. This building is going to be $6\frac{1}{2}$ units high. Ask, What does the building look like? Ask students to turn and talk to a partner and describe what they see in their minds. Invite students to offer descriptions of the building and what they see in their minds. Encourage descriptive language and gestures that help students communicate what they imagine. Perhaps this building actually reminds them of one they have seen.

Tell students that today their challenge is to find the volume of this building and the others that are similar to what they have already seen before. Ask, How can you reason about the volume of buildings that are not rectangular solids?

Explore

Students work with a partner or in a small group to develop methods for finding the volume of buildings that are not rectangular solids, starting with the U-shaped building. Provide partners with a copy of the U-Shaped Building Footprint sheet and make snap cubes available. Ask students, What is the building's volume? Develop a method for finding the volume of this building.

Once partners have found the volume of the U-shaped building, invite them to choose another footprint and find the volume of the building. Once all groups have found the volume of the U-shaped building, gather the class together for a discussion.

Discuss

Discuss the following questions:

- What is the volume of the U-shaped building? How do you know?
- What strategies did you use?
- How did you deal with the fractional height? How did you count partial cubes?

Come to consensus about the volume of the U-shaped building and ways of reasoning about volume with partial cubes.

Explore

Students return to their groups to investigate the volumes of the other buildings. For each volume students find, ask them to represent their thinking on the page as clearly as they can so that other groups can understand what they have done. For each building, create a display space in the classroom and have students post solutions on the wall or bulletin board clustered by building.

Once students have had the chance to work on several buildings, assign a group of students to curate each building's solutions. In their group, students can reorder or regroup the solutions. Ask students to look at what the solutions have in common or where they are different. In their curating group they need to decide, What is interesting for us to talk about for this building's volume and the class's solutions? The group should choose something to show and a question for the class to discuss.

Discuss

Invite each curating group to share something from the solutions they curated and pose a question that the class can discuss. Be sure to draw attention to places where groups disagreed or where they agreed but used very different strategies.

At the close of the discussion, tell students that each of these buildings is a *prism*. Pose the question, How do we find the volume of prisms?

Look-Fors

- **Are students drawing on their experience finding the areas of these footprints?** If you still have posters or student work available from the Visualize activity, it can serve as a useful reference for students. It is a conceptual stretch, however, for students to think of volume and area as related, particularly since teachers work hard to ensure that students don't get area and perimeter confused. The relationship between area and volume will require that students shift from thinking in square units used to cover the two-dimensional shape to cubic units used to cover and build up from the footprint. Don't underestimate the shift in conceptual thinking that this requires, and the relationship between area and volume will not be immediately obvious to all students. Encourage students to build using the snap cubes and ask them questions about how what they are doing is and is not related to the work they did to find area. You might ask, How is this like finding area? How is it different? Can area help you find volume? How?

- **How are students reasoning about partial cubes?** All of the figures we have created in this investigation require that students reason about partial cubes when they cannot build with partial cubes. Students may tackle this challenge by building figures too large and imagining shaving parts off, or by doing the opposite, building figures too small and imagining adding missing parts back on. How are students doing this? How are they mentally accounting for what is being added or subtracted? This requires both the conceptual understanding that such slicing is needed and the spatial relations to imagine what cannot be made concrete well enough to count the parts. Again, this is quite challenging work, and we encourage you to take that challenge seriously when students struggle. Ask them questions to support visualizing the building, such as, What kind of block(s) would you need to build this building so that it was accurate? How big would those blocks be in relationship to the cubes we have? How do you know? How could we count the volume of just those pieces?

- **Are students thinking about volume as layers of cubes?** A key part of understanding volume is thinking in layers of cubic units. Students may have had experiences with volume in the past that focused only on multiplying dimensions of rectangular solids. If this is the case, students will struggle with imagining the volume of nonrectangular solids, which require thinking conceptually rather than formulaically. You might ask students to construct the building from the ground up and ask them, What would the volume be if the building was only one unit high? Two units high? Three units high? And so on. Such questions may help students both attend to the pattern that is created by building in layers and reason about half-unit heights as well.

Reflect

How do we find the volume of prisms?

Shanghai Skyline

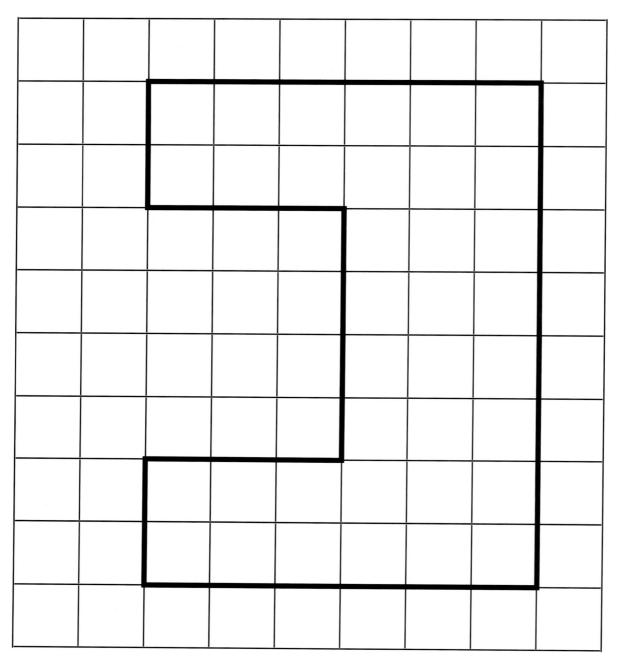

This building is $6\frac{1}{2}$ units high.

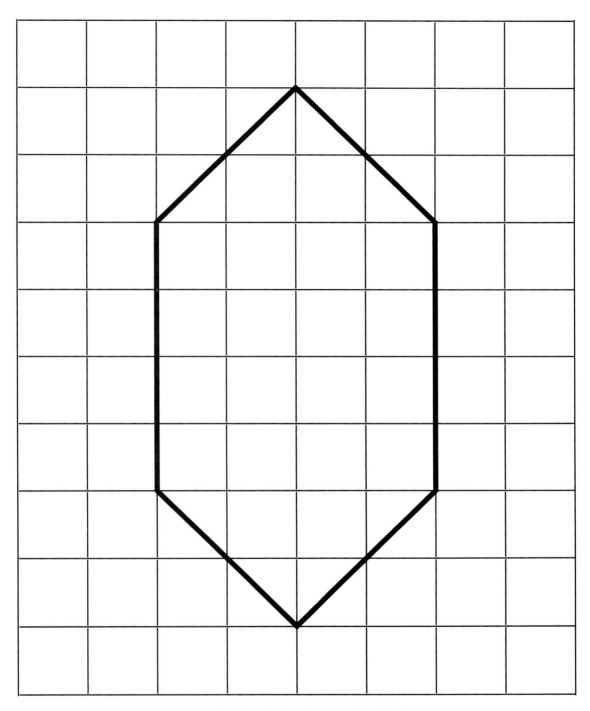

This building is 7 units high.

Building Footprint B

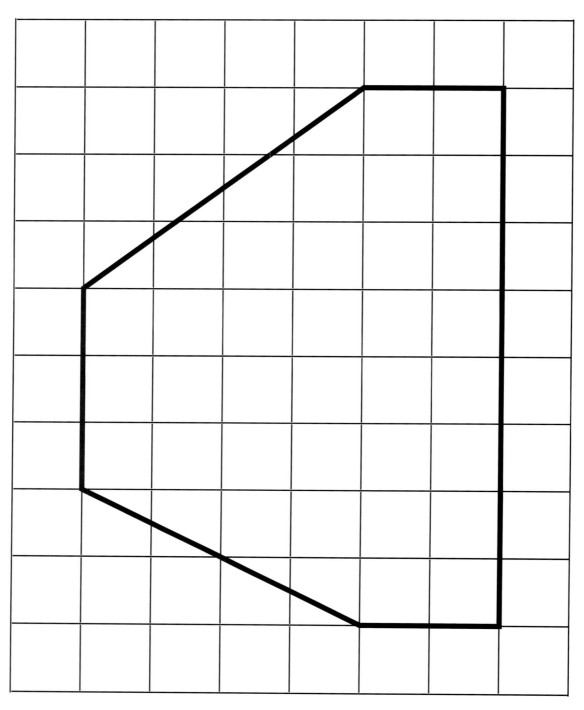

This building is 6 units high.

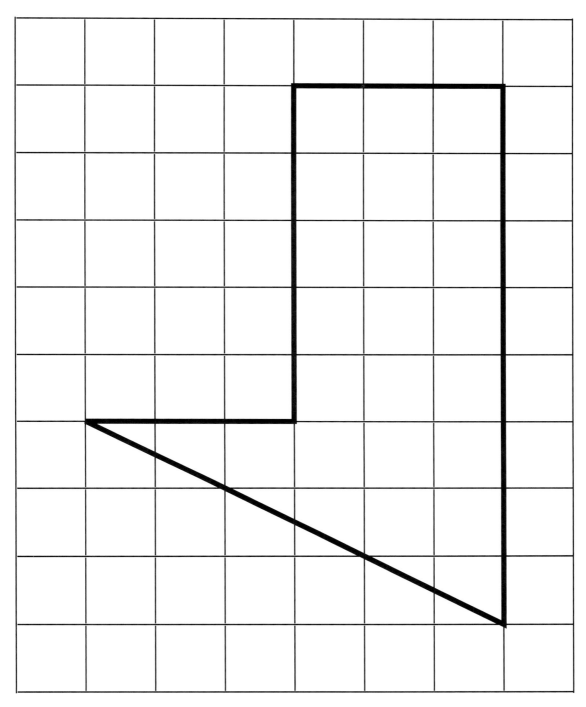

This building is 8 units high.

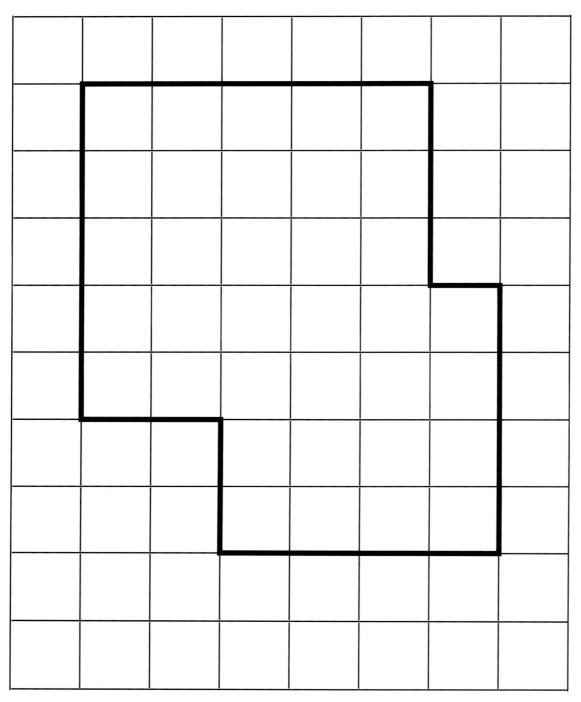

This building is $5\frac{1}{2}$ units high.

Folding and Unfolding Objects

This big idea follows from the last, in continuing a focus on volume and area, but this time offering students the opportunity to visualize, fold, and construct. When experts think about the most useful mathematics for the world, they often highlight estimation and number sense, but they also stress the importance of 3-D visualization and construction. Although this is a really critical area of mathematics, it is often neglected in schools. As we go through our daily lives, we frequently need to work out what will fit into a space—whether it is food items in a shopping bag, cars in parking spaces, or even people's bodies moving around. In employment in the STEM fields, 3-D visualization is even more central—in medical explorations, data science, brain imaging, and many other fields. Yet our traditional mathematics curriculum has offered few opportunities for students to visualize, build with nets, or investigate with 3-D shapes. These activities are all central to the tasks in this big idea and should engage students as well as help them understand deeply.

It is likely that students will have had little or no experience of visualizing or building with nets. This means there is plenty of opportunity for them to struggle, which we know is the most important time for brain growth. In the moments of struggle, it is important not to dive in and "save" students; that will take away the brain growth opportunity. Instead ask questions and encourage students to try ideas and refine them. I like the motto of Silicon Valley and of entrepreneurship in general, which is "Fail fast, fail often." This is a good approach to the activities in this unit, as students will be entering uncharted territory for them, and it is good for them to try out ideas, make mistakes, fix them, and move forward.

In the Visualize activity, students are provided images of three-dimensional nets that produce a cube with one side missing. The missing side is considered the top. The goal for students is to predict which of the squares making up the net will be the bottom of the cube. Students will be given the opportunity to visualize and make predictions and to try to convince themselves and one another, using 3-D and spatial thinking as they cut and fold the nets.

In the Play activity, students study nets that have faces for each side, and they are asked to visualize the 3-D shapes they will make. They are encouraged to share and discuss their 3-D thinking with each other. Students will first draw the objects they think each net will make. This is a really important step, as it will involve plenty of opportunity for struggle and hard thinking. Drawing takes time, and we often don't provide students enough time and space to sketch shapes. This is a great time for learning and one that should not be rushed. Once students have made conjectures and tried to convince their partners, they will then cut out the net and fold it to see how it matches up to their conjectures and their drawings. This is another good time to celebrate mistakes and talk about the positive brain activity that takes place at times of mistakes and struggle. Some of the nets we have provided will not fold into a 3-D shape, which was deliberate on our part and is more typical of a mathematical situation students will encounter in the "real world" when situations are not perfectly designed math questions that always work out! What will students think of these nets? It will be a good time to hold a discussion with them about the nature of real mathematical thinking in the world.

In the Investigate activity, partners investigate the question, What is the largest-volume box that can be made from 15 × 15 cm paper? When I was a teacher in London, I often gave students activities like this, where they investigated the maximum volume possible. Students will be able to design and test out different nets in order to explore the relationship between the design of nets and the volume that results from their different designs. As students test out different designs and calculate volumes, there will be a need for good organization of results. This is a perfect teaching time, when teachers can value and share good ideas for organization that different students come up with. Students are asked in the activity to make tables, graphs, and sketches and to calculate. These different ways of working draw on different brain pathways and will cause communication between different parts of the brain to take place. This is now known to be an important opportunity for the brain and one that leads to high achievement and thinking, so it is a nice time to value this multidimensional thinking and share with students that they are creating opportunities for brain communication.

Jo Boaler

Folding Cubes in Your Mind

Snapshot

Students build connections between two-dimensional and three-dimensional representations of cubes by folding nets, first mentally and then physically, to test their predictions.

Connection to CCSS
6.G.4

Agenda

Activity	Time	Description/Prompt	Materials
Launch	5–10 min	Show students the Folding in Your Mind sheet and tell them it is a plan, or *net,* for an open-topped box. Ask students to imagine folding it in their minds. Ask, Which square will be the bottom of the box? Come to consensus on one or more predictions.	Folding in Your Mind sheet, to display
Explore	20–30 min	In partners, students test their prediction for the image by cutting and folding. They repeat this process of predicting, agreeing, and testing on additional nets. Once students finish these, they can try to create their own nets to test.	• Folding in Your Mind sheet, one per partnership or per student • Scissors and tape • Open Box Net A–D sheets, one per partnership • 1" grid paper (see appendix)
Discuss	15–20 min	Discuss how students had to visualize to predict which square would be the bottom, the predictions students made, and what surprised them when they folded the nets. Students share the nets they designed and how creating their own was different from predicting.	
Extend	25+ min	Students design nets for open boxes that do not work, to determine what makes a net work (or not).	1" grid paper (see appendix) Scissors

To the Teacher

Celebrate mistakes! This activity will invite students to visualize three-dimensional motion and make predictions, a kind of mathematical thinking that students will use every day to navigate the world but that is rarely taught in school. Because students have likely had few experiences that challenge them to fold two-dimensional figures into three-dimensional solids, they will make lots of mistakes and be surprised by what they find. Encourage students to reflect on the differences between what they visualized and what they discovered when they physically folded the nets.

Another element that surfaces in this activity is the relationship among visualization, gestures, and verbal explanations. As students try to explain what they are visualizing, they may use gestures to communicate. Rather than seeing this as a failure of vocabulary, recognize the use of gestures as a signal that students are actively seeing the motion of the net being folded in their minds. These gestures also serve as a bridge between visualization and the words one might use to describe the spatial relationships students can see. Gestures can provide the listening audience access to what the speaker visualizes. Encourage students to imagine, show, and tell in multiple ways to build connections.

Activity

Launch

Launch this activity by showing students the Folding in Your Mind sheet on the document camera. Tell the class that this image is a plan for an object and that if we folded it, it could become a square box with no lid. Tell students that we call this kind of plan a *net*. Invite students to try to fold it in their minds. Ask, Which square would become the bottom of the box? How do you know? Give students a chance to turn and talk to a partner about what they see and the prediction they make.

Ask students to share their answers and reasoning, as in a number talk. You might mark the different squares students predict will be the bottom of the box and then ask if anyone would like to defend one of these answers. Students can come up to point at the figure and explain their thinking. Gesturing serves as a critical bridge here between visualizing and explaining. Draw attention to motions students are using to explain what squares are getting folded in their minds and what positions the squares will occupy once folded. Through a brief discussion, come to agreement on a class prediction or, if debate remains, identify two or more possibilities for the class to test.

Tell students that now they will test their prediction by cutting and folding this box and will do the same for other nets to explore how to fold two-dimensional plans in their minds.

Explore

For this activity, students work in partnerships, but you may want each student to have their own materials to get the experience of folding. Provide students with the Folding in Your Mind sheet, scissors, tape, and the Open Box Net A–D sheets. For each net, students work to

- Make a prediction of which square will be the bottom of the box by folding the net in their minds. Partners should try to come to agreement about what square they believe will be on the bottom. If they disagree, partners should work to convince one another before cutting the box out. Ask student to mark or color the predicted bottom (or base) on the sheet.
- Test their prediction by cutting out the net and folding it. Students can tape it together if they want, or they can leave it open, so that the net can be flattened and folded repeatedly.

When students finish with these nets, challenge them to design their own on 1″ grid paper (see appendix) and test them by cutting.

Discuss

Gather the class together to discuss the following questions:

- How did you make your predictions? What were you seeing in your mind?
- (Show each of the nets on the document camera.) What is the base or bottom of the box? How do you know? What did you see in your mind?
- Did you make any predictions that didn't work out? Why? What did you discover when you folded it?
- What nets did you design? What was challenging about designing nets? Did you design anything that didn't work?

Be sure to celebrate the mistakes that students made and the ways they learned to revise their thinking.

Extend

Invite students to make nets for open boxes that do not work. How do you design a net that won't fold into a box? How can you be sure that your nets don't work? Students can design nets on 1″ grid paper (see appendix) and then cut them out to prove why they do not work. Discuss what students have created and how they know, by looking at a net for an open box, whether it will work or not.

Look-Fors

- **Are students visualizing the shape the net will create?** Critical to getting started on this task is understanding that the nets all make the same three-dimensional shape, a cubic box with an open top. The questions we are asking in this activity are not about *what* shape will be created but rather about *how* the net will fold to make that shape. If you have a box that is this shape, perhaps a cardboard box left over from a delivery or a paper one you can make, you might want to show students this example during the launch if you anticipate that students will have difficulty in understanding what shape the net will become.

- **How are students communicating about their predictions?** Support students in using precise language and gestures to help them communicate about what they are imagining in their minds. Words like *face, edge, base,* and *vertical* may help students explain what they are thinking to a partner or to the class. Revoicing what they are saying using this language and checking if you've understood can be useful ways of encouraging the use of these words, as in, "So, are you saying that if you fold this face so that it is vertical, then this square will be the base of the box?" Also, remember the importance of gestures for making connections in the brain. Rather than using words to replace gestures, add language on to gestures so that even more connections are made. If students are attempting to explain without gestures what they see in their minds and the explanations are difficult to follow, encourage them to show with their hands what they are imagining.

- **Are students' predictions becoming more accurate?** This is an activity in which to celebrate mistakes and surprises. Students will make predictions that others disagree with and that may later turn out to be incorrect. As students try to visualize how the nets get folded, they should be using what they learn from their mistakes to become more accurate. When students' predictions do not match the folded box, encourage them to unfold and refold the box several times to see how the faces and edges come together. You might ask students then to lay the net flat again and try to visualize the folding they have just done with their hands. Connecting the visualized folding with the physical folding will support connections between two- and three-dimensional figures and lead to more accurate predictions.

Reflect

What surprised you the most when you were trying to fold the nets in your mind?

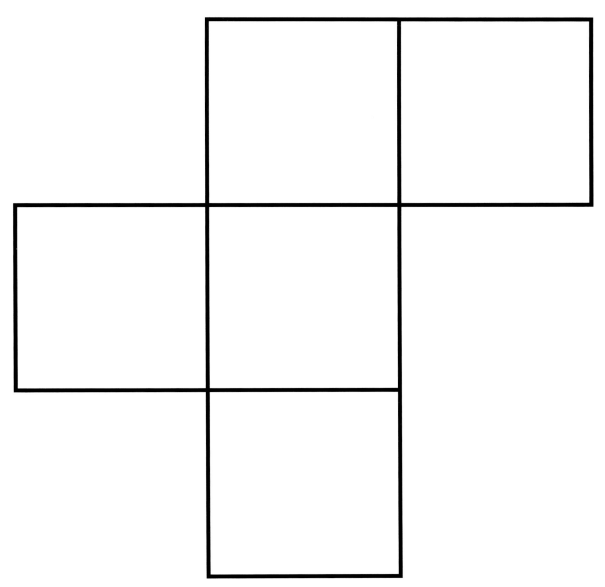

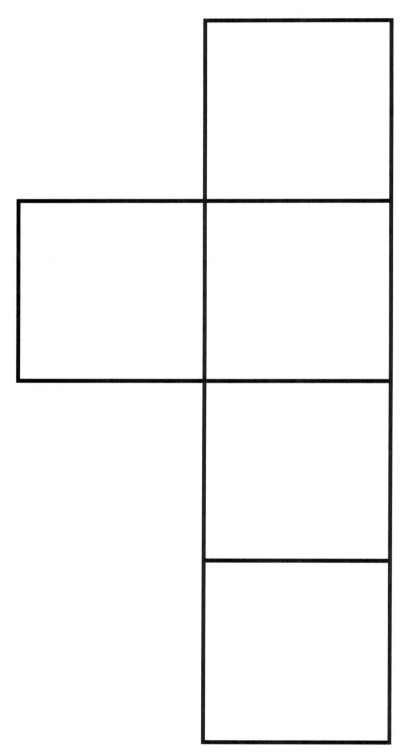

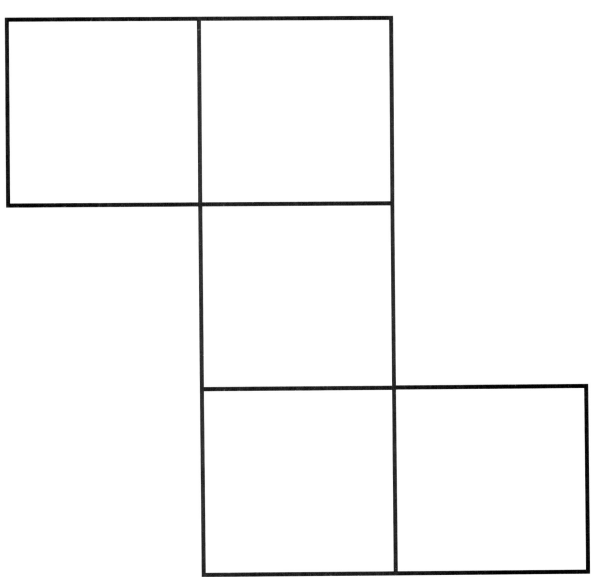

Open Box Net C

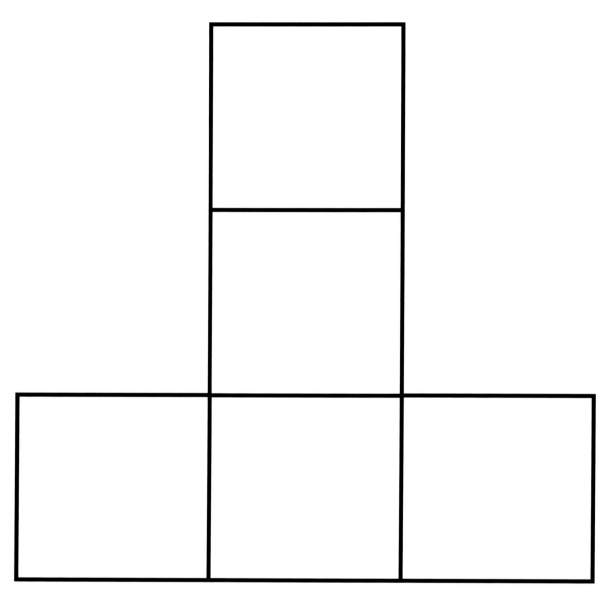

 **Open Box Net D**

Folding Nets in Your Mind
Snapshot

Students play with nets of different prisms and solids to predict what shapes the nets make, and test their predictions by cutting and folding. Students explore nets that do not work to understand how nets are constructed.

Connection to CCSS
6.G.4

Agenda

Activity	Time	Description/Prompt	Materials
Launch	10 min	Show students the Folding a Net in Your Mind image and ask them to visualize what shape would be made by folding this net into a solid. Discuss and come to agreement about a prediction.	Folding a Net in Your Mind sheet, to display
Play	20–30 min	Partners use the Net Set A–H sheets to make predictions about what shape each net will make when folded. Students sketch their predictions on dot paper. Some of the nets in the set do not work. Students explore which do not work and how they know.	• Net Set A–H sheets, one set per partnership • Dot paper and isometric dot paper (see appendix) • Optional: colors
Discuss	15–20 min	Discuss the predictions students made for each net and their reasoning. Come to agreement about these predictions and which nets do not work. Reflect on the challenges of trying to draw solids.	
Play	20–30 min	Partners test their predictions by cutting and folding the nets. For each net that does not work, partners develop a strategy for revising it so that it makes a solid.	Make available: scissors and tape

Activity	Time	Description/Prompt	Materials
Discuss	15–20 min	Discuss which of the predictions students made were accurate and what mistakes students made. Students share and compare the revisions they made to the nets that didn't work.	
Extend	25+ min	Partners construct a net to match a geometric solid manipulative. Students explore whether more than one net is possible for this solid and the challenges that emerge when trying to create nets.	• Geometric solids • Make available: dot paper and isometric dot paper (see appendix), scissors, and tape

To the Teacher

This activity serves as another opportunity to support students in using three-dimensional geometry and spatial relations vocabulary with meaning. As students are beginning to discuss their predictions and the shapes that are made, they are going to search for words to describe the sides and bottom of the figures. Support them by providing them with vocabulary—*face, base, edge, vertex/vertices, vertical, perpendicular*—when they need it to describe what they visualize and to convince others. Students should be encouraged to express their thinking in whatever words they know; having the correct mathematical language should not be a requirement for participation. However, through revoicing you can add in opportunities for everyday, descriptive language to be coupled with more precise mathematical language.

Activity

Launch

Launch the activity by showing students the Folding a Net in Your Mind sheet on the document camera. Tell students that, unlike the nets they explored in the Visualize activity, this is a net for a solid shape that is not a cube. Invite students to try to fold this net in their minds. Ask, What shape would this net make? How do you know? Give students the chance to turn and talk to a partner about what they visualize and why.

Ask students to share their answers and reasoning, as in a number talk. You might ask students to name all the different shapes they think this net might make, and list them on the board or on the Folding a Net in Your Mind sheet. Ask students to defend these shapes by explaining their reasoning and what they visualized. They can come up to point at the figure to help explain their thinking. Use this discussion to come to agreement on a class prediction.

Play

Students work in partners to make predictions about the kinds of shapes formed by different nets. Provide partners with Net Set A–H sheets to work with. For each net, students work together to make a prediction of what shape the net will make by folding the net in their minds. Partners should try to come to agreement about the shape that can be made. Encourage students to try to sketch their ideas on either dot paper or isometric dot paper (see appendix). Note that drawing three-dimensional figures on two-dimensional paper is very challenging work for the brain and will support making new connections by pushing students to think about how the different components of the figure are related.

In the Net Set A–H sheets, some of the nets don't work. That is, if students were to cut them out to fold them into a solid, the shape wouldn't close into a solid or would have leftover faces. Ask students to explore, Which nets don't work to make a solid? Why?

Discuss

Gather the class together to discuss the following questions:

- What shapes do these nets make? (Invite students to share, discuss, and debate their predictions by putting them on the document camera.)
- Which nets don't work to make a shape? How do you know?
- How did you make your predictions? What were you seeing in your mind?
- How did it feel to try to draw the figures on dot paper? What made it hard? Which ones do you think you drew the way you see it in your mind? (Invite students to share examples of their drawing on the document camera.)

In this discussion, students may need geometric language that they do not have to describe or name the shapes they imagine. Use this opportunity to provide names for solids that students might imagine and describe but cannot yet label, such as *pyramid, cylinder, prism, solid, cone,* and so on.

Play

Returning to work with their partners, students test their predictions for each of the solids by cutting out the nets and folding them. Students can tape them together or leave them open so that they can be flattened and refolded during the discussion. Partners gather evidence for which shapes they can make and which nets don't work. For any net that doesn't work, ask students to modify it so that it does. Ask, What does it take to make it work? Students may want to remove, add, or move a face to make the net work. Encourage students to color-code or diagram their revisions so that they can share them with others.

Discuss

Gather the class together to discuss the following questions:

- Did you make any predictions that didn't work out? Why? What did you discover when you folded the net?
- Which nets truly didn't work? Why? What was the problem with their design?
- What might it take to fix these nets so that they would make a solid? What different strategies did you come up with?
- Did you discover anything that surprised you?

Be sure to continue to use the vocabulary of the shapes students have made now that they have physical examples they can touch and see.

Extend

If you have a set of geometric solids, invite students to choose one or more and try to make a net to match. Ask, What could your net look like? Are different nets possible? Provide students with dot paper or isometric dot paper (see appendix) and scissors. After students have constructed different nets, hold a discussion of the following questions:

- What nets did you design?
- What was challenging about designing nets?
- Did you design anything that didn't work? What did you do to revise your design?

Look-Fors

- **Are students able to make predictions?** You may find that some students are simply baffled by the task of trying to fold a two-dimensional image into a three-dimensional solid. This task can create a high degree of struggle and frustration for students who have had little experience manipulating figures mentally. While we do not want students to get stuck and quit, it is important to acknowledge that this is very challenging work and that by struggling, students are making new connections in their brains. You might ask these students to focus in on parts of the image and make connections to the work they did with the open boxes in the Visualize activity. For instance, in that activity students saw that each line between two squares became a place to fold and then an edge to the box. You might ask students to look at a net and identify places where they will need to fold. Ask, What will happen to each of these faces when you fold along these lines? Students may not yet be able to fully construct a mental image of the solid, but each step toward that visualization is productive.

- **What words are students using or looking for to describe what they visualize or create?** Vocabulary should be purposeful. Students should learn words when they need them. This activity creates many opportunities to hear and assess what vocabulary students can already use comfortably, and instructional opportunities to provide just the words students need in the moment they need them. Consider the many kinds of words students might need: shape names (*prism, cylinder, hexagon*), attribute names (*edge, face, base, vertex*), positional names (*angle, perpendicular, vertical, horizontal*), and transformation names (*rotate, flip, turn*).

- **How are students managing the physical task of cutting and folding?** This is a second area for potential struggle. The fine motor skills necessary to cut and fold nets out of flimsy paper can leave some students frustrated. If you anticipate this frustration, you may want to copy the nets on card stock or heavier paper stock to make it easier for students to cope with errors and less likely that the nets will become accidentally torn or folded. Alternatively, you could have some nets precut (but not prefolded) so that scissors are no longer necessary. You will want to have plenty of copies of the Net Set A–H sheets available in case students do make mistakes and would like a fresh page to try again. It can also help students to simply name the challenge you are seeing and ask what they need, as in, "I notice that cutting these out is very frustrating. What could we do to make this more manageable?" Students may have a clear sense of what they need, and this is a prime opportunity to encourage them to exercise agency.

Reflect

How can you tell whether or not a net will work to make a solid?

Folding a Net in Your Mind

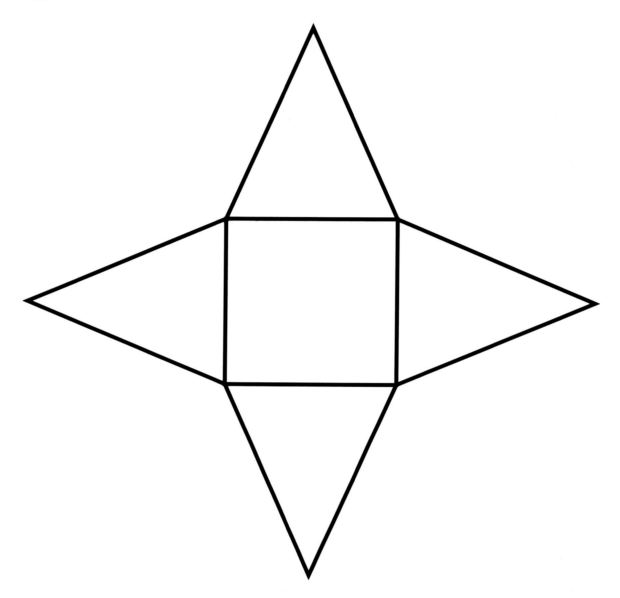

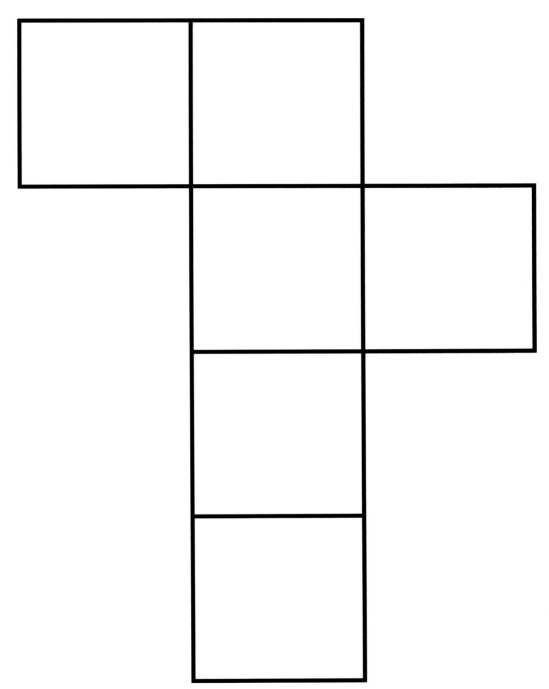

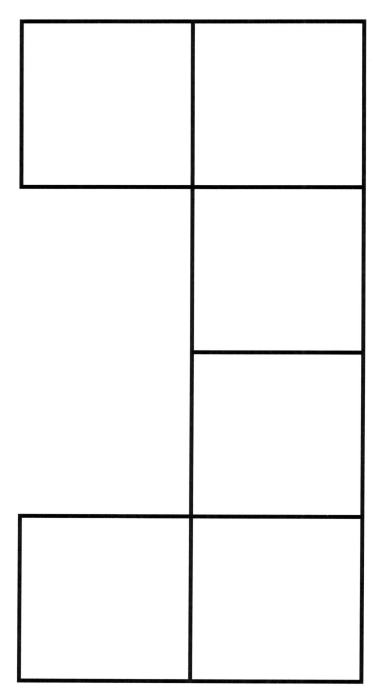

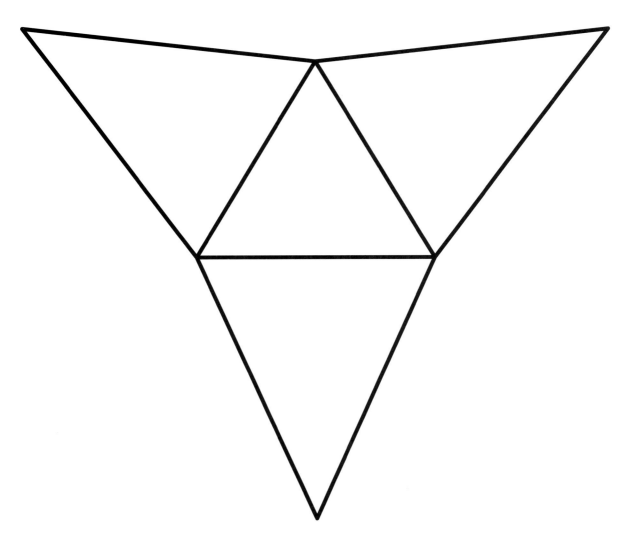

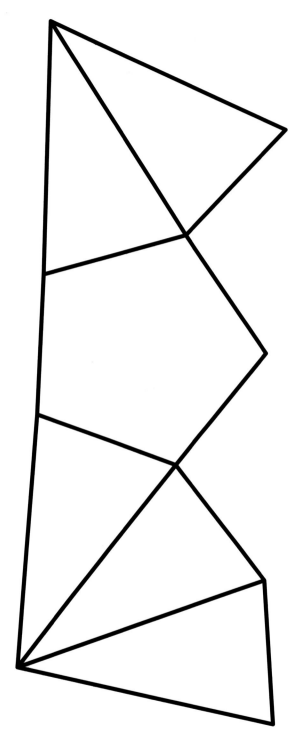

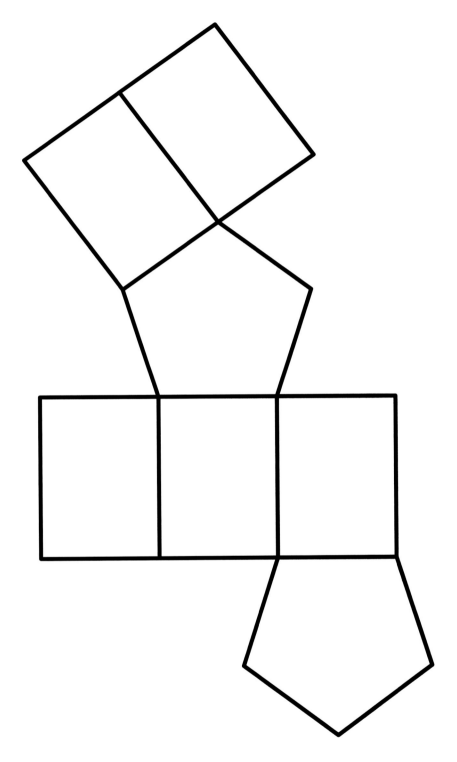

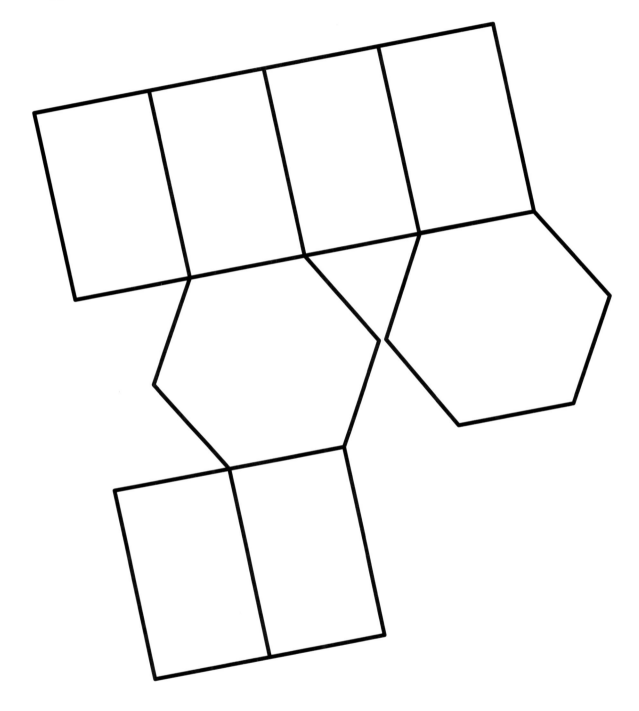

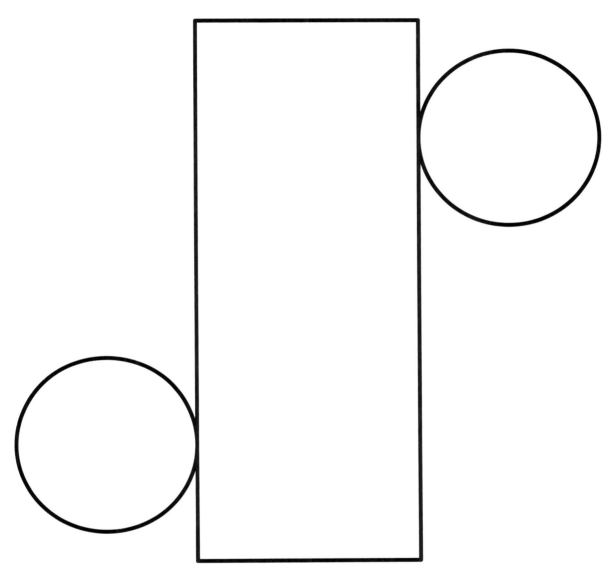

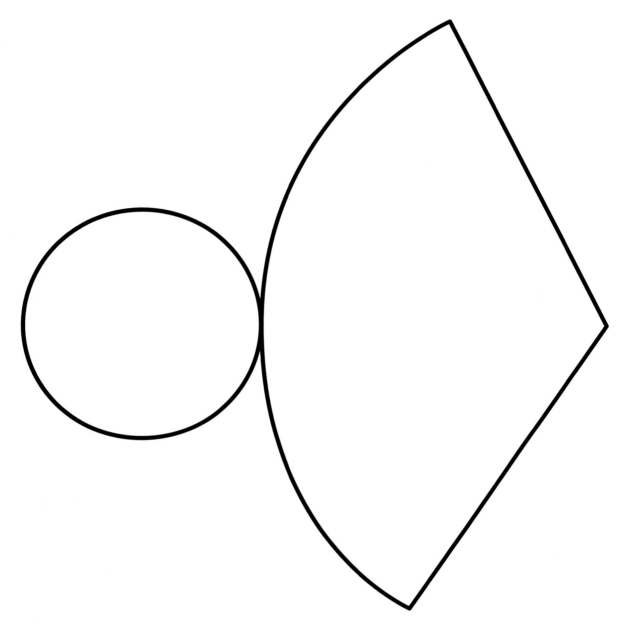

Filling Our Nets

Snapshot

Students connect nets to volume by investigating the volume of the different boxes that can be created from a 15×15 cm sheet of paper.

Connection to CCSS
6.G.4, 6.G.2

Agenda

Activity	Time	Description/Prompt	Materials
Launch	5–10 min	Show students a piece of 15×15 cm paper and the Net-from-a-Square sheet. Tell them you can make a net for an open box from the paper by removing squares at the corners. Pose the question for the investigation.	15×15 cm piece of paper Net-from-a-Square sheet, to display
Explore	30–45 min	Partners investigate the question, What is the largest-volume box that can be made from 15×15 cm paper? Students design and test different nets for an open box to find the largest possible volume.	Make available: 15×15 cm paper, centimeter grid paper (see appendix), rulers, scissors, tape, calculators, and centimeter cubes
Discuss	20+ min	Discuss what students noticed as they worked to create box nets and find their volume. Collect all of the class's attempts into a table and make observations about the data. Ask students if they think that they have found the largest volume possible and why.	Chart paper and markers

Activity	Time	Description/Prompt	Materials
Extend	30+ min	Partners develop ways of graphing the data to look for patterns and determine whether they have found the largest-volume box possible. Students may return to investigate boxes if they believe a larger-volume box could be constructed.	• Grid paper (see appendix) • Rulers • Calculators

(Continued)

To the Teacher

In this activity, materials are important. You'll want an ample supply of 15×15 cm paper. Origami paper is available in this size, and 6″ patty paper is close enough to 15×15 cm to work for this task. Alternatively, students can use centimeter grid paper (see appendix) to cut, count, and fold their own 15×15 cm sheets. Having centimeter cubes available that students can use to pack their boxes will make this activity even more concrete and support bridging the work done in this big idea about nets with the previous big idea on volume.

We encourage you to focus students on removing squares at each corner with whole-number centimeter side lengths to make exploring volume a whole-number affair. However, if students want to try fractional units, allow them to see what happens. It will be more challenging to model with cubes, but students have done just this in the Investigate activity for Big Idea 1.

When students investigate the maximum volume possible, a new kind of pattern will emerge from multiple trials: a parabolic pattern. Removing neither the smallest nor largest possible corner squares produces the box with the greatest volume. If students do use whole-number units, they may see a pattern like the one illustrated in the table shown here. This pattern might cause students to wonder whether they could get a larger volume by removing corner squares larger than 3×3 cm but smaller than 4×4 cm, and this is a worthy question to investigate. Even as they are working, you may want to encourage students to organize their trials in a table like this one, or one organized differently, to see patterns and draw conclusions.

Corner Squares Removed	Box Base Size	Box Height	Box Volume
1 × 1 cm	13 × 13 cm	1 cm	169 cm³
2 × 2 cm	11 × 11 cm	2 cm	242 cm³
3 × 3 cm	9 × 9 cm	3 cm	243 cm³
4 × 4 cm	7 × 7 cm	4 cm	196 cm³
5 × 5 cm	5 × 5 cm	5 cm	125 cm³
6 × 6 cm	3 × 3 cm	6 cm	54 cm³
7 × 7 cm	1 × 1 cm	7 cm	7 cm³

Activity

Launch

Launch the activity by showing students a 15 × 15 cm sheet of paper. Tell them that if you wanted to use a square piece of paper like this one to make a net for a box with no lid, you could cut out the corners and fold up the sides. Show the diagram on the Net-from-a-Square sheet to help students visualize how the sheet of paper could become a net.

Tell students that today they will be using pieces of paper like this one you've shown that is 15 × 15 cm. Pose the questions, If we want to use this paper to make an open box with the greatest volume possible, what would the net look like? What would its dimensions be?

Explore

Students work in partnerships to investigate what is the largest-volume open box they can create out of a 15 × 15 cm sheet of paper. Provide partners with 15 × 15 cm paper or centimeter grid paper (see appendix), rulers, tape, scissors, calculators, and centimeter cubes. Note that students will need lots of paper to test their ideas. Students investigate the following questions:

- What is the largest-volume open box that can be made from the 15 × 15 cm paper?
- What would the net look like for this box?

- What are the dimensions of this box?
- How do you know this is the largest possible volume?

Encourage student to record every trial so that they can see the different possibilities they have found. Ask, How could you record your findings so that you can see patterns?

Discuss

Gather the class together to discuss the following questions:

- What did you discover?
- What is greatest volume possible? How do you know?
- What are the dimensions of the box? How much paper gets cut away? What does the net look like?

Create a class display of all the data students have collected. Ask students what the table of data should look like. It might include columns such as the dimensions of the base, the height of the box, or the size of the squares cut away, and it should certainly include the volume of the box. Ask all the groups to contribute data from their trials until every box that students made is represented. Ask the class, What do you notice about our data? You may find that you want to reorder the data to help see patterns. Ask students, Based on this data, do you think we have found the box with the greatest possible volume? Why or why not?

Extend

Pose the question, How could we graph this data to help us see patterns? Invite groups to use grid paper (see appendix) and create some kind of graph of the data. Students will need to choose what values they are graphing. For instance, they may want to compare base length to volume, or they may compare the size of the squares removed to volume. Whatever students choose, they just need to be consistent. Students will likely struggle with how to set up the graph, including labeling the axes. You might lead a brief discussion in which the class thinks together about these issues before sending students off to create a graph.

After students have had a chance to create graphs of the class's data, gather them together to show their different graphs and discuss the following questions:

- What do you notice now?
- Do you still think we have found the largest volume?

If students think that there is a greater volume possible based on the graph, send them off to test this conjecture. This would involve exploring fractional side lengths for the squares removed and the base of the box. Using centimeters as we have here opens the possibility of using decimals, rather than fractions, which could make exploring incremental lengths more straightforward.

Look-Fors

- **Do students understand the task?** This task involves connecting the work students have done with nets to their prior work with volume. Building such connections is powerful for learning and can create moments where students are moving between—and potentially getting tangled up in—different ideas. It is worth spending time in the launch to ensure that everyone understands the relationship between the 15×15 cm paper, the net, and the volume they are seeking. Watch as students get started to see whether they are finding an entry point into the investigation or are immediately stuck. If students get stuck, you may want to show them the Net-from-a-Square sheet and have them describe what it shows. It may make sense to invite students simply to make any net they want and then return to ask them about its volume. After students have tried this task once, they will find iterating to compare volumes more manageable.

- **How are students thinking about volume?** Because the box being created here is a rectangular solid, students may be thinking about volume in one of three ways. First, they may simply think of volume as packing centimeter cubes inside the box, which is consistent with the concept though time consuming and potentially error filled when done with boxes this size. Second, students may be thinking in layers, either by constructing the area of the base and then multiplying or by finding the area of the base and multiplying. This is much more efficient and also grounded in the concept of area. Third, they may simply see volume as the product of the dimensions of the box. Be sure to probe students who are only multiplying to explain what they are multiplying and why.

- **How are students organizing their findings?** All trials of this task produce useful data. Be sure to encourage students to find some way of capturing each box they make and its volume. They may want to create a display, table, or set of sketches with labels. Ask, How will you keep track of the boxes you've made so that you can figure out which one has the biggest volume? Support students in coming up with a recording plan that makes sense to them. You may want to remind students that organizing in some way will help them try only new boxes and not repeat their trials.

Reflect

What surprised you when you made boxes of different sizes from the same piece of paper? What do you wonder now?

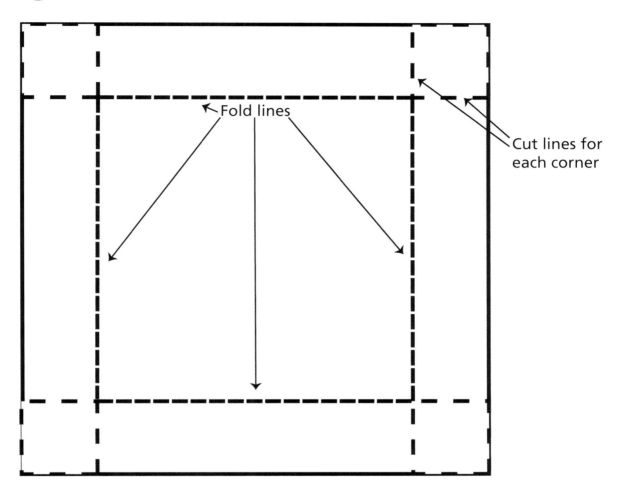

Fold lines

Cut lines for each corner

Expanding the Number Line

In this big idea, we choose to focus on the number line because our work with neuroscientists has helped us understand the benefits of having students encounter numbers on a line in order to match the way the brain is thought to perceive and hold numbers. In many classrooms, students are quickly introduced to negative numbers and expected to calculate with them, but we know that it is important for students to be introduced to them carefully and slowly. Tsang, Blair, Bofferding, and Schwartz (2015) also showed in an experiment that when students saw the symmetry of positive and negative numbers on a line, and worked with folding activities to observe the symmetry, they achieved at higher levels not only in work with negative numbers but also in pre-algebraic tasks. These researchers highlight the importance of symmetry as students learn about positive and negative numbers, and we have deliberately made symmetry a key part of students' learning in this big idea.

In the Visualize activity, students use adding machine tape to fold a number line with a center fold of zero. The students then construct a number line of positive integers and match them to their opposites; they also make observations about two different numbers on the line. As they make their own observations and conjectures, they are visualizing and seeing numbers, along with their position and their relationships with one another. As the activity progresses, students move two objects the same number of units in the same direction along the number line at the same time to make further observations. This is an introduction to some important algebraic concepts.

In the Play activity, students use the adding machine tape number lines they created in the first activity. In this game, students roll dice to determine the number of units they move their marker. As they navigate moving from positive or negative integers, in either direction, they practice the operations of addition and subtraction through movement. This activity will also help students understand operations visually and with movement.

The Investigate activity brings a horizontal and vertical integer number line together so that students experience the four-quadrant coordinate plane. Many activities start with students plotting points. In this activity, we ask students to identify points on two lines: $y = x$ and $y = -x$. As students identify points, record their findings, and study patterns, they will be asked to make conjectures that can lead to rich classroom conversations. Another reason we have structured the activity in this way is to give students a chance to make sense of patterns—this sense making will later support their learning of transformational geometry.

Jo Boaler

Reference

Tsang, J. M., Blair, K. P., Bofferding, L., & Schwartz, D. L. (2015). Learning to "see" less than nothing: Putting perceptual skills to work for learning numerical structure. *Cognition and Instruction*, 33(2), 154–197.

Folding around Zero

Snapshot

Students construct and explore number lines by folding adding machine tape to build understanding of negative integers through symmetry.

> Connection to CCSS
> 6.NS.6a, 6.NS.5, 6.NS.7c

Agenda

Activity	Time	Description/Prompt	Materials
Launch	15+ min	Together fold paper number lines and mark zero at the midpoint. Label the positive values and ask students, What does the first point on the line to the left of the zero represent? Students turn and talk and then discuss ideas to come to agreement that this value is −1.	• Adding machine tape, cut to approximately 30"–36", one per student and one to display • Markers
Explore	15–20 min	Students figure out how to label all the values on their number lines and then make observations. Partners then place two objects on one of their number lines: one at −3 and one at +5. Partners make as many observations as then can about the objects' positions.	• Students' number lines • Markers • Tape • Objects for marking positions on the number line, such as paperclips, two per group
Discuss	15 min	Discuss and chart students' observations about the number line and about the positions of the objects at −3 and +5.	Charts and markers

Activity	Time	Description/Prompt	Materials
Explore	20+ min	Students use their own number lines to explore the question, What might happen if we moved one of the objects 6 units? For each solution students find, they use the number line to make observations.	• Students' number lines • Objects for marking positions on the number line, such as paperclips, two per group
Discuss	15+ min	Discuss the solutions students found and their observations. Organize the four possible solutions and students' observations into a table and look for patterns or connections.	Chart and markers
Extend	20+ min	Students use their number lines to explore the question, What happens if you move both objects the same number of units in the same direction at the same time?	• Students' number lines • Objects for marking positions on the number line, such as paperclips, two per group

To the Teacher

In this activity, we draw on the research of Tseng, Blair, Bofferding, and Schwartz (2015), which suggests the importance of symmetry to understanding and working with integers. Unlike positive integers, which can be viewed as representing collections of individual objects, negative integers are most clearly described as positions on a continuous number line that is symmetrical at zero. Real-world models for integers, such as altitude and temperature, are nearly always arrayed on a number line. The number line's symmetry is most clearly seen when students can literally fold the number line at zero to see how the positive and negative values align. For instance, it is a key observation that −3 and +3 are both 3 units away from zero. By folding, students can begin to see this relationship of absolute value.

We believe that students need the opportunity not just to see an integer number line but to create one themselves. Anticipate that folding and labeling this paper number line will take students some time; we believe this is time well spent. As students fold, unfold, and refold the number line, they are building the physical relationships between integers and learning about the symmetry of the number line. When adults think about integers, they use this symmetry to decompose values, compare, and find solutions. Before students can fold the number line mentally, they need adequate opportunities to do so physically.

In this activity, we ask you to construct three different charts of students' observations, which can be used to help students as they make sense of the number line and integers. We recognize that this is quite a lot of information to chart, but these charts play a key role in making the structure of the number line and the values on it explicit to students. In the first discussion, you'll want to make a chart of students' observations about the number line and a chart of students' observations about −3 and +5. For these two charts, we encourage you to record all the observations students can make. Students may avoid making what seem like obvious observations, but all of the features of the number line and the values on it are meaningful for understanding numbers as a system that extends into negative territory. Students may make very concrete observations, such as, "Zero is in the middle," or "There are eight spaces between −3 and +5." Every one of these observations can be probed for the meaning behind it.

In the second discussion, you'll want to make a chart of students' solutions to the challenge of what happens when we move one of the objects 6 units. There are four possible choices students can make: either of the two objects can be moved to the left 6 units or to the right 6 units. Record on your chart both what movement students chose and what the result was. A table makes organizing these observations to see patterns much easier.

Activity

Launch

Launch the activity by telling students that they are going to make a number line to explore, and provide each student with a strip of adding machine tape. Tell students that their adding machine tape is going to be a number line, and ask them to fold it in half. Ask students to mark this midpoint as zero. Show students how to fold their paper into the number line that they will be using today by first folding their paper in half at the zero, then folding it in half four more times. This will make 16 segments on each side of the zero.

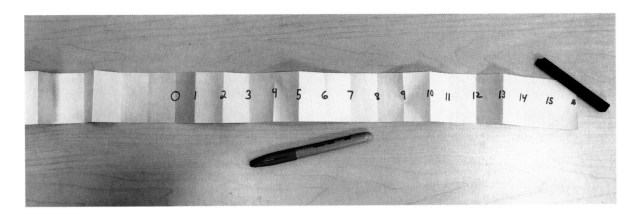

Folding adding machine tape five times creates 32 (or 2^5) segments, just enough for a number line from −16 to 16.

To the right of the zero, mark the values on the number line and ask students to do so on their own number line. Ask, What does the point on the line to the left of zero represent? What number might go on that point? Give students a chance to turn and talk to a partner about the value for the fold immediately to the left of zero. Discuss the ideas that students come up with. Note that students may have many different ideas about the value of the number to the left of the zero. As students share these ideas, ask them to explain the reasoning that underpins each idea. Encourage students to use the pattern represented to the right of the zero as data to support their thinking. For instance, for any point on the number line, the point to its left is 1 less, so the point to the left of zero should be 1 less than zero. Students may or may not know the name for such a number, but the reasoning is something the class should be able to agree on. Through this discussion, come to agreement that the number name we give to the fold immediately left of the zero is −1, which we call "negative one," which can be thought of as the opposite of 1.

Explore

Ask students to figure out how to label their number lines completely. Encourage students to fold their number lines to help them decide on labels for each point. Students should work with a partner, but each student should have their own number line so that each can fold and label. After students have labeled their lines, ask partners to discuss the question, What do you notice about the number line? Challenge students to come up with as many observations as they can to share with the class in the discussion.

Then tell students to choose one partner's number line to work on together. Provide students with two objects, such as paperclips, to mark positions on the number line, and tape to secure their number lines to their tables, if desired. Ask them to place one marker at −3 and one at +5. Ask students, What do you notice about the positions of the objects? What observations can you make? Note that not all students will want to tape their number lines down, as they may want to be able to continue to fold and unfold them. If you use paperclips as markers, then students can still use folding while marking these two points.

Discuss

Gather the class together to discuss the following questions:

- What do you notice about the number line? (Chart some student observations on a poster titled Observations about the Number Line.)
- If we put two objects at −3 and +5, what observations can we make? (Chart students' ideas on a poster called Observations about −3 and +5.)

Explore

Students use their own number lines to explore the question, What might happen if we moved one of the objects 6 units? Students generate possible solutions, and for each solution, ask partners to make observations. Students can think about the following questions:

- What happened?
- What do you notice?

Students record in their notebooks what they tried and what they found.

Discuss

Gather the class together to discuss the following questions and make a chart:

- What might happen if you moved one of the objects 6 units? (Ask students to share a solution.)
- For each solution, invite the class to make observations. What happened? What do you notice?

You may want to organize your chart in a table with a Solutions column and an Observations column to help the class see patterns. Students may make observations about the distance between the points, the distance from each point to zero, the midpoint between the points, or other features. After the class has generated all four solutions and observations to match, ask them to look at the chart. Ask, What do you notice about our solutions?

Extend

Pose the question, What happens if you move both objects the same number of units in the same direction at the same time? Invite students to explore using their own number lines and the markers you've provided.

Look-Fors

- **Are students using symmetry to help them label and see relationships?** Symmetry is a key idea in building understanding of integers and the number line. As you watch students labeling their number lines and thinking about observations, look for whether students are folding their number lines at the zero. Ask questions about how they know which value to place in each position. Even if students use patterning to simply count down, "$-1, -2, -3, \ldots$," you'll want to ask why this way of counting makes sense on the number line. Encourage students to fold the number line in half and reason about what they see.

- **How are students counting (and labeling) on the number line?** Even older students can struggle with whether to count the points or the intervals on a number line. It requires precision and intent to mark the creases as lines and label those lines, rather than the roomier spaces between the folds. Each line represents a 1-unit difference from the line on either side. As students label their number lines, pay attention for this common error. If you notice students labeling the spaces, ask them to explain their thinking. Ask students to explain their thinking to one another, and if you have several students labeling the spaces, it may make sense to pause the class to discuss which way of labeling makes sense and why. It is important that students collectively use the same mathematical conventions for recording and investigating distance.

- **Are students comparing values on the number line?** One of the ideas we hope students will explore in this activity is the relationship between the values on the number line. As students make observations, you'll want to listen for comparative language, such as *smaller, larger, greater than,* and *less than.* Encourage students to think about how the values change as they move left or right on the number line. There are several ways students might think about comparisons. They might think about the distance between two points so that they can say that one is 8 more than or less than another. They might compare each point to zero and say that one is closer to zero than the other. They might also find the midpoint and say that it is halfway between these two points. All of these ways of making comparisons help build students' ideas about the number line and our number system. If students are not comparing values, you might explicitly ask, Which one is bigger, and how do you know?

Reflect

What observations can you make about the number -4?

Bouncing around the Number Line

Snapshot

Students play Number Line Bounce, building connections among integers, movement on the number line, and addition and subtraction.

Connection to CCSS
6.NS.5, 6.NS.6a, 6.NS.7a,c

Agenda

Activity	Time	Description/Prompt	Materials
Launch	10+ min	Model for students how to play Number Line Bounce using a class number line for all to see.	• Adding machine tape number line showing values −16 to +16, to display • Paperclips, two of different colors • Dice, two of different colors • Target Number sheet, to display • Colored chip or coin
Play	20–25 min	Partners use their number lines made in the Visualize activity to play Number Line Bounce, in which they must choose a positive or negative distance to move on the number line with the goal of landing on a target number.	• Student's number line, one per partnership • Objects to use as markers, such as paperclips, two of different colors per partnership • Dice, two of different colors per partnership • Tape • Target Number sheet, one per partnership • Colored chip or coin, one per partnership
Discuss	10–15 min	Discuss what students noticed as they played, the strategies they developed, and how they determined where they would land on each of their moves.	

Activity	Time	Description/Prompt	Materials
Extend	20+ min	Students can play a version of the game in which they keep score using their distance from the target number.	• Student's number line, one per partnership • Objects to use as markers, such as paperclips, two of different colors per partnership • Dice, two of different colors per partnership • Tape • Target Number sheet, one per partnership • Colored chip or coin, one per partnership

(Continued)

To the Teacher

For this activity, students will need the number lines they created in the Visualize activity, one per partnership. We encourage you to have students hold on to these manipulatives as they work with integers and make meaning out of the number system. You will also need the model you created in the launch of that lesson to use when showing students how to play today's game.

In this game, we make connections between integers, addition and subtraction, and direction on the number line. While the game has simple rules, the most challenging aspect is for players to predict where they will land when they move their marker across the zero. For instance, if a player is positioned at +3 and decides to move 5 units in the negative direction, or to the left, that player must develop ways of deciding where they will land. Students might count the points on the number line one by one, or they might begin to develop mental strategies, such as decomposing the 5-unit move into 3 units to get back to zero and then 2 more units into the negative territory. The more students play and need to leap across the zero, the more they will have to think about ways to make that movement efficient and accurate. In the discussion after the game, we encourage you to support students in articulating the ways in which they thought about moving in the negative direction as being like subtraction and moving in the positive direction as being like addition. These connections will prime students for later work with integer operations.

Activity

Launch

Launch the activity by telling students that today they will be playing a game on the number lines they made in the Visualize activity. Using a class copy of the adding machine tape number line that extends from −16 to +16, show students how to play Number Line Bounce. Tape the number line to the board so that students can see the movements of game play. Show the Target Number sheet and dice rolls on a document camera. When you are confident that students understand how to play, send them off in partners to play the game.

Play

Students play Number Line Bounce in partners. Each partnership will need one student-made number line, two objects of different colors for marking locations on the number line (one for each player), two dice of different colors, tape, one colored chip or coin, and one copy of the Target Number sheet.

Set up the game by taping the number line down where both players can sit side by side and see it clearly. Both players begin by placing their markers on zero. The two dice are going to represent positive and negative values; partners decide which color is positive and which is negative.

Game Directions

- Set the target number by tossing the colored chip or coin onto the Target Number sheet. Whatever value the chip lands on is the target number, or the value that both players are going to try to move their paperclips to on the number line. The goal of the game is to place your paperclip on the target number.
- Player A rolls both dice. One represents a positive value, or the number of units the player can move to the right. The other represents a negative value, or the number of units the player can move to the left. The player can move to either the left or the right. Player A decides which die they want to use to get closer to (or land on) the target number and moves their marker that number of units.
- Players alternate turns rolling and moving.
- The first player who lands on the target number wins the round.

- To play the next round, players stay where they are on the number line and simply set a new target number. Play begins again, starting with the player who did not win the previous round.

As partners play the game, encourage them to think about the strategies they are using to get closer to the target number.

Discuss

Gather the class together to discuss the following questions:

- What did you notice while playing the game?
- How did you decide how to move? How did you know where you would land?
- What strategies or shortcuts did you develop?
- What made the game challenging? Why?

In the discussion, be sure to draw attention to the strategies students were using to predict where their paperclips would land. While some students will count by touching the number line, others will begin to develop mental strategies for moving across the zero.

Extend

Students can play a variation of this game that includes scoring each round, with the goal of having the lower score after several rounds. At the end of each round, each player scores their distance from the target number. For instance, if the target number is −2 and Player A lands on the target number while Player B is on +4, then Player A scores 0 and Player B scores 6, or the distance between −2 and +4.

Look-Fors

- **How are students determining where they should place their paperclips?** Watch students on their turn figure out where to place their paperclip on the number line. Do they count the points using their fingers? Are they decomposing the numbers in some way? Are they doing work entirely mentally? Ask questions about how they figured it out and probe for the strategies students are using, particularly when students cross zero.

For instance, how does a student decide where to land when they begin at +1 and move 5 units in the negative direction? The student may be decomposing using the zero as a benchmark number to move 1 unit back to zero and then 4 units to −4. Using zero as a benchmark is a critical tool for thinking about movement on the number line, symmetry, and, later, integer operations.

- **Are students connecting negative numbers and subtraction?** Students may make the implicit connection between moving in the negative direction and subtraction when working with positive integers. For instance, if a player's paperclip is on +8 and they move 3 in the negative direction, they will likely think of this as $8 − 3 = 5$. This is mathematically accurate, and it has implications for later work with integer operations. Ask students to describe how they were thinking about this move and how it works when the numbers are not all positive. Students may not be sure, but if you pose this question to students as they play, they can investigate, Can we always think of moving in the negative direction as subtraction?

Reflect

What was the most useful strategy you developed for playing the game? Why?

Target Number

-7	-3	11	5	-10
10	-2	-5	12	6
8	-8	-6	4	9
0	-9	-11	-1	3
7	-4	2	1	-12

Going 2-D

Snapshot

Students investigate lines on a coordinate plane and look for patterns in the integer ordered pairs of the points on those lines. Students build connections between the integers on the number line and the two number lines that make the coordinate plane.

Connection to CCSS
6.NS.6abc, 6.NS.8

Agenda

Activity	Time	Description/Prompt	Materials
Launch	10–15 min	Show the class the Coordinate Plane sheet and ask them to make observations about the plane's structure. Highlight connections with the number line. Show students the Two Lines on a Plane sheet and ask them to look for points on the lines. Mark these and show students how to use the (x, y) convention for points on the plane.	• Coordinate Plane sheet, to display • Two Lines on a Plane sheet, to display
Explore	20 min	Partners use the Two Lines on a Plane sheet to explore what points they can find on the lines and what patterns they notice in these points. Students mark up their sheet to make these clear.	• Two Lines on a Plane sheet, one per partnership • Colors
Discuss	15 min	Invite students to mark on the class sheet all the points they identified on the two lines. Discuss patterns that students observed and collect these in a chart.	Chart and markers

Activity	Time	Description/Prompt	Materials
Explore	30+ min	Partners investigate what happens to the patterns in the points on a line if the line is moved. Students mark new lines on the coordinate plane and investigate which patterns remain and what new patterns emerge. Partners try this with several lines and create a chart with their findings.	• Coordinate Plane sheet, multiple copies per partnership • Ruler, one per partnership • Colors • Charts and markers • Tape
Discuss	15–20 min	Do a gallery walk of all the evidence partners collected. Discuss the patterns that students noticed and any connections they see between groups' work. Discuss any conjectures the class can develop about the points on a line.	Chart and markers
Extend	30+ min	Students investigate what happens when they transform a line using a rule, such as shifting every x value 2 units to the right or swapping the x and y values.	• Coordinate Plane sheet, multiple copies per partnership • Ruler, one per partnership • Colors

(Continued)

To the Teacher

In this investigation, we extend students' thinking about integers to the coordinate plane, which is simply two perpendicular number lines used to mark two-dimensional space. Positive and negative values for the horizontal (or x) and vertical (or y) positions tell where to locate a point in that space. Instead of values being one-dimensional distance on the number line, they now represent positions on a two-dimensional plane and can be used to navigate that space. This is yet another way we use integers, and it is important to remember that students need time to learn this particular conception of integers and to build critical connections between the coordinate plane and the number line.

As students investigate patterns, support them in using increasingly precise mathematical language to communicate about those patterns. Students may want to use visual words to describe the lines they observe. For instance, in comparing the two lines in the first part of the investigation, they may want to say they are the same, only flipped. You might provide the term *reflected* or *rotated* to describe the motion students are referring to. Students may want to use other kinds of movement words to describe the points, such as moving two over and two down. Provide students with additional words, such as *horizontal, vertical, positive direction,* and *negative direction.* Students may look for ways to describe the angle of the line, and it would make sense to offer the term *slope* for this attribute. Students learn vocabulary in a meaningful way when they are provided with a term that they need in order to communicate an idea they understand or have observed. Throughout this investigation, look for such opportunities to provide language just when students need it.

Activity

Launch

Launch the investigation by showing students the Coordinate Plane sheet on the document camera. Ask, What do you notice? Give students time to turn and talk with a partner about what they notice on the coordinate plane. Collect students' observations by annotating the Coordinate Plane sheet, using arrows, notes, and colors to highlight the structures that students notice. Be sure to draw attention to observations that connect the plane to the number line. If students do not yet have a name for this structure, tell them this is a *coordinate plane,* and show students how this is two number lines that are used together to mark off two-dimensional space.

Show students the Two Lines on a Plane sheet on the document camera, and tell them that on this coordinate plane, two different lines are shown. Ask, What points can you see on these lines? Give students a few moments to turn and talk to a partner about the points they notice. Collect a few points that students observed on each line and mark them on the plane. Use the convention of marking each as (x, y) and point out to students, if they have not seen this already, that this is how we indicate points on a coordinate plane. You might also want to record these points in a table of values of x and y, so that students can see this representation of points on a line.

Explore

Provide partners with the Two Lines on a Plane sheet and colors for marking up their observations. Partners investigate the following questions:

- What points are on these lines? Mark up the lines to show what you notice.
- What patterns do you see in the points on these lines? Keep a list of patterns to share.

Encourage students to hunt for as many patterns as they can. They can record these patterns either in writing on the back of their sheet or by annotating the lines themselves.

Discuss

Using the class copy of the Two Lines on a Plane sheet, mark all the points that students noticed. Invite students to come up to mark them and explain how they know that the name for that point is accurate.

Discuss the question, What patterns did you see in the points on these lines? Make a chart of patterns that students noticed. These patterns are likely to include some purely numeric patterns, and you may need to ask students to develop some ways of communicating these. For instance, how might you record the pattern that the horizontal (or x) value is the same as the vertical (or y) value? Other patterns students identify may be visual, involving movement horizontally and vertically. For these you may want to annotate the Two Lines on a Plane sheet to make the pattern clear.

Explore

Partners investigate, What happens to the patterns we've noticed in the points on a line if you move the line? Provide students with copies of the Coordinate Plane sheet, a ruler, colors, tape, a chart, and markers. Students mark new lines on the coordinate plane, label the points, and look for patterns. Students can place their lines wherever they like in order to investigate what happens, and they can do this as many times as they'd like, trying different sorts of lines. Encourage students to make lines by selecting two points to connect and extending the line to the edge of the plane. As they work, students investigate the following questions:

- Which patterns remain the same? Why might they stay the same?
- What new patterns can you find? Why did the patterns change?
- What patterns do different kinds of lines make?

Be sure to refer students back to the class chart that you made in the previous discussion as a reference for the patterns they are investigating. Partners make a chart with their findings, taping their marked-up coordinate planes to the chart and labeling the different patterns they found.

Discuss

Ask partners to post their evidence on the wall, and have the class do a gallery walk. As students circulate around the room looking at the evidence collected, ask them to consider, What do you notice about the patterns the class found? What connections can you make across the charts that groups made?

Gather the class together to discuss the following questions:

- What do you notice about the patterns the class found?
- What connections can you make across the charts that groups made?
- What conjectures can we make about the patterns on a line on the coordinate plane? (You may want to make a new chart called Conjectures about the Points on a Line.)
- What are you wondering now?

Extend

Students can extend their investigation by exploring a few ways of transforming a line and the patterns generated by these transformations. Ask partners to draw a line on a coordinate plane with clear points and then mark the points on the line. Explore the following questions: What new line is created if you

- Make each value its opposite? For instance, if $(2, -4)$ became $(-2, 4)$.
- Swap the x and y values for each point? For instance, if $(2, -4)$ became $(-4, 2)$.

- Shift every *x* value 2 units to the right? For instance, if $(2, -4)$ became $(4, -4)$.
- Shift every *y* value 2 units down? For instance, if $(2, -4)$ became $(2, -6)$.
- Make your own rule to investigate?

After transforming the line, what does it look like? What changed? Why?

Look-Fors

- **Are students able to distinguish which points are on a line and which are merely close?** In the two lines we have provided in the first half of the investigation, seeing the points where these lines intersect with the grid on the coordinate plane is relatively straightforward, if students understand what we mean when we say that "a point is on a line." If students are struggling, they may not know how to interpret this language and may need you to be more explicit about what it means for a point to be on, or not on, a line. However, when students are placing their own lines on the coordinate plane, the lines may not be as crisply drawn, and it may be genuinely challenging to tell. Ask students to backtrack by asking, What were the two points that you started with in constructing your line? How can we mark those? Using the ruler as a straightedge to look for other points that would be on this line may also help students. Notice whether students are thinking about the value of the non-whole number points on the line. Students often do not think of these as points on the line, and if students do notice them, be sure to highlight this in your discussion.

- **Are students struggling to see patterns in the points?** If you notice that students are struggling to identify any pattern in their lines, it may be that they simply need to mark more points to be able to see patterns. You might ask, How can you record these points to help you see patterns? While many students will find it easiest to record these directly on the coordinate plane, some students may better see patterns if they record the points in a list, column, or table. You may also ask students, How do you move from point to point on the line? What are some ways to describe what is happening? Students may want to mark on the coordinate plane the horizontal and vertical motions that get them, step-by-step, from one point to another. There are patterns in this movement that may provide a better entry point than numerical patterns.

- **How are students drawing their own lines? Are they precise?** Students can certainly plunk any line down on the coordinate plane and look for patterns; however, given the size of the plane we've provided, students will be set up for success if they select two points to connect and extend the line they create to the edge of the plane. You may want to encourage students to explicitly premark these two points and connect them as precisely as they can to make it clearer what patterns exist. This may pose fine motor challenges for some students. Encourage students to work with their partners to hold the ruler and draw the line, and you may also want to provide physical assistance so that students can draw the line they intend.

Reflect

If you know some of the points on a line, what can you predict about that line? For instance, if you know that the points (3, 1) and (0, 0) are on a line, what else can you tell about the line?

Coordinate Plane

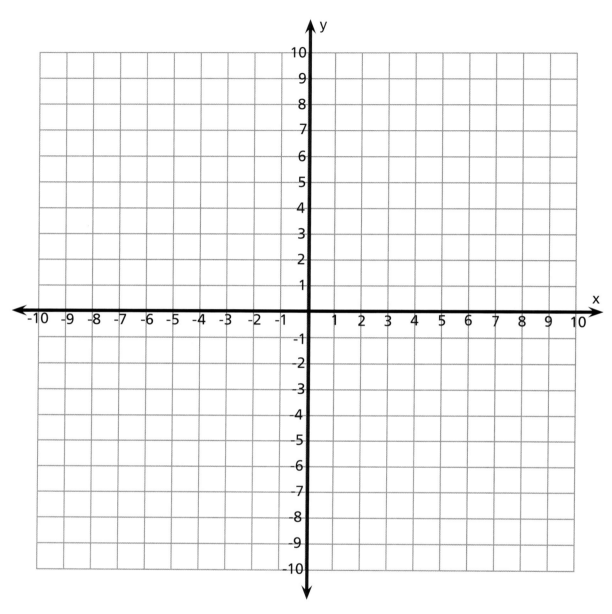

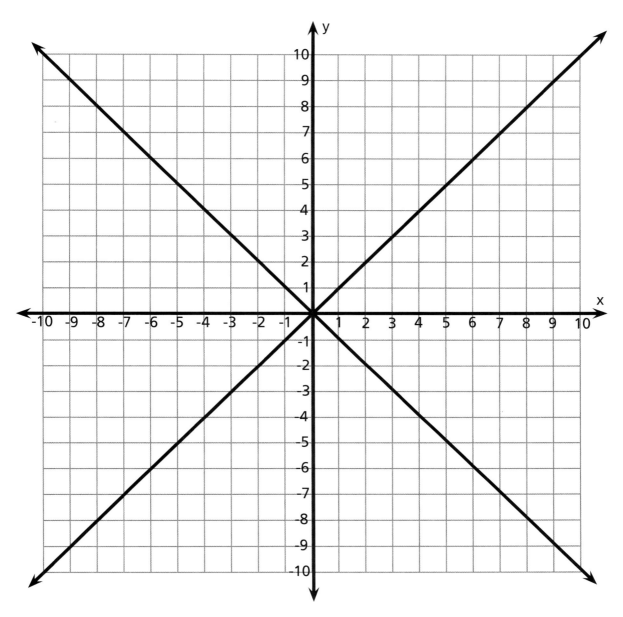

BIG IDEA 4

Finding and Using Unit Rates

Unit rates are all around us in the world, and when students learn about them and start to see and use them in different ways, they will have a mathematical lens to use in their lives and in their future study of mathematics. The idea of a unit rate is one that can be difficult for people if it is introduced procedurally; students get the idea that they need to divide something by something, but they are often confused as to what they should be dividing. We try to help with this potential confusion by giving students the space to think about what the unit rate really means. In my teaching of unit rates, I have found that students often ask which number is the number to divide by. I always answer this question with a question! I ask students to estimate what they think the unit rate should be. This encourages them to move away from a procedure and think about the idea of the unit rate. In our Play activity that involves the price of bottles, for example, students are told that single bottles cost $1 and that six bottles cost $3. At this point, if students are asked to find a unit rate, some students will wonder whether to divide 6 by 3 or 3 by 6. The two possibilities give different results of $2 and $0.50. This is a good time to ask students the sort of cost they would expect for bottles sold in groups of six. This orients them to think of the big idea: What should the rate be?

Unit rates are most often seen and used when buying items or thinking about scaling up supplies. But unit rates exist all around us in architecture, nature, and even our bodies. We want students to be able to visualize unit rates first before we ask them to think about numerical relationships. In the Visualize activity, we invite students to explore unit rates in tiling patterns to support students in seeing the relationship between different shapes that repeat in continuous and predictable ways. We then invite them to think about numerical relationships.

In the Visualize activity, we ask students to consider a two-dimensional tiling pattern with a finite border. Students are asked to work out what the base unit is that is repeating and that tiles the space. We have designed this activity so that there are different possible base unit rates, which allows for mathematical choice. Students can work to identify some that work and some that don't. We ask students to complete a table of values quantifying the number of base unit tiles and the shapes that make up those tiles. The table of values will be different depending on the unit tile they identify, but the totals of the values will be the same because all the students are working on the same image. Students may want to use pattern blocks, other shapes, and dot paper as tools for constructing these patterns and patty paper or transparencies to check their unit.

In the Play activity, we move on from a unit as a geometric figure to a unit that is connected to an item as cost. Students will look for the best deal in relationship to a unit rate. We hope that students will see unit rate as a strategy that is useful for comparing items in their lives. This activity is one where it is important to ask students to estimate what they think their unit price will be. Groups are encouraged to create a What's the Best Deal? chart with the choices on top and a visual proof of the solution on the bottom. Other students can then rotate around the classroom trying to figure out the best deal at each station and then discuss the group's visual proof.

In the Investigate activity, students work together on finding a method to identify a unit rate to express speed. Students use spaces and tools to collect walking speed data. They then work together to find a way to measure and quantify how fast they walk. This should help students realize that a rate is a comparison of two different measures that can be put together. A guiding principle to remember with all unit-rate work is that students should think carefully about what the unit rate means, and what they should expect as a result, before jumping into any calculations.

Jo Boaler

Seeing Unit Rates

Snapshot

Students visualize the concept of unit rates by exploring tiling patterns that repeat infinitely across space.

Connection to CCSS
6.RP.2, 6.RP.3a,b, 6.RP.1

Agenda

Activity	Time	Description/Prompt	Materials
Launch	10–15 min	Show students the Tiling Pattern sheet and ask them to make observations. Tell students that the pattern is composed of *base units*, or clusters of shapes that can be repeated infinitely to make the pattern. Invite students to find and justify different possible base units in this pattern.	• Tiling Pattern sheet, to display • Colors • Optional: transparency or patty paper
Explore	20 min	Partners explore how many tiles of each shape would be needed for an increasing number of base units. Students look for patterns in their findings that might help them predict how many tiles they need for any number of base units.	• Tiling Pattern Recording Sheet, one per partnership • Optional: colors
Discuss	15–20 min	Collect students' findings into a class table and look for patterns. Discuss how they might use these patterns to predict how many tiles of each shape would be needed for 100 or 500 base units. Name the relationships between the number of tiles and the number of base units as a *unit rate*.	Chart and markers

Activity	Time	Description/Prompt	Materials
Explore	25–30 min	Partners design their own tiling patterns that repeat a base unit infinitely.	Make available: pattern blocks and/or other shape sets, regular and isometric dot paper (see appendix), colors, and patty paper or transparencies
Discuss	20+ min	Do a gallery walk of the patterns students created and ask students to find the base unit in each pattern, which they can sketch on patty paper for the creators of the pattern to see. Students examine the different ways others saw their pattern and discuss what surprised them. Discuss the different unit rates represented in the patterns.	• Patty paper, several sheets per partnership • Optional: file folders or envelopes

To the Teacher

Unit rates are most often seen and used when buying items or thinking about scaling up supplies. For instance, bananas sell for $0.60 per pound, or we predict students will use 15 pencils per year. But unit rates exist all around us in architecture, nature, and even our bodies. We want students to be able to visualize unit rates before we dive into thinking about them as a numerical relationship. In this activity, we explore unit rates in tiling patterns to support students in seeing the relationship between different shapes that repeat in continuous and predictable ways forever.

To see the unit rates in tiling patterns, students first must see the unit of the patterns itself, what we're calling the *base unit*. In the examples here, possible base units are marked. Notice how each of these units can be repeated to create the whole pattern.

Different tiling patterns with base units identified for tiling

In most tiling patterns, there are multiple ways to decompose the pattern into a base unit. In the examples here, you'll see how the pattern that we explore in this lesson can be decomposed into base units in different ways.

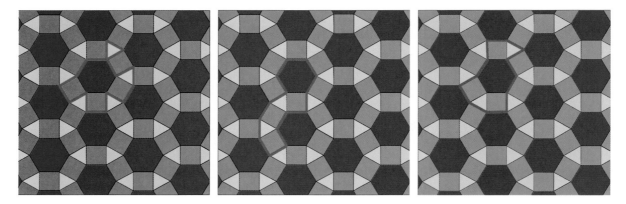

Three different base units for tiling the pattern. Can you find more?

In the launch, we invite students to see these base units in different ways and to use patty paper or a transparency to confirm that iterating this unit will fill in the pattern continually. We have deliberately chosen a pattern in which seeing the base unit is challenging. The rings of shapes make it easy to assume that the hexagon fully encircled by triangles and squares is the base unit, but if you try to iterate this unit, you will discover that it does not cover the surface. Encouraging multiple ways to see this base unit builds flexibility and acknowledges the many ways that the pattern can be decomposed. But regardless of the particular way that students identify the base unit, they will find through exploration that each base unit is composed of the same relationship, or ratio, of pieces. Unit rates allow for a great deal of flexibility, because they can be scaled up or down to suit one's needs, while also maintaining a consistent relationship. It is this duality of flexibility and constancy that we explore in this lesson.

There are several ways of conceiving of the unit rates in the tile patterns. One way is to see how the number of squares or triangles relates to the number of hexagons. If students want to explore this relationship, it is reasonable to frame the unit rates as, How many squares (or triangles) *per hexagon* are needed to build the pattern? But we have chosen to focus most of our questions on how many of each kind of shape are needed *per base unit*. We think that this is the most transferable way of thinking about unit rates in tiling patterns, because some tiling patterns may require more than one of each kind of shape to make a base unit. The relationship between the different types of shapes is a *ratio*, and you may want to use this language with students if it comes up in discussion.

Finally, a note on creating tiling patterns. This is challenging work, which can be made more manageable with manipulatives. Pattern blocks are particularly helpful here, and if you have them available, we highly recommend giving students access to them in the second half of the lesson. However, pattern blocks are also constraining. With pattern blocks, students can use only one kind of triangle, and they cannot use pentagons or octagons. Given the advantages and the limitations, we recommend making available a wide variety of tools for creating tiling patterns, including pattern blocks, other shape sets you may have, and regular and isometric dot paper (see appendix). You may also want to give students opportunities to look for tiling patterns in the real world that they might emulate, particularly if you have tiles in your school.

Activity

Launch

Launch the activity by showing students the Tiling Pattern sheet on the document camera. Ask, What do you notice? Give students a chance to turn and talk to a partner about what they see. Discuss students' observations and draw attention to the shapes students see and how the pattern continues in every direction infinitely.

Tell students that there is a *base unit* to this pattern, or a part of the pattern that repeats again and again to make the pattern continue across space forever. Ask, Where do you see the base unit in this pattern? What cluster of shapes repeats to make the pattern? Give students a chance to turn and talk to a partner about what they see. Invite students to share the base units they see, and color-code them on the sample tile pattern. Celebrate the different ways students see the base unit. Students may need to trace the unit on a transparency or patty paper so they can slide it over to see whether it iterates or to convince others that it works as a base unit.

Tell students that they're going to explore how to use this unit to predict how many tiles they would need to cover any space.

Explore

Provide partners with the Tiling Pattern Recording Sheet. Ask, How many tiles would you need in order to repeat the base unit any number of times? Students use the tiling pattern to explore this question and complete the table showing how many of each shape students would need for different numbers of base units. Some students may want to color-code the pattern to help them see the iterating units, so we suggest offering students colors.

To help students see patterns, we have prefilled the number of base units for students to explore as they begin, but we have also provided some blank lines so that students might either continue this pattern or try to predict how many tiles would be needed for a much larger number of base units.

After students have completed at least the first five rows of the table, ask, What do you notice? How is the table connected to the tile pattern?

Discuss

Gather the class together and use the class's data to create a class version of the table on a chart. Come to agreement on the values for each of the first five rows and ask students to justify the rows they added. You may want to ask students to add these rows in increasing order so that they help students see patterns.

Discuss the following questions:

- What do you notice?
- How is the table connected to the pattern?
- How would we predict how many tiles we need if our space needed 100 base units? Or 500 base units?

Together name the pattern that helps us predict how many tiles are needed: for every one unit, there are one hexagon, two triangles, and three squares. Tell students that this is a *unit rate*, or rather it is three unit rates: one hexagon per base unit, two triangles per base unit, and three squares per base unit. These unit rates help us predict the shapes that will be needed to cover larger or smaller surfaces.

Explore

Partners design their own tiling pattern that has a base unit that can repeat forever in every direction, like the one the class has just explored. Students may want to use pattern blocks, other shapes, and dot paper (see appendix) as tools for constructing these patterns, and patty paper or a transparency to check their unit.

Ask partners to make a table for their tiling pattern to show how many tiles would be needed to cover a surface of any size. Students explore the following questions:

- What do you notice in your table?
- What is your unit rate?
- How is it similar to or different from the first pattern we explored?
- What do you wonder?

Students can design more than one tiling pattern to explore how the answers to these questions change (or do not) with different patterns.

Discuss

Invite students to post their patterns in different stations around the room. Provide partners with several sheets of patty paper. Ask students to do a gallery walk to look at others' patterns. As they walk, ask students to look for, Where is the unit in each pattern? How many different ways can you see it? Partners record how they see the base unit for each pattern on a piece of patty paper, which they can leave behind at that pattern station. You may want to provide a folder in which students can place their paper so that each visiting partnership has a fresh chance to see the base unit without being influenced by the ways others saw it.

After students have had a chance to visit all the patterns, partners return to their own pattern and sort through the patty papers to find all the different ways people saw the unit. Partners discuss, Do they all show the same base unit? Why or why not? Partners can cluster together base units that are identical and look for different base units. Partners post these different base units next to their pattern.

Discuss with the class the following questions:

- What surprised you about how others saw your pattern?
- What did you find interesting about the patterns you saw during the gallery walk?

- What did you notice about the different unit rates in the patterns the class created?
- What do you wonder now?

Look-Fors

- **Are students identifying an accurate base unit?** Seeing the base unit in a tiling pattern is not straightforward, and we have selected a pattern that draws the eye toward a cluster of shapes that is not a base unit. Students will need to decompose the figure and test whether the portion they have identified can be iterated infinitely to create the entire pattern. Patty paper or transparencies can be useful for helping students to try, test, and revise base units. Some students may simply want to color in a base unit and then see whether they can repeat it in different colors across the surface. Some students may even want to cut out the base units to see whether they can literally be decomposed in the way they see in their minds. If students are struggling, emphasize all the options they have and that students are safe to try multiple times, make mistakes, and revise. Ask, What might be the base unit? How could you test that idea to see what happens? If students find that their idea for a base unit does not work, encourage them to revise rather than start over. You might ask, Why didn't this base unit work? Was it too large or too small?

- **Are students attending to multiple patterns in the table they have constructed?** The table sets up multiple comparisons that could lead to patterns. Students might attend to the relationships across the row, noting that for one base unit there is a given number of each shape. This relationship could lead to thinking about different unit rates. Students might also attend to patterns vertically, noting how the number of shapes increases with each additional base unit in multiples of 1, 2, or 3. With four columns, students may have trouble isolating different patterns because there is so much data, or they may identify one pattern and not seek others. You may want to focus students' attention on different parts of the table to help them see patterns. You might say, "I see you noticed a pattern in this column. What about the other columns?" or "You noticed how the hexagons relate to the number of base units. How do the other shapes relate to the number of base units?"

- **How are students extending or predicting using rates?** When extending the table, some students might continue to step up the number of base units one by one, and if they are doing so, you'll want to pay attention to how students are completing each row. Are they simply adding a new set of shapes—adding one more hexagon, two more triangles, and three more squares? Or are students moving down the rows skip-counting or thinking in multiples? When students focus on the pattern as additive, rather than multiplicative, they will struggle to predict the number of shapes needed for a number of base units unless they count up from one. This is tedious and inefficient. Encourage students to think multiplicatively about the relationships. You might ask, If you know the number of base units, how could you predict the number of triangles? What is the relationship between the number of base units and the number of triangles (or squares or hexagons)? Support students in naming this relationship in a way that they can act on to make predictions, such as, "For each base unit, we need two triangles," or "The number of triangles I need is double the number of base units."

Reflect

What is a unit rate?

 **Tiling Pattern**

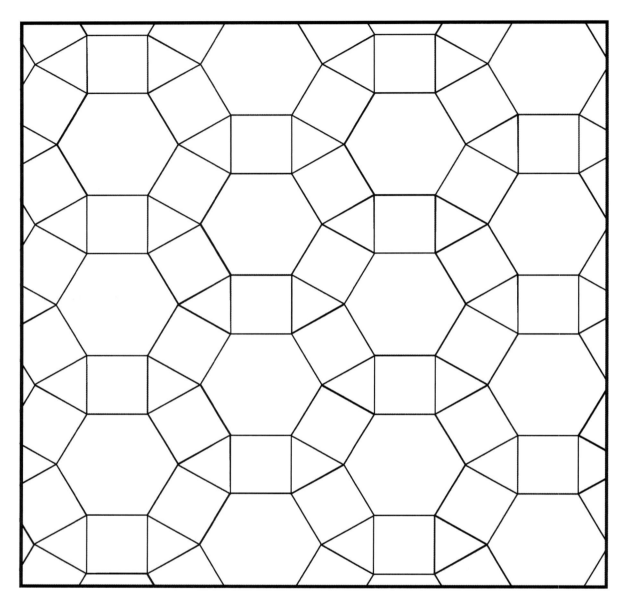

Mindset Mathematics, Grade 6, copyright © 2019 by Jo Boaler, Jen Munson, Cathy Williams.
Reproduced by permission of John Wiley & Sons, Inc.

Number of Base Units	Number of Hexagons	Number of Squares	Number of Triangles
1			
2			
3			
4			
5			

Tiling Pattern Recording Sheet

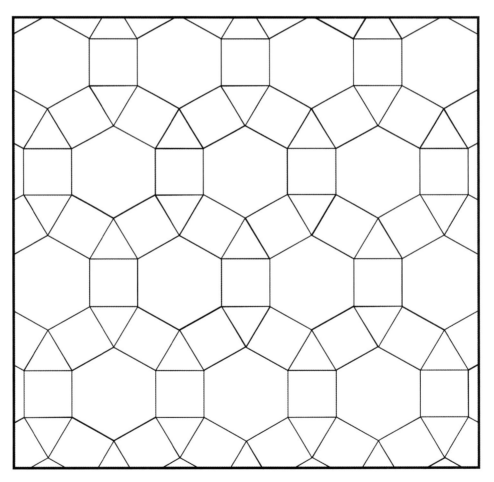

Mindset Mathematics, Grade 6, copyright © 2019 by Jo Boaler, Jen Munson, Cathy Williams. Reproduced by permission of John Wiley & Sons, Inc.

Seeing the Best Deal

Snapshot

What's the best deal? Using this frequently asked question, students explore how to use rates to make comparisons while playing a shopping game at stations they create.

Connection to CCSS
6.RP.1, 6.RP.2, 6.RP.3b

Agenda

Activity	Time	Description/Prompt	Materials
Launch	10 min	Show students the Water Bottle Price Sheet and ask them, Which is the best deal? Students turn and talk and then share their reasoning. Ask students how they saw this in their minds.	Water Bottle Price Sheet, to display
Explore	20–30 min	In small groups, students determine the best deal from choices on a task card. Groups then create a What's the Best Deal? chart with the choices on top and a visual proof of the solution on the bottom.	• What's the Best Deal? Cards, one card per group • Chart and markers, for each group
Play	20–30 min	Each group hosts a What's the Best Deal? station with their poster, with the visual proof covered. Others rotate around the classroom trying to figure out what the best deal is at each station and then discussing the group's visual proof.	Tape
Discuss	15+ min	Discuss the strategies that students developed for making comparisons, and which deals were the hardest to see. Discuss what made a convincing visual proof and what surprised them as they played.	

To the Teacher

In this activity, we first ask students to explore as a small group the best deal among some choices, and then they use the evidence they have gathered to make stations for others to try to find the best deal. The design of the posters students create is important. Students need to present the choices for the deal at the top of the chart. They may want to title their chart What's the Best Deal? They need to record their visual proof underneath this so that it can be folded up to hide the proof. This will allow the students visiting the station to come to their own ideas about the best deal before they see the visual proof. You may want to ask students to fold their charts up before they start making them so they can see which parts of the poster will show and what will be hidden.

For the deals, we have created cards that involve different contexts in which students might need to decide what the better deal is from among several choices in which the unit rate would be a useful tool for comparing. However, your students likely encounter these decisions in many different contexts every day. We encourage you to create your own cards like the ones we've provided using contexts familiar and relevant to your students. Perhaps your school cafeteria prompts students to make decisions about the best deal every day. Students may encounter these decisions when getting to and from school, buying supplies or groceries, buying tickets for events, or in their recreation. Making these decisions parallel to the kinds they must make in their home lives will support students in seeing how very useful and relevant unit rates can be.

Activity

Launch

Launch the activity by showing students the Water Bottle Price Sheet on the document camera. Tell them these are the prices for water at a local store. Ask, What's the best deal? Give students a chance to turn and talk to a partner about what they think is the best deal and why. Ask students to share their thinking and draw attention to those ideas that think in terms of rates, rather than absolute cost. Ask, How did you see the best deal in your mind? Students likely did some interesting kinds of mental work to make comparisons, scaling up or down the number of water bottles. Be sure to invite students to share not just the numerical work they did but also how they saw these comparisons in their minds.

Tell students that they are going to be exploring unit rates today to find the best deals and how to make visual proofs of those deals. The goal of a visual proof is to create a convincing picture, diagram, flowchart, graph, or other image with numbers or other labels that explains why your solution makes sense.

Explore

Students work in small groups to determine the best deal among the choices on a task card. Provide each group with a different task card from the eight different task cards. Each group then works to

- Figure out what the best deal is for their card.
- Design a visual proof of why this is the best deal.
- Create a poster that shows the choices on the top and the visual proof on the bottom, so that the proof can be folded over and masked in the game.

Play

Set up to play What's the Best Deal? Ask each group to post their deal chart with the proof folded over and taped up. These should be in locations where the group members can reach them to show their proof later. Designate a group member to stay with the chart and host the station. You can rotate these hosts during the game so that everyone gets a chance to see others' charts.

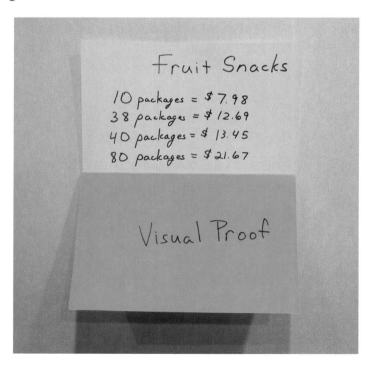

A student display of their What's the Best Deal? task with their visual proof behind the folded paper

Rotate groups around to visit each deal station. When they are at the station, the host poses the deal question shown at the top of chart. They ask, What's the best deal? The visitors can use whatever tools they like to come up with their decision about the best deal. When the visitors are ready, they tell the host what they think is the best deal and why.

The host shows the visual proof their group has developed. The host asks, Does this proof confirm your estimate? Is it different? Why? Are you convinced? Why or why not?

Make sure students have the chance to visit several stations before bringing the class together for discussion.

Discuss

Gather the class to discuss the following questions:

- Which deals were hardest to see? Why?
- What strategies did you use? Which were most effective? Why?
- How did you use unit rates? When were they helpful and why?
- What mistakes did you make? What did you learn from those mistakes?
- Which proofs were most convincing? What made a proof easy to understand or convincing?
- Which deals surprised you? Why?

Make connections between the kinds of strategies students used at different stations. Be sure to discuss whether different kinds of deals required different kinds of strategies. For instance, it may be that scaling up made the most sense for some deals, but finding the unit rate made the most sense for others.

Look-Fors

- **How are students making comparisons based on rate?** To make valid comparisons, students will need strategies that allow them to compare different prices for the same thing. Students can do this by scaling up the units so that they are buying the same large number of items. For instance, students could compare the price of the water bottles by imagining that they need to buy 24 bottles of water and seeing what that would cost if they purchased single bottles or packs of 6, 8, or 12. This is a mathematically valid way of making comparisons, but it demands finding the larger number where comparison is possible, a common multiple. Alternatively, students can make comparisons with a unit rate, which will always work, but requires division or thinking in equal groups. Students may also combine these efforts to compare individual deals in pairs. For instance, students might note immediately that $1 for a bottle is a worse deal that $3 for a six-pack, because it would cost $6 to buy six bottles at the single-bottle rate. Others may use the unit rate to see that $3 for a six-pack is $0.50 per bottle, which they can then scale up to say that an eight-pack should be $4, not $4.50. When discussing these different methods, be sure to draw attention to how scaling up and scaling down using rates can be used flexibly to make comparisons.

- **Are students' visual proofs showing convincing evidence?** Push students to show their evidence, not just make calculations. That might include drawing pictures to show the ways rates scale up or down or making diagrams to show comparisons. Encourage students to be creative with these visual proofs. You might want to ask students questions about what they see in their minds when they are comparing different values. For instance, they might see a six-pack of water as two quarters inside each bottle, or they might imagine three dollar bills cut in half, or a stack of six blocks with pairs in three colors. You might then ask, If this is what one deal looks like, how can you show the other deals using the same kind of picture so that we can compare? Be sure that students don't show just the best deal but why it is the best in comparison to the other choices.

Reflect

When would you use unit rates outside of our class? Why?

Water Bottle Price Sheet

$1.00

$7.00

$3.00

$4.50

What's the Best Deal? Cards

Candy Bar	**Fruit Snacks**
1 bar = $.89	10 packages = $7.98
6 bars = $16.48	38 packages = $12.69
48 bars = $35.89	40 packages = $13.45
	80 packages = $21.67
Glue Sticks	**Origami Paper**
4 sticks = $2.71	120 sheets = $3.00
8 sticks = $5.40	200 sheets = $4.99
12 sticks = $7.89	500 sheets = $9.99
30 sticks = $14.99	750 sheets = $12.99
48 sticks = $18.99	

Socks	Fountain Drink
1 = $9.00	Small, 16 oz = $1.00
3 = $16.00	Medium, 21 oz = $1.29
6 = $20.00	Large, 32 oz = $1.49

Post-It Notes	Mechanical Pencils
12 pack = $9.99	6 pack = $4.15
18 pack = $29.99	12 pack = $9.99
24 pack = $37.11	32 pack = $11.79

How Fast Do You Walk?

Snapshot

How fast do you walk? Students collect data and develop ways of expressing speed to explore speed as a unit rate.

Connection to CCSS
6.RP.2, 6.RP.3a,b,d

Agenda

Activity	Time	Description/Prompt	Materials
Launch	10 min	Pose the question, How fast do you think you walk? Record on a chart the ways students describe their speeds. Discuss the different ways students communicated speed, and name speed as a rate.	Chart and markers
Explore	45–60+ min	Groups choose one member's walking speed to explore, and develop a plan for what data they need to collect to describe that person's walking speed. Students use spaces and tools to collect walking speed data. Using this data, students develop a way of expressing the person's walking speed and present their data and conclusions in a chart.	• Space for walking (classroom, hallway, gym, or outdoor space) • Measurement tools, such as meter sticks or yardsticks, tape measures, rulers, string, and timers or stopwatches • Marking tools, such as masking tape or sidewalk chalk • Chart and markers, for each group

Activity	Time	Description/Prompt	Materials
Discuss	20–30 min	Groups present their processes and results. Discuss the strategies students developed for finding speed and the units they selected. Discuss which choices make the most sense, why, and whether different ways allow the class to make comparisons. Discuss what made the process of finding speed challenging.	
Extend	45+ min	Students investigate other ways that speed is expressed in different contexts, such as Olympic running or whale migration. Students explore why different ways of expressing speed are needed and how they would decide on units for speed.	• Information resources, such as nonfiction texts or access to web-based information • Optional: chart and markers

To the Teacher

In this investigation, we turn attention to a particular kind of unit rate that students encounter in the everyday world: speed. Although students are familiar with expressing speed in miles per hour, these particular units are not the only way of measuring walking speed, and indeed may not be the most appropriate. This investigation requires students to make decisions about how to measure both distance and time. In choosing units for time, students may have to consider whether or how they will express speed as a unit rate. For instance, if students measure distance in feet, they have to choose whether to express speed in seconds, minutes, or hours. But feet per second may be difficult to measure, or lead to fractional measures for distance. Given this conundrum, students might choose a different unit for time, such as minutes, or choose not to use a unit rate and express speed as feet per 10 seconds, for example. These decisions should give the class lots to talk about and give you many probing opportunities to ask about their processes. With that in mind, we encourage you to focus conversations with students on the process of finding foot speed, rather than on the speed itself. The investigation should not be a competition for the fastest walker, rather an exploration of what it means to find a rate for expressing distance over time.

Students will need access to a buffet of tools to make the decisions necessary for this investigation. Given this focus on decisions, we encourage you to deliberately provide students with options for tools so that they need to make conscious choices. When confronting yardsticks and meter sticks, tape measures, string, and masking tape, students will need to actively decide what makes the most sense to them; you, in turn, can ask about those decisions.

Activity

Launch

Launch the investigation by posing the question, How fast do you think you walk? Give students a chance to turn and talk to a partner. Collect some of the students' answers or estimates on a chart titled How Fast Do You Think You Walk? It is important that at this point you focus the conversation not on the quality of the estimates, or even the strategies students used to arrive at them. Instead notice the ways that students use rates to describe speed. Tell students that speed is a *rate*, a comparison between distance and time. Make connections between speed as a rate and the other rates you have been exploring recently, such as tiles per base unit and cents per bottle of water. Speed is a relationship between some unit of distance and some unit of time. Pose the investigation and explain the resources you have for students to use as they work.

Explore

Students work in small groups to develop ways of expressing their foot speed. The group must first decide whose walking speed to investigate, since each person will have a slightly different speed. The group discusses the question, What data will we need to describe how fast a person walks? Each group collects the data they need to develop methods for describing walking speed. Groups investigate the questions, Can you find multiple ways to express the same speed? Which do you think is the best way? Why?

Provide students with the following:

- Space for walking, such as a classroom, hallway, gym, or outdoor space
- Measurement tools such as meter sticks or yardsticks, tape measures, rulers, string, timers, or stopwatches
- Marking tools appropriate for your space, such as masking tape or sidewalk chalk

Each group works together to make a poster to show the data they collected and how they found their walking speed. If students found multiple ways, they should indicate which they think is the best way of expressing foot speed and why. You may want to invite students to choose a destination (a part of the school, a local shop, home, etc.) and to estimate how long it would take their walker to arrive; have them include this information in their chart.

Discuss

Post the groups' charts and invite each group to share their process and results. When discussing students' work, focus attention on the following questions:

- What strategies did you use to find the speed?
- How did you decide what units of measure to use? What made the most sense? Why?
- What was hard?
- What did you find that surprised you? Why?
- If we look across our charts, can we tell who is the fastest walker? Why or why not?

During the discussion, be sure to draw attention to the choices that students made about units, the ways in which rates were important to describing speed, and the connection between the speeds students articulated and unit rates. Students very likely reported their speeds in the form of a unit rate; some of these may have been standard measures of speed, such as feet per minute, while others may have been improvised measures of speed such as floor tiles per minute. Compare the utility of these different measures and why students made the particular choices they did.

Extend

Invite students to investigate other ways of expressing speed in the world. For instance, how is speed measured for Olympic runners? Cars on the highway? Space exploration? Sound? Whale migrations? The flight of a bumble bee? Provide students access to information resources, such as nonfiction texts or the internet, to gather data. Students explore the following questions:

- What different ways of expressing speed are used?
- Why are rates expressed differently?
- How would you choose a rate to express speed?

Ask students to come up with other instances where speed could be expressed and to develop an appropriate way of measuring the speed. What units would you use and why? You may want to ask students to create a chart of their findings or contribute speeds to a class chart as a shared resource for discussion.

Look-Fors

- **How are students planning their work?** Decisions are a crucial part of this investigation. As you observe students getting started, you might see some groups rushing to collect data, estimate, or start making a chart. Ask questions about their plan to help students slow down and attend to the decisions they are making. You might simply ask, What is your plan? What data are you going to collect? How will you do that? Why are you going to collect data in that way? What will you do next? Why? Support students in acting intentionally so that they collect data they can use and have a plan for how to use it.

- **What data are students collecting?** As students' plans unfold, observe the kinds of data students are collecting and ask questions about their intent. Students will need to collect data simultaneously in two dimensions: distance and time. Are students measuring both? How are they doing so? Students might choose to fix one of these measures and then examine the other. For instance, students might decide to measure the distance a person can walk in one minute, using a stopwatch to tell the walker to start and stop, and then measuring the distance walked. Alternatively, students might measure out a distance, such as 100 feet, and then time how long it takes to walk that distance. This second approach makes it more challenging to arrive at a unit rate for speed as we typically express it. Ask students how they decided on their approach and what they will do with their data next in order to come to a speed. You might ask, How will you express the speed when you are finished?

- **What units are they selecting?** Units are some of the most important choices that students make in this investigation. Students might select any number of units for distance—centimeters, meters, kilometers, inches, feet, yards, miles, floor tiles, sidewalk segments, lockers. They also must choose from several measure of time, particularly seconds, minutes, and hours, but they may also select less typical units such as days or weeks. Ask students about the units they are selecting and why these make the most sense for walking speed. If students select nonstandard units, such as sidewalk segments, you might ask them how they know that these units are all the same and why they think that is the best way.

- **What unit conversion issues emerge?** As students work, they may confront that the ways they collected data do not match the ways they want to express walking speed. For instance, students may have recorded feet and seconds, but they want to express speed in yards per minute. This poses challenges for unit conversion that we encourage you to embrace. This is an authentic opportunity for working with unit conversion, and students may struggle with thinking about converting in both dimensions simultaneously. Ask, How can you organize your data so that you can see equivalence? You might encourage students to convert first one unit and then the other to avoid confusion. You might also want to pose the problem of unit conversion to the class, asking, This group wants to change their units. How could they do that? Such a challenge could become a class investigation of its own.

Reflect

Why do you think we use unit rates for speed?

BIG IDEA 5

Reasoning with Proportions

There's an instructional strategy I really like, one that I now use in all of my teaching and that can be put to good use in this big idea. I show students a visual of a mathematical idea—which can be as simple as a collection of dots (https://www .youcubed.org/resources/jo-teaching-visual-dot-card-number-talk/)—and ask them what they see. I then collect all of the students' ideas on a board at the front, no matter how good or correct they seem to be, usually putting the student's name onto the idea for later reference. In the activities in this Big Idea we encourage you to engage students in similar ways, collecting their ideas and naming them so that they feel ownership for them. In this big idea, we are encouraging quantitative literacy by asking students to, at first, make sense of a complex and interesting graph. The students are asked to make sense of data that is shown through multiple representations in the first two activities in the big idea. This is a good time to encourage students to come up with their own ideas of what they see in the graphs, and to accept those ideas without judgment, using them as a source for discussion. Being able to read and make sense of complex data shown through different representations is one of the most important areas of mathematical literacy that students need to develop.

In the Visualize activity, students are invited to read a graph of animals' jumping distances, which we think they will find really interesting. The graph presents data in a way that students are likely to be unfamiliar with, and this is an excellent time to invite students to tell you what they see. You can lead a class discussion on what the graph is showing. We intend that after an initial opening, students read the graph in pairs, annotate it so that they can think and write, and then discuss what they see as a class. Once they have worked out what the graph shows, they can, if they want to, add their own data to the graph.

In the Play activity, students are presented with task cards that show two different pieces of data for some animals. They are then invited to make their own proportion from the data they choose and create a graph illustrating the data—similar to the graph they saw in the Visualize activity. This will give students an opportunity to make choices—an important part of mathematics—and create a graph with information that they have decided, together, to show and collect. We expect that this activity may prompt interesting conversations because some groups may choose the same task card but present the data in different ways.

In the Investigate activity, we ask students to consider a pattern based on a square table with four seats around it. In the previous lessons, students have looked at unit rates and proportions. In this activity, they will consider a unit rate that they develop for the tables and chairs in a restaurant. Students will be making and exploring patterns, and they will need to pay attention to certain constraints; both exploring patterns and considering constraints are intrinsically mathematical acts. The constraint in this investigation is that there is only one chair for each square side of the table. Instead of focusing on a single answer, they will be asked what they think is the most efficient way of seating people. Different table arrangements will yield different results. Students will be asked to justify their reasoning. We conclude by asking students to think about the ways this activity is connected to the ideas of area and perimeter.

Jo Boaler

Jump! Jump!

Snapshot

Students visualize proportions by exploring a graph of animal jump length in proportion to body length. As they make sense of the data, students explore how proportions change the way they understand the animals the data represents.

Connection to CCSS
6.RP.1, 6.RP.2

Agenda

Activity	Time	Description/Prompt	Materials
Launch	10 min	Show students the Animal Jump Graph sheet and ask, What does this graph show? Discuss students' interpretations and be sure they understand the different information being communicated by the two kinds of bars. Tell students that comparing body length to jump length is a rate called a *proportion*.	Animal Jump Graph sheet, to display
Explore	25–30 min	Partners explore the Animal Jump Graph sheet and annotate it with their observations. Students explore how the proportion data changes their thinking about the animals. Students add themselves to the bar graph, collecting the length and height data they need.	• Animal Jump Graph sheet, one per partnership • Colors • Measurement tools, such as rulers, yardsticks or meter sticks, or tape measures
Discuss	15–20 min	Discuss what students noticed in the graph and annotate a class copy of the graph with all observations. Discuss the way the proportion data changed their thinking about the animals and what they discovered when they added themselves to the graph.	• Animal Jump Graph sheet, to display • Markers

To the Teacher

The double bar graph of animal jump lengths that is the focus of this lesson is based on one created by Steve Jenkins (2016) in his spectacular book *Animals by the Numbers*. We've included some less accomplished jumpers than he did to encourage interesting comparisons and to help students see how humans fit into the animal jumping world. This book is an outstanding resource for data about animals, presented in novel infographics, and if you have the book on hand, consider making it available to students as you explore proportions, ratios, and rates.

When you present the Animal Jump Graph sheet to students, resist the urge to tell them how to read the graph. Let them make some observations and struggle with it in their groups. It is important that they understand that the two different types of bars communicate different kinds of information, and that the pairs of bars are each about a single animal. But they may not understand all of the kinds of data embedded in the graph, the kinds of comparisons they can make, or why having these two kinds of bars is useful. As you circulate while students grapple with the graph, you may find it useful to simply point at individual bars and ask, What is this bar saying? Students will need to examine individual data points before they can make sense of the whole.

Activity

Launch

Launch the activity by showing students the Animal Jump Graph sheet on the document camera. Ask, What does this graph show? Give students a chance to turn and talk to a partner about what they notice and how they interpret what they see. Collect a few student ideas and make sure students understand what the two bars represent. You may want to specifically point to the two bars for one animal and ask what each bar shows. Point out that the bars that compare jump length to body length are a kind of rate that we call a *proportion*. This discussion is not meant to be exhaustive. Rather you want to make sure students have enough understanding to explore the graphs further.

Explore

Provide each partnership with a copy of the Animal Jump Graph sheet. Students explore the question, What observations can you make about this graph? Students annotate the graph with observations, comparisons, and questions. As students explore the information in the graph, they try to answer the following questions:

- What does this graph mean? What does it tell us?
- What statements can you make about the data?
- How do the proportions change the way you think about comparing the animals?
- What does the graph teach you about the animals?

Once partners have explored the data in the graph, ask them, Can you add yourself to the graph? Invite students to collect whatever data they need to figure out what their human jump would look like on the graph.

Discuss

Gather students together to discuss the following questions. Be sure to display a copy of the Animal Jump Graph sheet as a shared reference.

- What did you notice in the graph that helped you make sense of it? Did you make mistakes in reading it? What did you learn?
- What observations did you make? (Annotate the class copy of the graph.)
- What's the most surprising thing you noticed?
- How did the proportion data change the way you thought about the data and comparisons?
- What did you find when you added yourself? How do you compare to other animals?

Look-Fors

- **Are students making observations, or are they stuck?** As long as students can make sense of the graph, allow them to work. But if students seem stuck or overwhelmed by the data, focus attention on one bar, one animal, or one comparison. Ask, What does this bar mean? What does this part of the graph tell us? How can this help you read the rest of the graph? For each bar students interpret, encourage them to write down next to the bar what they think it means. This will help them compare different bars and see patterns.
- **Are students noticing contrasts in the graph?** The graph shows some interesting contrasts, in which an animal's jump appears either long or short

in absolute length, but then has an opposite appearance in proportion to its body length. Interpreting these competing meanings requires students to understand each of the individual bars, see that they are in conflict, and then make sense of that conflict. You might simply ask, Why are these bars so different? What does that mean?

- **How are students finding the proportion between their own body length and jump length?** Regardless of individual variation in both body and jump lengths, your students should be noting that they can jump approximating one body length. However, students may get so absorbed in measuring with precision and trying to achieve the longest jump they can that they lose the proportional thinking necessary. In fact, less precision is better in this circumstance, because it makes little difference in the graph whether a student can jump 0.89 or 1.04 body lengths. At the level of precision of the graph, these are both equivalent to 1 body length. Similarly, if students use calculators to determine the rate of body lengths per jump, they may see an answer with a long string of decimals that immediately confuses. You might simply ask, About how many body lengths did you jump? Focusing students' attention on the body length as a unit, rather than inches or feet, may help them simplify the comparison.

Reflect

What do proportions help us see? When might a proportion help you see something new?

Reference

Jenkins, S. (2016). *Animals by the numbers*. Boston, MA: HMH Books.

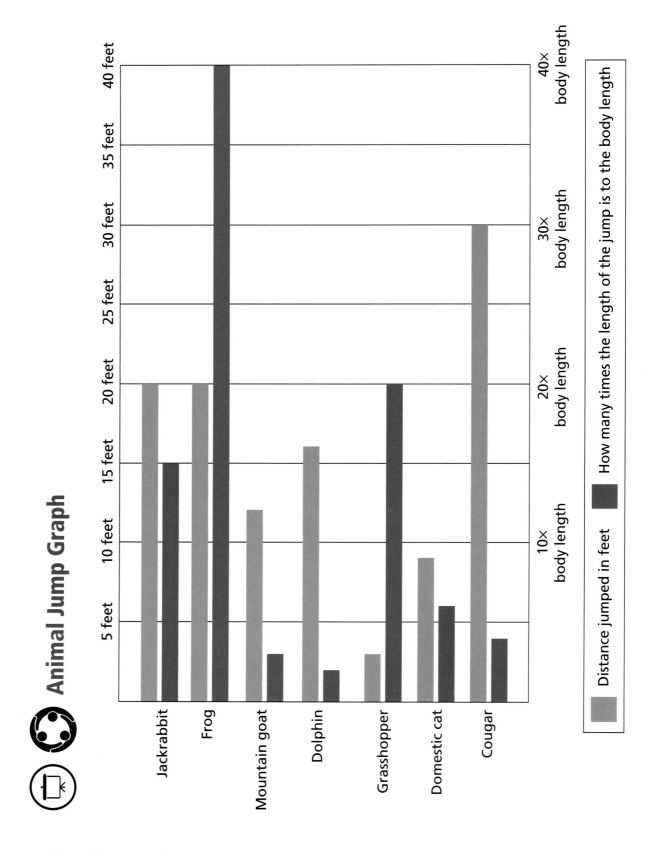

Animal Jump Graph

Distance jumped in feet

How many times the length of the jump is to the body length

Seeing Animals in a New Way

Snapshot

Building on the Animal Jump Graph in the Visualize activity, students play with ways to represent animal data that use proportions and help readers see the animals in a new way.

Connection to CCSS
6.RP.3a,b, 6.RP.1, 6.RP.2

Agenda

Activity	Time	Description/Prompt	Materials
Launch	10 min	Remind students of the work they did with the Animal Jump Graph sheet and how the observations they made using proportion data changed their thinking about the animals. Tell students that today they will develop ways to display proportion data about animals. Show them the Animal Data Task Cards, and invite them to choose one to work with.	• Animal Jump Graph sheet, annotated from the Visualize activity, to display • Animal Data Task Cards, to display
Play	40–45 min	Partners choose one Animal Data Task Card and work together to develop a visual way of presenting proportion data based on the information on the task card. Students find proportions based on the data, create a display that illuminates the data, and present their findings on a chart.	• Animal Data Task Cards, multiple copies, cut apart for partners to choose from • Chart, one per partnership • Make available: markers and colors, grid and dot paper (see appendix), rulers, calculators, and tape
Discuss	20+ min	Partners post their charts and the class does a gallery walk, focusing on the ways the data displays change their thinking about the animals and on the connections they see between displays. Discuss what students noticed. Debrief how students designed their displays, what challenges they faced, and how they thought about precision.	

To the Teacher

This lesson builds on the work students did to interpret the Animal Jump Graph in the Visualize activity. We encourage you to use the artifacts you and the class created during that lesson as a jumping-off point for this activity. Students will likely want to refer back to the Animal Jump Graph to think about how it was constructed to convey the proportion data or how two kinds of bars can be placed side by side. We ask students in this activity to think creatively about a data set, find proportions, and then display that data. Students may want to make a display that mimics the structure of the Animal Jump Graph, or they may want to create something different, simpler, or more innovative. If possible, we encourage you to have a copy of Steve Jenkins's book available for students to browse the different ways he chooses to display animal data. Once students have found the proportions they want to display, they'll need to make decisions about how to display that data for clarity. Jenkins's book provides useful ideas that students may not have encountered and can spark creative ways to communicate data. Be sure to celebrate the ways students try, even if they are not successful. Ask students to talk about what they were trying and what made displaying the data challenging. Do not expect beautiful graphs like Jenkins's; rather, expect and spotlight students' messy attempts and the risks they took.

Activity

Launch

Launch the activity by reminding students of the work they did with the Animal Jump Graph in the Visualize activity. Show the class the annotated graph from that activity. Tell students that this was a visual way of displaying animal data and a proportion that allowed us to see jumping in a new way. You may want to remind students of the interesting observations they made using the proportions, and the things that surprised them.

Tell students that today they are in charge of creating a display to show animal data. These displays could be similar to the Animal Jump Graph or they could be a new way of seeing the data, but they need to include some proportional data that will help us see the animals in a new way.

Show students the four Animal Data Task Cards on the document camera. Invite them to turn and talk to their partner about which data they would like to work with today.

Play

Students work in partners with the task card of their choice. Invite students to create a way to display the data that includes proportions and helps us see the animals in a new way. Each task card contains a blank column for students to add proportion data.

Students will need to think about what proportion they want to display. For instance, the data would look different if students found the number of tongue lengths per body length, versus the number of body lengths per tongue length. Finding this data will require some rounding, and students will need to reason about how precise they need or want to be in this kind of data display.

Partners discuss how to display their data and how they want to organize it to draw attention to surprises or interesting contrasts. For instance, does it make sense to organize the animals from greatest to least in some measure? What measure matters?

Partners make a chart to show what data they have found and how the data can be made visual. Provide students access to charts, markers and colors, grid and dot paper (see appendix), rulers, calculators, and tape. Students may want to make their graphs on grid or dot paper and tape them onto a larger chart, or they may want to draw their graphs much larger, directly on the chart.

Discuss

Ask partnerships to post their charts around the room. You may want to cluster them by the data they display. Invite the class to do a gallery walk, and as they walk students should discuss with a partner the following questions:

- What surprises you about the animals?
- How do the displays help you see new things?
- How do the proportions change your thoughts about comparisons?
- What do you wonder now?
- Where do you think you would fit on the graphs?
- What connections do you see across the graphs?

Discuss with the class the questions they considered as they examined the different charts. Then focus the conversation on the following questions:

- What did you have to do to design your displays?
- How did you find your proportions?

- How precise do you think the proportion data needs to be to communicate differences accurately and effectively?
- What was challenging and why?

Look-Fors

- **Are students thinking about iterating units to find proportions?** When thinking about proportions, students will need to consider what unit they want to iterate. For instance, in the tongue length data, students could use body length as the core unit and iterate tongue lengths to ask, How many tongue lengths make one body length? It is conceptually useful for students to be thinking about iterating units, rather than simply thinking about the rate as division. When students focus on dividing numbers, the numbers often lose their meaning, and students simply read the digits on the calculator display as the answer. Students can lose sight of what they are dividing, why, and what it means. Encourage students to think about the units they are using and what they are imagining. You might ask, So, are you thinking about how many tongue lengths make a body length, or how many body lengths make a tongue length? When you look at the data, about how many tongue lengths would you expect make a body length for this animal? Encourage students to estimate, imagining iterating the tongue length repeatedly down the length of the animal's body, before they use the calculator. Estimating with meaning before calculating will help students make sense of the precise answer when it is displayed.

- **Are students rounding data?** The proportion data that students find will include many decimal places, as naturally occurring data often does. Although students could choose to display data with all its decimal places, it does not make sense to do so when comparing different kinds of animals. Students will need to determine how to round the data so that it is still reasonably accurate, but it also makes it simpler for the reader to make comparisons between the animals presented. Ask students, How will you round this data to make it easier for the reader? If you round it in that way, is it still accurate? How do you know? Students often want to present the most accurate picture and may refuse to round, because in their view, rounding makes the data less correct. It can be difficult for students to see why presenting less accurate data is advantageous. You might ask, What's the big idea you want the reader to understand from this data? How accurate does your data need to be for your reader to see this idea?

- **What innovative ways are students creating to display their data?** Students may want to emulate the Animal Jump Graph, and we think this is a fine entry point for displaying proportion data. This graph can serve as a useful model for students, and you may want to give students access to this graph again so that they can see how it is constructed. However, this is not the only way to display this kind of data. Students may want to orient bars vertically, show only the proportion data, or turn the display into a pictograph. Draw attention to innovations that students design in their data displays, even if they are only modestly different from the model. Ask, Why did you make this choice? How do you think it helps the reader? What were you trying to help the reader see? In the class discussion, you may want to specifically highlight the differences among displays and what they allow the reader to see in the data. Ask the class what features helped them most or what made it easier for them as a reader to understand the data.

Reflect

What do proportions help us see? When might a proportion help you see something new?

Animal Data Task Cards

Bodies and Tongues			
Animal	Body Length in Inches	Tongue Length in Inches	
Giant Anteater	84	24	
Pangolin	18	16	
Hummingbird	3	1	
Sun Bear	50	9	
Giraffe	168	19	

Hearts and Weights			
Animal	Heart Rate in Beats per Minute	Body Weight in Pounds	
Giraffe	150	2,200	
Sun Bear	75	150	
Tiger	70	400	
Saltwater Crocodile	3	1,000	
Cow	65	2,000	

Animal Data Task Cards

Speeds and Weights			
Animal	Speed in Miles per Hour	Weight in Pounds	
Tiger	35	400	
Horse	30	1,500	
Saltwater Crocodile	15	1,000	
Giraffe	37	2,200	
Giant Anteater	31	80	

Bodies and Tails			
Animal	Weight in Pounds	Tail Length in Inches	
Giant Anteater	80	30	
Giraffe	2,200	36	
Saltwater Crocodile	1,000	90	
Tiger	400	36	
Cow	2,000	36	

A Seat at the Table

Snapshot

Students investigate the relationship between seats and tables at a restaurant, developing ways to communicate this relationship using proportions, ratios, and unit rates.

Connection to CCSS
6.RP.1, 6.RP.2, 6.RP.3a,b, 6.G.1

Agenda

Activity	Time	Description/Prompt	Materials
Launch	10 min	Show students the Restaurant Table Unit sheet and explain that a restaurant uses these tables to seat customers. Ask, If each person needs one side length, how many people can be seated at two tables pushed together? Discuss what this will look like, what students notice, and why doubling the number of tables does not double the number of seats.	Restaurant Table Unit sheet, to display
Explore	30–40+ min	Partners explore how many people can be seated at different numbers of tables, and what arrangements are possible. They record their findings in a Table Table sheet and develop ways of communicating the relationship between seats and tables. Students work to answer, What is the most efficient way of seating customers?	• Table Table sheet, one per partnership • Make available: square tiles, grid paper (see appendix), and colors
Discuss	15+ min	Discuss the class's findings, the patterns they observed, and what makes the most efficient arrangement of tables. Ask, What ways did you develop to communicate the relationship between seats and tables? Name these methods using the language of *proportion*, *ratio*, and *unit rate*. Discuss the connection between the seats and tables and perimeter and area.	

Activity	Time	Description/Prompt	Materials
Extend	20–30 min	Partners investigate how many people could be seated at a restaurant that had 36 square tables, generating all the possible combinations and looking for the most and least efficient ways.	Make available: square tiles, grid paper (see appendix), and colors

To the Teacher

In this activity, we shift from animal data to other ways proportions are seen in the world, to encourage students to see that rates are everywhere. At this point, students have had experience with both unit rates and the concept of proportions, so in this investigation of seats around tables at a restaurant, we invite students to develop ways of communicating that relationship. Students may develop a unit rate, such as 4 chairs/table, 3 chairs/table, $2\frac{2}{3}$ chairs/table, and so on. Students may develop a proportion, as with the animal data, such as that chairs are 4× the number of tables. Alternatively, students may invent a relationship that could be called a ratio, in which two quantities are compared, such as that the relationship between chairs and tables is $\frac{4}{1}, \frac{3}{1}, \frac{8}{3}$, and so on. Ratios can be communicated like this, as fractions, or as a comparison using a colon (such as 4:1) or words (such as 4 to 1). In your closing discussion, highlight all the ways students developed to communicate this relationship, and name each of these using the terms *proportion, rate, unit rate*, and *ratio*, so that students can see how all of these conventions could be used to communicate the same data in different ways.

In the closing discussion, we invite students to consider the connection this investigation has to area and perimeter. Each table can be considered an area unit of 1, with a perimeter of 4. As the number of tables increases, the perimeter increases, but at different rates depending on the arrangement. For instance, four tables arrayed in a line have a perimeter of 10 units (or seats); the same number of tables arrayed in a square has a perimeter of 8 units (or seats). In previous grades, students have explored the relationship between perimeter and area, and this investigation gives students an opportunity to draw connections between those concepts and proportions, rates, and ratios. By making these connections, students develop these concepts of proportional reasoning as simply extensions of previous thinking, rather than new, isolated ideas.

Activity

Launch

Launch the activity by showing students the Restaurant Table Unit sheet on the document camera and telling them that at a restaurant, there are a large number of these square tables that can seat four people. At a table, each person needs one side length of space to have enough room to eat. The restaurant can put tables together to seat larger groups.

Ask students, What do you think will happen if the restaurant puts two tables together? What will it look like, and how many seats will there be? Give students a chance to turn and talk to a partner, then invite students to come up and draw what two tables together could look like. Use this opportunity to make sure students understand that each chair needs a side length of space and that the two tables must adjoin along a side. This means that the only solution for joining two tables will look like the image shown here.

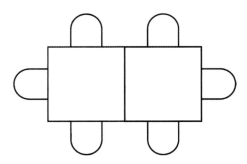

Arrangement of two tables and six chairs

Ask students, What happened to the number of chairs? What do you notice? Collect some student observations, and draw attention to the idea that doubling the number of tables did not double the number of chairs. Ask students why they think that happened. You may want to have students turn and talk or to discuss this question as a class.

Tell students that today they are going to be exploring what happens when the restaurant puts tables together to seat larger groups and what different arrangements can be made.

Explore

Students work in partners to investigate the different arrangements of tables possible at a restaurant. Provide students with square tiles, grid paper (see appendix), colors, and a copy of the Table Table sheet for recording what they find. Students investigate the following questions:

- For any number of tables, what different arrangements of the tables are possible?
- How many chairs will fit for each arrangement?
- What is the relationship between the number of tables and the number of chairs?

- What patterns do you notice?
- The restaurant wants to be able to seat people as efficiently as possible, getting the most chairs per table. What is the most efficient arrangement possible?

For each arrangement of tables students find, they record it in the Table Table sheet. Students sketch the tables and chairs, record the number of tables and chairs, and develop a way of communicating the relationship between the tables and chairs in the arrangement. Note that while one and two tables have only one possible arrangement, three or more tables can be arranged in multiple ways, not all of which seat the same number of people. Encourage students to consider all the ways of arranging these tables.

Discuss

Gather students together to discuss what they have found. You may want to collect the data students have generated into a class table so that you have a shared document to discuss and use for pattern seeking. Discuss the following questions:

- What patterns did you notice as you put tables together?
- How can you see those patterns in your table?
- What ways did you develop for expressing the relationship between the number of tables and number of chairs?
- What is the most efficient way of seating people? How can you tell?

During this discussion, draw attention to and name the different ways students thought about the relationship between tables and chairs. For instance, some students may have used unit rates to make comparison easier, while others may have written theirs as a proportion or ratio. These are related but different ways of thinking about the relationships, and it will be useful to have names for each as they emerge.

Finally, ask the class to consider how this investigation is connected to area and perimeter. Some students may have already made some connections during the investigation. You may want to give groups time to talk about the connection before discussing this as a whole class. Discuss the following questions:

- How are the tables and chairs connected to area and perimeter?
- What does our investigation of tables and chairs tell us about area and perimeter?

Extend

If the restaurant has 36 tables, how many people could it seat? How would the tables be arranged to seat the greatest number of people? How would the tables be arranged to seat the fewest number of people? How do you know? Explore the combinations possible. How could you record your thinking so that others can see your evidence and patterns?

Look-Fors

- **Are students seeing multiple ways of arranging tables?** Students may be tempted to simply array the tables in an ever-growing line. However, once students have three or more tables to connect, a line is not the only way of arranging the tables. Ask students, Is this the only way the restaurant could join the tables together? What else could they do? Do different arrangements of the same number of tables seat the same number of people? How could you find out?

- **What ways of communicating the relationship between seats and tables have students developed?** We have left this column of the Table Table sheet open to different ways of communicating the relationship between seats and tables so that students can develop ways to represent this idea. As discussed in the To the Teacher section, students may draw on the work with animal data to use a proportion, or on the work in the previous big idea to use a unit rate. Both of these are appropriate and could be used with accuracy to communicate and compare relationships. However, some students may develop new ways that could be called rates or ratios, and students are likely not to use conventional ways to do so. They may simply want to say that there are "8 seats for 3 tables" or "8 seats/3 tables" or "8 to 3." Encourage students to be consistent within their own data, and ask how they chose this particular way of capturing the relationship. Ask questions that prompt them to think about using these to compare, such as, How can you tell which is the most efficient way to arrange the tables using these relationships? It is not necessary that students revise their methods or all use the same method. In fact, a diversity of methods will give the class more to discuss and help them form conclusions about what methods seem to be the most useful in this context.

- **Are students connecting seats and tables to perimeter and area?** Each table can be seen as 1 unit of area, with a perimeter of 4 units. Students may use the language of seats and tables as they work through this investigation, but you may also hear some students using language that connects to the concepts of perimeter, such as how many seats we can place "around the table," or that an arrangement has more or fewer edges. Listen for language that connects to area and perimeter so that you can highlight and draw on these ideas in the class discussion.

Reflect

Where do you see proportions, rates, or ratios in the classroom right now? Draw pictures to help explain your thinking.

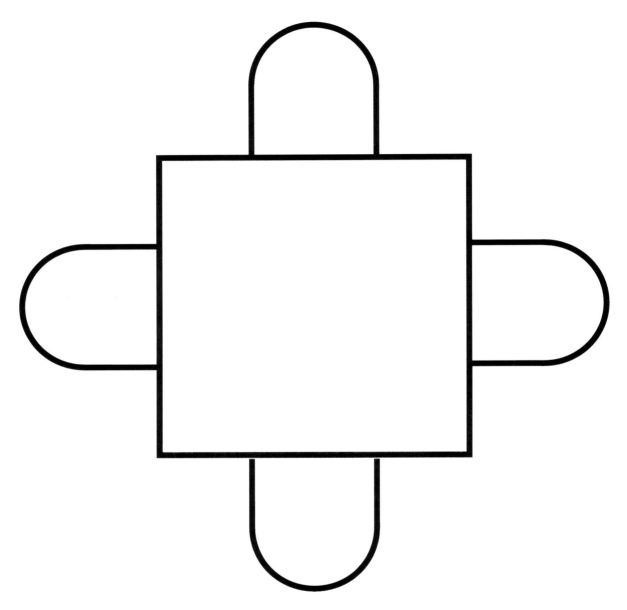

 **Table Table**

Image	Number of Tables	Number of Seats	Relationship between Seats and Tables

BIG IDEA 6

Visualizing the Center and Spread of Data

Mean, mode, and median are three measures of central tendency; if you think back to your learning of them in school, you will probably remember different numbers and calculations that had one correct answer. In our designing of tasks for this big idea, we have chosen tasks that focus on the meaning of the three measures and that ask students either to see them visually or to work with the measures conceptually. We have again chosen to present data in different ways to help students develop quantitative literacy. It is ideal if students approach any data set knowing they have learned a set of tools and a mathematical mindset that they can bring to the data, exploring them to see what they mean and what they reveal.

Mean, mode, and median are three tools that can be applied to any set of data to reveal different, interesting properties of the data set. Often the mean is the best average to use, and it is one that many people use in their lives when they want to work out an average, but it isn't always the best average to use. Sometimes there are numbers in a data set that are wildly out of synch, and when that happens, the mean may give a value that is unlike the other data in the set. The median and the mode do not get thrown off by unusual data values. The mode—the number that occurs most frequently—is a term used in life, often in fashion. When something is "in mode," it means it is regularly seen, as with the modal numbers in the data set. One time that the mode is really useful is when the data are not numbers but names. For example, if we looked at the most common baby names in the US, we might say that the mode is Emma. Mode is also used with sets of numbers, when the mean and the median do not make as much sense. The median value is the one in the middle of the data set when it is ordered, and the average of the two in the middle when there is an even number of data points. It is good to have students think about the meaning of the three different averages, or measures of central tendency, and consider when one is more appropriate than the others.

In our Visualize activity, students will be given real data on hurricanes in the Atlantic Ocean to analyze. The opening activity starts with the 2017 data, which it shows in a line plot. Students will discuss the shape of the data in small groups and then in pairs. After the class discussion, groups will choose from four different data sets of hurricanes in the Atlantic for different years so that they can analyze the data and share their findings. The different representations of data we are focusing on are line plots, bar graphs, a data table, and a list. Different groups may be analyzing the same data set but displaying it in different ways. In the final discussion, they analyze the different ways they have displayed the data as well as analyze the data across the years for 1977, 1987, 1997, 2007, and 2017. The time frame shows the way the weather is changing, which connects to the idea of climate change.

In the Play activity, students will get an opportunity to see the concept of the mean visually. So many times, students only see concepts numerically, missing an important time to develop brain connections and to understand more deeply through visual engagement. In this activity, students will also be able to move with their hands and use models, which has also been shown to enhance understanding of mathematics at all grade levels. They will be asked to build a representation of different data sets with snap cubes and then represent the mean. We anticipate that students will balance out the cubes by moving different ones so that the representation shows a rectangle. After the class has discussed this, they will collect their own data by rolling a die and seeing how they can average out the representation when they roll the die a different number of times. Students will get a lot of opportunities to think physically and visually about averages and what they look and can feel like.

The Investigate activity gives students an opportunity to think conceptually about the three averages and the differences between the three ways of measuring central tendency. I really like that this activity asks students to think deeply about the relationships between the three measures and not just perform a calculation. It is an open investigation, which means that students will be able to explore patterns, and the patterns they explore can extend to the sky, as students can keep moving onward with different sets of numbers. The investigation is conceptually difficult, as students have to consider different constraints at once; that is good, as it will give them important times of struggle and will offer opportunities for the teacher to give positive messages about the benefits of struggle for brain growth. Teachers can also remind students that looking for patterns is a mathematical act; it is really the essence of what mathematics is.

Jo Boaler

The Shape of Data

Snapshot

Students explore the shape, center, and spread of data by examining hurricane data sets and describing what they see.

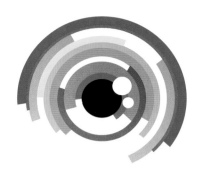

Connection to CCSS
6.SP.2, 6.SP.3, 6.SP.4, 6.SP.5

Agenda

Activity	Time	Description/Prompt	Materials
Launch	10 min	Show students the Atlantic Hurricanes of 2017 line plot and ask, What do you notice? Collect students' observations and annotate the graph. Tell students that today they will be exploring the shape of data.	Atlantic Hurricanes of 2017 sheet, to display
Explore	20 min	Partners explore the Atlantic Hurricanes of 2017 line plot to determine the shape, center, and spread of the data. Students explore what this shape tells us about hurricanes that season.	Atlantic Hurricanes of 2017 sheet, one per partnership
Discuss	15 min	Discuss the shape, center, and spread of the data students explored. Annotate the graph as students offer observations. Create a chart called Ways We Describe the Shape of Data to capture vocabulary that arises in the discussion.	• Atlantic Hurricanes of 2017 sheet, to display and annotate • Chart and markers
Explore	20–30 min	Partners choose from four different data sets, each from a different year and displayed differently, to explore the shape, center, and spread of the data. Students can transform the data into a different display to help them see these features. Partners compare this data set to the 2017 data.	Atlantic Hurricanes of 2007, 1997, 1987, and 1977 sheet, multiple copies for partnerships to choose from

Activity	Time	Description/Prompt	Materials
Discuss	20 min	Each group presents their conclusions about the graphs, from 1977 to 2007. Looking at all of the data, compare the data sets and how different displays allow or inhibit seeing the shape of data. Discuss the conclusions the class can draw or questions that can be posed based on the five years of data.	

(Continued)

To the Teacher

For this activity, we have drawn on actual hurricane data from five years spread across four decades. If your students are not familiar with hurricane categories, it will make sense to spend some time addressing what the categories mean in the broadest sense, particularly that a larger number means a more powerful hurricane. For the sake of the data presentation, we have added a Category 0, which refers to tropical storms and depressions, or storms that could have become hurricanes but did not reach sufficient intensity. Naming these as 0 will allow students to use measures of central tendency, such as median, mode, and mean, which can only be used with quantitative data. However, this is not a standard naming of these storms, and students familiar with hurricane naming conventions will likely want to understand what this invented term means.

The goal of students' exploration of these data is to create a need to express qualities related to the shape and spread of data, in order to describe and compare data sets. Students are often asked to find measures of center but without those measures being needed, useful, or well understood. In this activity, students may use these terms, or they may use the ideas without the language, such as describing one category as being the *most common* rather than the *mode*. Capitalize on opportunities to label the features of the data using the language of statistics, but focus on the meaning of these terms and what they tell us about the data set. The big idea here is that the data sets have a shape and that these shapes communicate something about a phenomenon in a way that helps us understand it. Rather than having students generate a rote report on the data set's measures, encourage them to simply describe what the data shows and what it might be telling us about hurricane seasons across time.

Activity

Launch

Launch the activity by showing students the Atlantic Hurricanes of 2017 line plot. Ask, What do you notice about this data set? Give students a chance to turn and talk to a partner about their observations. Collect student observations and annotate the graph. If students are unfamiliar with the ways hurricanes are categorized, this is a good moment to discuss the meaning of this system. When you collect observations, students may make statements about what is most common, or what kinds of hurricanes there are few of. Students may ask questions of the data, such as, Why are there so many Category 0 hurricanes? We encourage you to record these, too, as they may inspire interesting comparisons later in the lesson. Tell students that today they are going to explore the shape of data.

Explore

Students work in partnerships to explore the data. Provide each partnership with a copy of the Atlantic Hurricanes of 2017 line plot. Students explore the following questions, annotating on and writing statements about the graph:

- How would you describe the shape of this data?
- Where is the center of the data? How do you know?
- How far does it spread?
- What does that tell you about Atlantic hurricanes in 2017?

Discuss

Gather students together and show the class version of the Atlantic Hurricanes of 2017 line plot that you began to annotate in the launch. Discuss the questions students explored, and continue to annotate the evidence for their observations on the graph:

- How would you describe the shape of this data?
- Where is the center of the data?
- How far does it spread?
- What does that tell you about Atlantic hurricanes in 2017?

When discussing the data, students may use either formal or informal language to describe the center and spread of the data set. As students name these ideas in whatever words they choose, begin a chart called Ways We Describe the Shape of Data. Terms that may come up include *range, mode, median*, and possibly *mean* or *average*. It is not necessary that all of these terms be defined at this point. Rather, if an opportunity presents itself to name that the highest bar, or the most common, is called the *mode*, then we encourage you to seize that moment.

Explore

Provide students with the choice of four different data sets: Atlantic Hurricanes of 2007, 1997, 1987, and 1977. Each of these data sets is displayed differently. Invite students to explore the shape of the data set using the same questions:

- How would you describe the shape of this data?
- Where is the center of the data?
- How far does it spread?
- What does that tell you about the data?

To explore these questions, students can transform the data set into another form. For instance, students looking at a list may prefer to see the data in a line plot, while students looking at a line plot may want to explore what they can see if the data were in a table.

Ask students to compare the shape of this data set to the 2017 data they explored at the beginning of this activity. Ask, What do you notice about the shapes of the two data sets? How are they alike or different?

Discuss

Focusing on each data set one at a time, invite groups to share what they noticed about the shape of the data. Invite students to show on the document camera how they transformed the data and what that allowed them to see. You may want to ask students to arrange these data sets in chronological order to make comparisons over time easier.

As a whole class, look at the five data sets—the 2017 hurricane data and the four years students have just explored—and discuss the following questions:

- How are the shapes of these data sets similar? Different?
- How can you see the similarities and differences in the data sets in different data representations (line plot, bar graph, list, and table)? Which makes it easiest to see the shape of the data? Why?
- What conclusions can you make about hurricanes based on these different data sets?
- What questions do the shapes of the data sets raise? What do you wonder now?

If any additional vocabulary for describing the shape, center, or spread of data arises in this discussion, be sure to add it to your Ways We Describe the Shape of Data chart.

Look-Fors

- **Are students attending to shape, center, and spread?** Students may focus on one of these dimensions, particularly shape, to the exclusion of the others. Students may describe shape in ways that don't help draw conclusions or comparisons. For instance, saying that the data looks "like a house" doesn't tell us much about what is happening, but saying that the data is "all bunched up on one side" does help provide insight into a particularly weak or powerful year. You may want to ask, Where is the center of the data? How do you know? How is the data clustered? Colloquial terms, such as *bunched* or *flat*, can help describe what is going on. You may also want to prompt students by asking, What does that shape mean about the hurricanes that year? For instance, if the graph is flat, what does that mean about the kinds of hurricanes that occurred that year?
- **Are students transforming the data to better visualize it?** Some of the measures of spread and center are easier to visualize in different forms. For instance, shape is easiest to see in graphs, but the median is best visualized in a list. In order to see multiple dimensions of data, students may need to transform the data into different forms. In the second half of this activity, we open the door for students to do just that, and it is critical that you observe

whether students recognize the need to see the data in different forms to draw conclusions. You might say to a group, "I notice that you can see several things about the data when it is displayed this way. What do you think you might see if the data was displayed differently? What could you try?"

- **Are students considering the number of data points represented?** One dimension of the data that is worthy of comparison is the number of data points that are represented. In this case, such an observation would allow students to compare how many hurricanes occurred in each of the five years under investigation, and this quantity does vary. Depending on the form in which the data is represented, determining the number of data points could be simple or far less obvious. Students may not even consider this a question to ask. If anyone does count, be sure to draw attention to this in the discussion and ask the class how the number of hurricanes compares across years. If no one does, you might pose the question, How come all the bars are low for 1997? What does that mean?

- **Are students making larger statements about what the shape of the data communicates?** We don't want students to go so far down the path of analyzing the data that they lose sight of what it means. For instance, students might catalog the median, mode, and range, and describe the shape, but in the end the question is, What do these tell us about the data? Encourage students to return to the idea that this data represents hurricanes during one year on the Atlantic and that higher category numbers indicate more powerful storms. Students will not be able to make comparative statements until the second half of the activity, but they can say things like, "Most of the hurricanes this season were not strong" or "There were hurricanes in every category this season." Later, when students can look at the data from five years, they may be able to make conjectures about what constitutes a bad or mild hurricane year, or whether they perceive any trends across the 40-year period. Encourage students to keep making these connections by asking, What does this tell us about the hurricanes that year?

Reflect

What do the shape, center, and spread of data tell you?

Atlantic Hurricanes of 2017

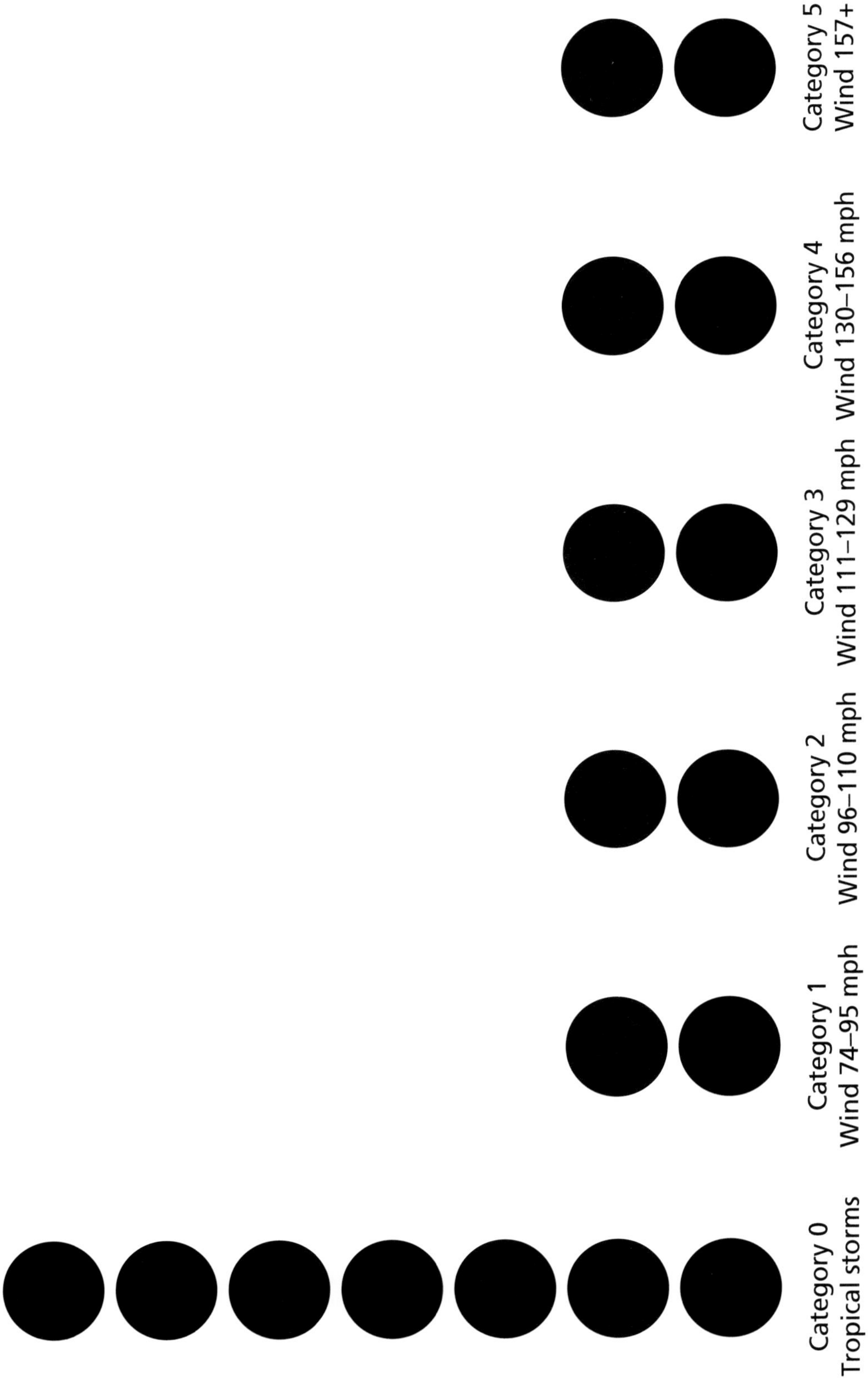

Category 0
Tropical storms

Category 1
Wind 74–95 mph

Category 2
Wind 96–110 mph

Category 3
Wind 111–129 mph

Category 4
Wind 130–156 mph

Category 5
Wind 157+

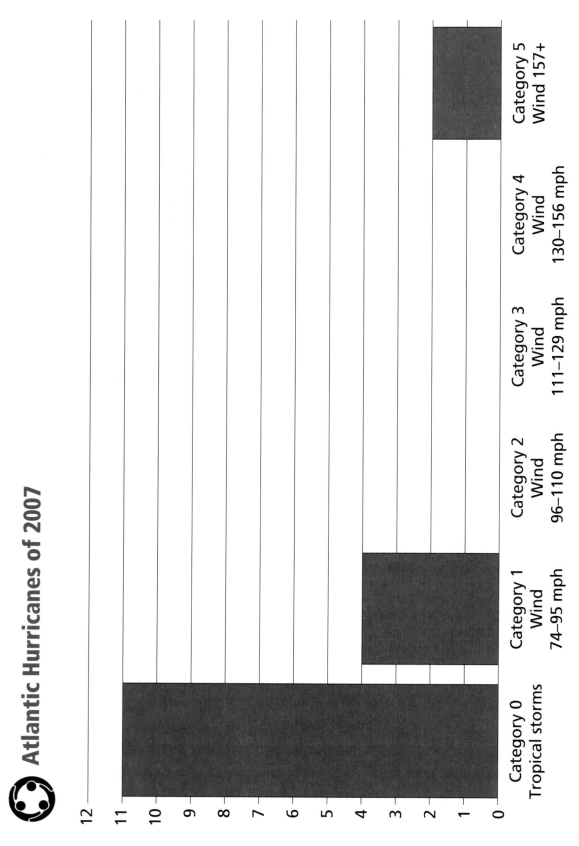

Atlantic Hurricanes of 2007

Atlantic Hurricanes of 1997

| Category 0 Tropical storms | Category 1 Wind 74–95 mph | Category 2 Wind 96–110 mph | Category 3 Wind 111–129 mph | Category 4 Wind 130–156 mph | Category 5 Wind 157+ |

Atlantic Hurricanes of 1987

11 Category 0 storms with winds less than 74 mph

2 Category 1 storms with winds between 74 and 95 mph

0 Category 2 storms with winds between 96 and 110 mph

1 Category 3 storm with winds between 111 and 129 mph

0 Category 4 storms with winds between 130 and 156 mph

0 Category 5 storms with winds 157 mph or greater

Atlantic Hurricanes of 1977

Category	Number of Storms
0 Winds < 74 mph	22
1 Winds 74–95 mph	3
2 Winds 96–110 mph	1
3 Winds 111–129 mph	0
4 Winds 130–156 mph	0
5 Winds 157+	1

What Does *Mean* Mean?

Snapshot

Students explore the meaning of mean by evening out data represented in stacks of cubes.

> **Connection to CCSS**
> 6.SP.5c, 6.SP.3, 6.SP.2

Agenda

Activity	Time	Description/Prompt	Materials
Launch	5–10 min	Tell students that a women's hockey team wants to determine their average, or mean, score from their first six games. Show students the goals scored in the first six games represented in stacks of cubes and ask how they might use these cubes to find the average.	Cubes in six colors, stacked to replicate the data set (1, 6, 3, 2, 4, and 2 goals)
Explore	20 min	Partners work together to reconstruct the data using cubes and figure out how to use the cubes to find the mean number of goals scored in the six games.	Cubes, six in each of six colors, per partnership
Discuss	15 min	Discuss the strategies that students developed and what the mean means. Ask students to develop conjectures for how to find the mean of any set of data.	• Ways We Describe the Shape of Data chart, started in the Visualize activity • Markers
Play	20–30 min	Students test the conjectures they developed for finding the mean of any set of data by generating their own data with dice. Partners explore what to do when they cannot even out the number of dots exactly.	• Cubes, six in each of six colors, per partnership • Dice, one per partnership

Activity	Time	Description/Prompt	Materials
Discuss	15 min	Discuss whether students' conjectures for finding the mean worked and how to find the mean for any set of data. Discuss the meaning of extra dots or cubes that cannot be evened out. What do these mean for the mean?	

To the Teacher

At the heart of this activity is building a physical and intuitive sense of what mean, or average, represents. Too often mean is reduced to a formula: finding the sum of the data and dividing that by the number of data points. But what does that actually mean? What does such a procedure represent? In action, mean is the value if you evened out all the data and made each data point the same. This means that any data set with six data points and a total value of 18, such as the one presented here, will have a mean of 3, because if all six data points were the same, each would have a value of 3. This evening out of the data is precisely what we are encouraging students to do in this activity so that they can imagine what is happening when they find the mean of any data set.

We've selected a context for thinking about the mean that we think many students will find engaging, but the same data could be used in a variety of contexts. We encourage you to consider what contexts for the data your students might find most compelling and adapt this task to their interests. For instance, this data could represent

- The number of letters in people's first names
- Scores for a soccer, softball, or baseball team
- The number of people in different families
- The number of pencils in kids' backpacks
- The number of puppies or kittens in different litters or eggs in nests
- Rolls of a die in a game

You may have other ideas based on your students' interests. While we have written this lesson to discuss a women's hockey team, you can revise the language to suit whatever context will most engage your students.

Activity

Launch

Launch the activity by telling students that a women's hockey team is trying to improve their scoring. They want to look at their scores over their first six games of the season to see what their average number of goals scored in a game is. Using blocks or snap cubes, make six towers to represent the scores for each of the first six games: 1, 6, 3, 2, 4, and 2 goals. Be sure that each stack is made from a different color of cube. You may also want to record this data on a board or chart as a shared reference.

Data illustrated by snap cubes. How would you evenly distribute them?

Ask, How could we use these cubes to figure out what the average number of goals scored per game is? Give students a chance to turn and talk to a partner about what they could do with the cubes to find the average, or mean, number of goals scored by the hockey team.

Explore

Provide partners with enough cubes of different colors to model the data set: 1, 6, 3, 2, 4, and 2. Using the cubes, students explore the following questions:

- How can you use the cubes to figure out the average number of goals scored per game?
- How can you see the average, or mean, using the cubes?

- What does *mean* (or average) mean?
- How could you find the mean of any data set?

Discuss

Gather students together to discuss the following questions:

- How did you use the cubes to help you see the mean?
- What is the mean number of goals scored by the women's hockey team? How do you know?
- What does *mean* mean? (Record a class definition of mean on a chart, along with your previous definitions of other measures of center from the Visualize activity.)
- How could we find the mean of any data set? (Record student ideas publicly so they can test them.)

There are several ways that students might even out the cubes. Two such examples are shown here. Regardless of the way students distributed the cubes into even stacks, all stacks will be three cubes high.

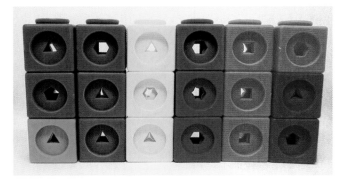

Two different ways to evenly distribute the snap cubes

Play

Partners test their ideas about how to find the mean of any data set by creating their own sets to play with. Provide each partnership with a die. Students roll the die to create a set of six data points. Students can again use cubes, if they want, to help them explore the following questions:

- What is the mean number of dots per roll in your data?
- How do you know?
- What do you do if the number of dots can't be evened out? What happens to the leftovers? Why?

As students work, they should record their data sets and draw pictures or show in numbers or words how they are finding the mean. Once students have developed a strategy, ask them, Will your strategy for finding mean work if you roll the die five times? Or eight? Or four?

Discuss

Gather students together to discuss the following questions:

- What strategies for finding the mean did you develop? What patterns did you notice?
- How did you organize your data to help you see the mean? What was helpful? Not helpful? Why?
- Did you have any data set where you couldn't even out the number of cubes [or dots]? How did you deal with the leftovers? What do these extra dots mean?

Pay specific attention in this discussion to instances in which the values could not be evened out, leaving extras or groups with uneven numbers. Making sense of what to do with these values will help students understand what it means when we say that, for example, the mean number of goals scored in a set of soccer games is 3.5, when it is not actually possible to score half a goal.

Look-Fors

- **How are students representing the data?** In the first part of this activity, you will have modeled with the cubes in the launch how to represent the hockey data. When students head off to represent this data, the first challenge they will face is replicating this representation. It is important that students interpret each cube as a goal (or point) scored and each stack as a game. If students' representations do not match the data, you may start by asking, What does each cube represent? What does each stack represent? They could be struggling with meaning or have simply made a counting error. When students generate their own data, they may represent it with stacks of cubes again. In this case, the stacks each represent a roll of the die, and the cubes each represent a dot on the face of the die. Again, if students are not representing their rolls accurately, ask them what the stacks and cubes represent. If students do not use cubes, ask questions about how they have decided to represent their data so they can find the mean.

- **How are students using the cubes to find the mean?** The cubes allow students to see physically and concretely what is happening when we find the mean, but students may not know how to represent averaging the data with the cubes. If they are struggling to model the mean physically, ask questions about what the average means to help students find language that might describe what to do with the cubes. For instance, ask, What does it mean to find the average number of goals scored in each game? Or, When we say we found the average number of goals scored, what does that mean? Students may say that the average is what's "typical" or "normal," to which you might reply, How could you move the cubes so that you could see what's typical or normal for the team to score in a game?

- **How are students dealing with extra cubes or dots when trying to find the mean?** It is particularly challenging to deal with extra data that cannot be shared equally as a whole number when fraction units don't make practical sense, as with our data. It is not possible to score a fractional goal, have a fractional number of people in a household, have a fractional number of puppies in a litter, or roll a fractional value on a die. So, when students end up with extra dots, it can be difficult to interpret what to do with these or what they represent. Students may be tempted to simply disregard them, but they do have meaning. Even if students simply want to conclude that the mean is "more than 3 but less than 4 dots per roll," then this conclusion maintains the meaning of the dots. More precisely, students can divide or represent the extra dots as decimals or fractions, such as 3.17 or $3\frac{1}{6}$ dots per roll. To encourage students to think in this way, you might ask, We know we cannot cut these cubes, but if we could, how many would end up in each stack?

Reflect

What does *mean* mean?

When Does Mean = Median = Mode = Range?

Snapshot

Students investigate and create data sets where the mean, median, mode, and range have particular relationships.

Connection to CCSS
6.SP.5c, 6.SP.2, 6.SP.3, 6.EE.5, 6.EE.8

Agenda

Activity	Time	Description/Prompt	Materials
Launch	10–15 min	Show students the following data set: 2, 5, 5, 6, 7. Ask, What do you notice about the center and spread of this data set? Discuss the center and spread of the data until the class notices that the mean, median, mode, and range of this data set are the same: 5.	• Ways We Describe the Shape of Data chart, for reference • Optional: cubes to model the data set
Explore	30+ min	Partners explore the question, What other sets of five positive whole numbers can you find where the mean, median, mode, and range are all equal? Students use tools to create and justify data sets that satisfy these criteria.	Make available: cubes, square tiles, grid paper (see appendix), and colors
Discuss	15–20 min	Students share the data sets they created and their justifications. Discuss the strategies students developed for creating and revising data sets so that they met the criteria. Discuss the patterns students noticed and used as they worked.	

Activity	Time	Description/Prompt	Materials
Explore	30+ min	Partners investigate and create data sets in which the mean, median, and mode have different relationships, each provided on a different task card. Students post the data sets they create for each set of criteria in a different spot in the classroom, along with evidence to support their claim.	• Data Set Challenge Task Cards, multiple copies, cut apart, to distribute to partners • Make available: cubes, square tiles, grid paper (see appendix), and colors
Discuss	15–20 min	Discuss the strategies students developed or adapted to find data sets meeting different criteria. Discuss which criteria were more or less challenging to meet and any patterns students noticed along the way.	
Extend	30+ min	Partners investigate how their strategies change when they try to satisfy the same criteria they have already explored, this time with a data set of four or six data points.	Make available: cubes, square tiles, grid paper (see appendix), and colors

(Continued)

To the Teacher

This investigation challenges students to juggle several data constraints at once and leans on an understanding of the measures of center and spread that we have been developing in the previous activities in this big idea. We encourage you to have available for reference the Ways We Describe the Shape of Data chart the class has been building.

Creating data sets that meet criteria is difficult work, particularly because each measure requires a different kind of strategy. For instance, if you focus on the median, you might place a value in the center and build out from there by adding values on either side until you have five in total. But focusing on the mode means attending to repeated values, and the mean requires thinking about how the data gets transformed when evening it out. Embrace the struggle and frustration inherent in this investigation and focus students on how they can revise data sets that meet some, but not all, criteria. This is an opportunity to encourage students to make the data sets visual so that they can manipulate, check, and revise them, whether that representation is with cubes, line plots, lists, tables, or square tiles.

Activity

Launch

Launch the activity by showing students the following set of numbers on a chart, board, or document camera: 2, 5, 5, 6, 7. Be sure to have your Ways We Describe the Shape of Data chart available for reference. You may also want to model this data set as stacks of cubes, as in the Play activity.

Ask students, What do you notice about the center and spread of this data set? Give students a chance to turn and talk to a partner. Collect student observations and record them for all to see. Allow students enough time to think and discuss for the class to notice that this data set has a range, median, mode, and mean of 5.

Explore

Students work in partnerships to investigate data sets where the mean = median = mode = range. Partners work to answer the question, What other sets of five positive whole numbers can you find where these measures are all equal? Provide students with tools to model and investigate sets of data, such as cubes, square tiles, grid paper (see appendix), and colors. Encourage students to find as many sets of five positive whole numbers that fit the criteria as possible and to record evidence to support each.

Discuss

Gather the class together to discuss the following questions:

- What sets of five numbers did you find in which the mean = median = mode = range? How do you know they satisfy these criteria? (Create a space to display all the data sets that students share.)
- What strategies did you use for creating these data sets?
- What patterns or structures in the data did you use to help you?
- What made creating these sets challenging? What mistakes did you make? What did you learn from those mistakes?

Focus attention in this discussion on the strategic thinking students developed to find data sets that satisfy the criteria. Be sure to probe how students took a data set that satisfied some, but not all, of the criteria and revised it so that all measures were equal.

Explore

Ask students to create data sets of five positive whole numbers that satisfy the criteria on a task card. There are six task cards provided, each of which is a challenge, so we suggest that you distribute the cards one at a time; teams may spend the entire investigation period on one card. You may decide to distribute all six to different groups, or the same card to all groups. We leave this up to you. The six relationships students might explore are as follows:

- Mode < median < mean
- Mode < mean < median
- Mean < mode < median
- Mean < median < mode
- Median < mode < mean
- Median < mean < mode

Create a display space around your classroom for each set of criteria you choose to distribute. This space may be a chart for each or a part of a board, where students can record the data sets they find as they go. Students should also post evidence that their set satisfies the criteria. For each data set students find, ask them to create an "evidence page," or a sheet of paper with the data set and their evidence or visual proofs for the relationship between the mean, mode, and median that they found.

Discuss

Gather the class together to discuss the following questions:

- What patterns did you notice as you worked to create data sets?
- What strategies did you develop?
- Were there criteria that were easier or harder to satisfy? Why?
- What did you learn about the relationship between these different measures of center?

Extend

Students investigate the question, What would happen if you tried to create data sets to satisfy the criteria the class has just explored, but with only four numbers in the set? Or six numbers? How does changing the number of data points change the strategies you use to create the sets? Why?

Look-Fors

- **How are students getting started?** While some students may dive right in, creating a set and seeing what its properties are, others may try to begin strategically by assigning a value they want all of the measures to have, such as 4. If students seem stuck, struggling to enter this task, you might encourage them to model the data set that the class examined together and explore it. First, students might explore, How does this data set work so that all of the measures of center and spread are equal? Then they might consider, How could we revise this set to find another set where these measures are all equal?

- **Are students attending to all the criteria?** The mode is the easiest value to visualize in the many different forms students might use to construct their data, whether they use cubes, a line plot, or a list. The median can be seen in a small set of five values, provided they are in order. But seeing the mean requires transforming the data set. Attending to the range means focusing on the difference between the lowest and highest value. These represent many different ideas to juggle simultaneously. Ask students, What measures are you focusing on? How will you test the other measures once you create a set?

- **How are they finding the mean?** In the Play activity, students built an understanding of mean as the value when the data is evened out among all data points. Students may have found ways to calculate mean by adding up all the values and then dividing to redistribute these evenly among the data points, or they may have focused on a concrete meaning of mean that involved redistributing the data physically. Either will work for this activity, but finding mean concretely requires representing the data with objects. If students are not representing their data with objects, ask, How will you find the mean of this data? Students may have figured out that they only need to determine the total necessary to start with and work backward, a key strategic notion. For instance, students may realize that for a data set of five points to have a mean of 6, it needs to have a total value of 30, or 5×6. If students know the total, they can distribute that total in any way they want. If students find a fractional mean, you might ask, How many more (or fewer) cubes would you need to make that mean a whole number?

- **How are students visualizing the data sets?** Students may choose a variety of ways to make the data sets visual and manipulable. They may represent them with cubes or square tiles so that they can move the data around and add or subtract value easily. They may draw a graph, such as a line plot or bar graph. They may decide to create numerical representations in lists or tables. Each of these makes parts of the data visible and may obscure other aspects of the data or make revision more challenging. Ask students about how they are choosing to display the data for themselves and why they have chosen this method. You might encourage them to consider what this method allows them to see or do, and what will be harder to see or do if they use only this method. You might ask, What other way might you like to see the data so that you can see all the measures we're working with?

Reflect

What did you discover about the relationships between mean, median, and mode?

Mindset Mathematics, Grade 6

Mode < median < mean	Mode < mean < median
Mean < mode < median	Mean < median < mode
Median < mode < mean	Median < mean < mode

BIG IDEA 7

Using Symbols to Describe the World

Algebra is a very important part of mathematics for expressing relationships, but students' approach to algebra and their chance of enjoying and appreciating algebra are often destroyed by the ways it is taught in traditional textbooks. Algebra is a language—a way of describing relationships—but textbooks introduce it as a set of methods and rules to memorize. When students are introduced to variables, they should learn that they are used to represent unknowns and can stand for different numbers, as illustrated in the following pattern.

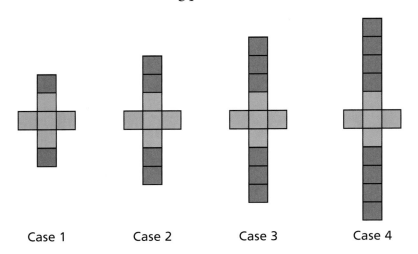

Case 1   Case 2   Case 3   Case 4

The shape has a constant value of 5, shown by the green cross in the middle. But the tails of the cross grow each time, and the growth is always $2x$, two times the case number. In case 1 there are 2 squares; in case 2 there are 4. For this reason, the linear expression that describes the growth is $2x + 5$. One reason that we know this growth is linear is that a graph of the pattern growth, showing case number against number of squares, would be a straight line.

In the expression illustrated here, the value of x changes depending on the case number. In case 1, $x = 1$, and in case 2, $x = 2$. This shows the meaning of the word *variable*: the value of x varies.

The problem comes in US classrooms when students are taught, at the beginning, to solve for x. They do repeated exercises solving for x. They get the idea that x has to be one number that does not vary. This is not a good representation of a variable. In the artificial situation set up by the textbook question, there is only one number that satisfies x, but in most uses of algebra, x is a variable representing something that varies. When students have solved for x for enough hours, they become resistant to seeing algebra as something that can describe patterns and growth, with variables that vary, when this is arguably the most important part of algebra.

In the Visualize and Investigate activities in this big idea, we encourage students as they investigate relationships to use variables as symbols whose value can vary. In the Play activity, students will meet a situation where the variable is one number. These are the different uses of variables. Students should know that variables can vary and that in some situations like the one presented in the mobile activity each of the variables represents one number. In the Visualize and Play activities in this big idea, we encourage students to think about equivalency in interesting puzzles and patterns. We ask them to build, draw, write, and discuss the relationships they see. We stress this type of work so that they can engage themselves in deep thinking about balance and what the equal sign means. We are focusing on flexibility with numbers as students work to create multiple representations of equivalent expressions.

In our Visualize activity, we bring in Cuisenaire rods, one of my favorite manipulatives, which shows numbers visually and physically. In this activity, students use two rods to define a whole and then choose rods to represent half of the unit. There are different possibilities, as students may choose one rod or a combination of rods to represent the half. The goal of this activity is for students to use multiple representations for what they are defining as a fraction $(\frac{1}{2}, \frac{1}{4}, \frac{1}{3})$ or mixed number $(1\frac{1}{2})$. We also ask them to make 1 in another way, which will require different rods. They may say that if light green + yellow = 1, then dark green + red = 1. This can lead to interesting questions, such as: "If purple + brown = 1, then what is $\frac{1}{4}$?" Students are asked to sketch the Cuisenaire rod proof they build, describe the relationship with words, and then describe the relationship with symbols. We anticipate that students will develop their own symbols because they are tired of writing the words for the rod colors over and over again.

In the Play activity, there is an opportunity to focus on equality. It is always good to remind students that the equal sign (=) means that whatever appears on one side of it is equal to whatever appears on the other. Some students get the mistaken idea that the equal sign means, "Do something; perform a calculation!" In this activity, students will get the chance to think of equality through balance in visual puzzles. There are multiple different ways that students can come up with for finding values of shapes that create balance. We think this will lead to some good classroom discussions.

In the Investigate activity, students will see a growth pattern using pattern blocks. We chose hexagons, trapezoids, squares, and rhombuses to make the growing pattern. Students are given the first three cases and asked if they can see how the pattern is growing and whether they can predict how many of each tile there would be in the different cases. This is an opportunity for students to use variables to represent the *changing* number of shapes and to describe growth. This is an important use of algebra: a way of describing patterns and growth. It is also an opportunity for students to see algebra visually and create brain connections when both visuals and symbols are used.

Jo Boaler

Cuisenaire Rod Equivalents

Snapshot

By developing symbols to represent the relationships between Cuisenaire rods, students explore the ways that symbols can be used to efficiently and clearly communicate relationships.

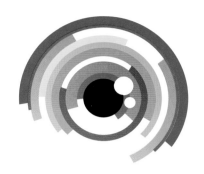

Connection to CCSS
6.EE.2a, 6.EE.4

Agenda

Activity	Time	Description/Prompt	Materials
Launch	5–10 min	Introduce Cuisenaire rods if students have not seen them before. Show students the purple and brown Cuisenaire rods and tell them that we are going to consider these two rods together to add to 1 unit.	Purple and brown Cuisenaire rods, to display
Explore	10 min	Partners explore the question, If purple + brown = 1, then what is $\frac{1}{2}$? Ask students to develop ways to communicate in writing the relationships they find.	Cuisenaire rods, one set per partnership
Discuss	10–15 min	Discuss the ways the class can use words and symbols to record the relationships they found. Discuss which ways are most effective and clear. Make sure students focus not just on communicating the answer but on the relationship between rods.	• Chart and markers • Cuisenaire rods, to display
Explore	20–30 min	Partners explore the relationships between rods on the Cuisenaire Rod Equivalents sheets, with a focus on recording these relationships in pictures, words, and symbols.	• Cuisenaire Rod Equivalents sheets, one per partnership • Cuisenaire rods, one set per partnership • Colors

Activity	Time	Description/Prompt	Materials
Discuss	15 min	Discuss the ways that students developed to communicate the relationships they found and the symbols they used. Discuss why symbols were useful. Tell students that this is what mathematicians do to develop ways of communicating clearly with one another.	Chart and markers
Extend	20+ min	Students create their own Cuisenaire rod relationship questions, which they record and solve on the sheet provided.	• Design Your Own Cuisenaire Rod Equivalents sheets, one per partnership • Cuisenaire rods, one set per partnership • Colors

(Continued)

To the Teacher

The intent of this activity is somewhat different than many of our others. Students are asked to do many tasks rather than one long one. We want these tasks to be challenging, but the recording should become a bit tedious so that students have a reason to invent variables out of their own need to make writing equations more efficient. When students invent the variables, the variables all clearly represent something students understand. Students will typically use the first letter of the colors to stand for that block, but this can create additional challenges, such as what to do with two different greens or the blue, brown, and black rods, which all begin with *b*. These challenges are themselves motivations for having a common system for naming the rods that can help students communicate with each other. This is how mathematical conventions of all kinds arise, and it is worth highlighting to students in the closing discussion that they have engaged in the authentic work of mathematicians as they invented a common language for communicating mathematical ideas.

We use fractions in this activity to give students a chance to think with fractions, which are critical to developing algebraic thinking but are not well represented in sixth grade overall. Note that there are multiple solutions to the tasks we've posed. When students can provide evidence and communicate it clearly, celebrate these diverse ways of thinking about the tasks and use these multiple correct solutions to promote thinking about equivalence.

Activity

Launch

Launch this activity by telling students that today they are going to explore the relationship between different blocks, or Cuisenaire rods. If students have never seen Cuisenaire rods, you may want to show them the entire set and ask them what they notice about the structure of these blocks.

Show on the document camera the purple and brown rods side by side, and tell students that we are going to consider these two rods added together to be 1 unit. Tell students that recording relationships clearly is important to our work. Write out this relationship on the board or chart: purple + brown = 1. Ask students, If purple + brown = 1, then what is $\frac{1}{2}$?

Explore

Provide partners with a set of Cuisenaire rods to explore the question, If purple + brown = 1, then what is $\frac{1}{2}$? Ask students to focus on developing ways to record the relationship between these rods clearly. How could you do it with words? How could symbols help you be clear? Students will likely need only a brief time for this part of the exploration.

Discuss

Once students have developed some ideas, come together to discuss briefly what students found and how they recorded the relationship. Ask students, If purple + brown = 1, then what is $\frac{1}{2}$? Invite students to share their answers and come to agreement that the dark green rod is $\frac{1}{2}$. They may have also found other smaller rods that can be summed to the same length. The focus of this discussion, however, is on how to record this relationship clearly and precisely. Ask students, How did you record what you found? Record horizontally on the board or a chart all the different ways students came up with so that they can see them side by side.

Discuss the following questions as a class:

- Which ways are the clearest? Why?
- Which ways are precise? Which are not? Why?

Draw attention to the ways of recording that are the most accurate and take into account not just what dark green represents as a number ($\frac{1}{2}$) but what it is $\frac{1}{2}$ of, such as dark green $= \frac{1}{2}$ of purple + brown.

Explore

Provide partners with the Cuisenaire Rod Equivalents sheets and ask them to continue to develop both verbal and symbolic ways of recording. Students should build, sketch, and record all the relationships in each task. Students will likely begin to substitute letters for the color words simply to make recording easier. Be sure to push students toward precision in the use of these symbols. For instance, there are two different greens. How will they indicate each? There are multiple colors that begin with the letter *b*. How will they handle this?

Discuss

Gather students together to discuss the following questions:

- What ways to communicate the relationships did you develop?
- Which ways do you think are clearest? Which are the most precise?
- Why did we use symbols to communicate? How do the symbols help us?

Record the ways students developed for communicating that they think are the clearest and most precise. Tell students that mathematicians use symbols to help them communicate relationships clearly and precisely, just as students did today. You might ask students when they have seen similar equations with letters to represent quantities. They may name formulas for area, volume, or other measurements they have seen in the past. Students may think of these as abbreviations. Name for students that in mathematics, we consider these *variables*, since we don't always know the value of things or that values may *vary*.

Extend

Invite students to pose their own Cuisenaire rod relationship questions and to record what they find using words, numbers, and symbols. Provide students with the Design Your Own Cuisenaire Rod Equivalents sheets to record the questions they create and solutions they find. Students will need access to the full set of Cuisenaire rods and colors.

Look-Fors

- **Are students communicating the full relationship, or just the answer?** Students may be tempted to make recording simpler by only writing the answer, such as green $= \frac{1}{2}$. However, this does not capture the full relationship, in that green only represents $\frac{1}{2}$ when brown and purple are 1 unit. Hold students accountable to recording this full relationship in words and using symbols to make the recording more efficient. After students have recorded a precise relationship in words, ask them, How could you show this same idea using some symbols? What would be an efficient way of recording the relationship?

- **Are students writing the relationships in words first?** As students move down the Cuisenaire Rod Equivalents sheets, you may notice that students are skipping the writing column. This is not inappropriate as long as students are capturing the relationship in symbols accurately and completely. In fact, the tedium of recording in words is intended to motivate the use of symbols as a more efficient representation of the relationship. If you see students skipping the words, ask them why and encourage them to articulate why symbols seem more useful.

- **How do students' symbols relate to their words and sketches of the relationship?** One challenge of representing an idea in multiple forms, as we have asked students to do here, is that these representations can end up not being equivalent. If students discover that one form does not match another, they may also be confused about which one is accurate. Be sure to probe students to explain how their pictures connect to the words they have written, and how both of these are reflected in the symbols they have used. You might point to parts of the equation and ask, What does this represent in your picture? What words do these symbols represent? If students do encounter errors, ask them, How will you decide which makes sense? How can you decided which relationship you want to represent in the rods?

- **Are students inventing or using variables?** The goal of this activity is to support students in developing symbolic representations, including variables, for relationships. Students may do this in ways that are not conventional for mathematics, and this is appropriate at this point. For instance, students may deal with the challenge of having a light green and a dark green by abbreviating them as "lg" and "dg." In mathematics, we would not conventionally use two symbols to stand for a single quantity, but this decision makes sense for students who are inventing variables. If in the discussion it comes up from students themselves that the use of two letters could be confusing, spend time discussing why. This can support students in refining the conventions they are developing.

Reflect

How do symbols help you communicate mathematical ideas?

Cuisenaire Rod Equivalents

Build the Problem	Sketch It	Describe the Relationship with Words	How Could You Record It with Symbols?
If purple + brown = 1, what is $\frac{1}{3}$?			
If purple + brown = 1, what is $\frac{1}{4}$?			
If red + orange = 1, what is $1\frac{1}{2}$?			
If red + orange = 1, what two other rods together = 1?			

Build the Problem	Sketch It	Describe the Relationship with Words	How Could You Record It with Symbols?
If light green + yellow = 1, what is $\frac{1}{4}$?			
If light green + yellow = $\frac{1}{3}$, what is 1?			
If red + white = $\frac{1}{6}$, What is 1?			
If red + white = $\frac{1}{6}$, what is $\frac{1}{6}$?			

Design Your Own Cuisenaire Rod Equivalents

Design a Problem	Sketch It	Describe the Relationship with Words	How Could You Record It with Symbols?

Math Mobiles

Snapshot

Students play with math mobiles, which show relationships of balance and equivalence, to determine the value of each shape in the mobile. Students explore how they might represent these relationships with symbols.

Connection to CCSS
6.EE.2, 6.EE.3, 6.EE.4, 6.EE.5, 6.EE.6

Agenda

Activity	Time	Description/Prompt	Materials
Launch	10 min	Show students the Math Mobile Puzzle sheet and ask students what they notice. Use words to annotate features that students notice.	Math Mobile Puzzle sheet, to display
Play	20+ min	Partners work with the Math Mobile Puzzle sheet to determine the value of each shape. Students explore what they notice that helps them find these values and how they might represent these relationships symbolically.	Math Mobile Puzzle sheet, one per partnership
Discuss	15+ min	Discuss what students found in the Math Mobile Puzzle sheet and how they used what they noticed to find the values of the shapes. Focus on the ways students represented relationships and how they used symbols.	Math Mobile Puzzle sheet, to display
Play	30+ min	Partners choose from Mobile Puzzles 1–4 to explore the relationships in the mobiles, how they might represent these symbolically, and the value of each shape.	Mobile Puzzle 1–4 sheets, multiple copies for partnerships to choose from

Activity	Time	Description/Prompt	Materials
Discuss	15–20 min	Discuss the observations students made about the relationships in the puzzles, how they represented those relationships, and how they used these to figure out the value of shapes. Celebrate students' observations, questions, challenges, and surprises.	Mobile Puzzle 1–4 sheets, to display
Extend	30+ min	Partners design their own math mobile puzzles, providing their audience with enough information to solve the puzzle. Students can swap puzzle drafts with another group to test them and get feedback.	

To the Teacher

The mobiles in this activity are based on puzzles designed by Lou Kroner (1997) in his book *In the Balance* for grades 4–6, which, sadly, is out of print. If you do find a copy of either of his books in this series, we highly recommend these puzzles for algebraic thinking.

When looking at these math mobiles, we are reminded of mobiles created by sculptor and painter Alexander Calder. If possible, we recommend finding some images of his work to share with students and asking them what they know about mobiles. The central idea that students need to understand and draw on in this activity is *balance*. The components of a mobile must be in balance so that it does not tip over or collapse. The mobiles in these puzzles all balance, and this balance creates the opportunity to use symbols and equations to express relationships between the different pieces within the mobile.

For the first puzzle, the entire structure is based on balance and halving. The "weight" of the mobile, or the sum of the shapes, is 16. Sixteen is a particularly flexible and advantageous number for halving, and we hope this task will give students an entry point to finding that the shapes are worth 4, 2, and 1, each a result of halving repeatedly. We have not provided answer keys for the puzzles students explore in the second half of the activity. We highly recommend that you sit down, perhaps with colleagues, and try to solve these yourselves to see how students might do so. One last note: Mobile Puzzle 4 has multiple solutions. Be sure to push students to consider what the shapes might represent and to figure out different ways to solve this puzzle.

Big Idea 7: Using Symbols to Describe the World **205**

Activity

Launch

Launch the activity by showing students the Math Mobile Puzzle sheet on the document camera. Tell students that this is a *mobile* and ask them what they know about mobiles. Use this as an opportunity to ensure that students understand that mobiles must balance to work. Tell students that this mobile is perfectly balanced and has a total weight of 16 units.

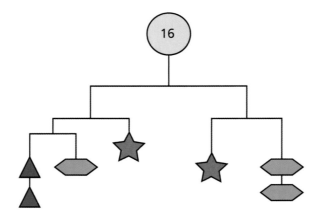

Can you find the weight of each shape to balance this math mobile?

Ask students, What do you notice about the mobile? What observations can you make? Invite students to turn and talk to a partner about their observations. Collect and record some observations from the class and ask students to justify what they see. Record these observations using words, as you recorded relationships in the Visualize activity. Pose the question that students will explore today: What do you think is the value of each of these shapes? Ask students to think about how they could represent these statements using symbols and how symbols could help them solve the puzzle.

Play

Partners work together using the Math Mobile Puzzle sheet to try to find the value of each of the shapes in the mobile, remembering that the mobile must balance and have a total weight of 16. As students work, they explore the following questions:

- What relationships do you notice in the mobile?
- How could you represent these relationships using symbols?
- How could these equations help you solve the puzzle?

Discuss

Gather students together to discuss the following questions:

- What was the first thing you noticed that helped you figure out the value of one of the shapes? How did it help you?
- What strategies did you use to find the values of the shapes?
- What equations did you write to describe the relationships in the mobile? How did these help you?

Be sure to highlight the ways students are thinking about the mathematical relationships of equivalence in this puzzle and how those might be represented with symbols and any examples of where these symbolic representations were *equations*. Representing relationships in some way provides evidence for the values students find and can help students remember their chain of reasoning.

Play

Partners choose from Mobile Puzzles 1–4. Some groups may work through several puzzles, while others may spend their time focused on one puzzle. Expect struggle and be sure to celebrate every observation students make about the mobiles, as each observation moves students along on their journey. Partners work on one or more puzzles, recording their thinking on the puzzle sheets and exploring the following questions:

- What relationships do you notice in the mobile?
- How could you represent these relationships using symbols?
- How could these equations help you solve the puzzle?
- What is the value of each of the shapes in the mobile? How do you know?

Discuss

Gather the class to discuss the following questions:

- What were the most useful observations you made about the puzzle you tried? Why?
- How did you use symbols to represent the relationships you found? How did that help you?

- How did you use the different clues, observations, or relationships together to reason about the value of the shapes?
- What was the hardest part of the puzzles you tried? Why? How did you tackle that challenge?
- What mistakes did you make? What did you learn from them?

Be sure to discuss any interesting strategies, observations, or moments you noticed as you observed students at work. Invite students to share their realizations, questions, and surprises.

Extend

Invite students to create their own math mobiles. These are challenging to make because students will need to think about how to balance the mobile and how to make sure that there is enough information in the puzzle so that others can figure it out. When students have a draft of a puzzle, have them ask another group to try it and give feedback. Students will likely make many mistakes in designing these mobiles, but the opportunity to create a puzzle engages students in kinds of reasoning that are different from those used in solving puzzles. When students have created and tested their puzzles, they can swap with other groups or create a puzzle bulletin board or display for others to engage in.

Look-Fors

- **Are students using equivalence?** The central idea in this lesson is using equivalence to determine relationships and find the missing values. As you watch students working, look for students decomposing the mobiles into parts where equivalence is visible and useful. They may isolate one branch of the mobile and locate the relationship inside—for instance, that two triangles are the same as one rectangle. Students may not know yet what to do with these individual observations, but making them is the first step. Encourage students to start by simply noticing the relationships they see to help them locate an entry point into the task. Students may be overwhelmed by the full mobile. You might encourage decomposition by saying something like, "Is there a part of the mobile where you can see a relationship? Choose a section and let's talk about what you see."
- **How are students representing relationships?** After students notice relationships, they may not know how to coordinate them in order to find the

values of the shapes. But we don't want students to lose these observations. This is one reason that recording and representing the relationships students see is crucial. If you hear students discussing equivalence or other relationships, ask, How could you record that relationship so you don't forget it or so you can use it later? How might you represent it? What symbols would help you capture what you just said?

- **Are students using variables?** It is not necessary that students use variables to represent the relationships they see, but we expect that some students, following the Visualize activity, will choose to represent the shapes with variables. It makes sense that students may want to designate triangles as t and squares as s to make it easier to record how they are related. If so, look for students making a key of some kind to track what the letters stand for. You might ask, How will you remember what each letter stands for? Or, How would someone else know what each letter stands for? However, you may also see students simply using the shapes themselves, drawing triangles to represent triangles. This is entirely appropriate, and it makes sense to ask students to discuss these decisions and their reasoning behind them in the whole-class discussions.

Reflect

What strategies were most helpful in finding the values of the shapes in the mobiles? Why?

Reference

Kroner, L. (1997). *In the balance: Algebra logic puzzles grades 4–6.* New York, NY: McGraw-Hill.

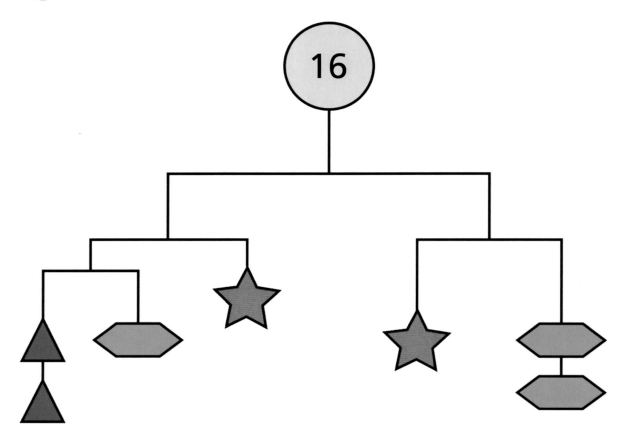

Mobile Puzzle 1

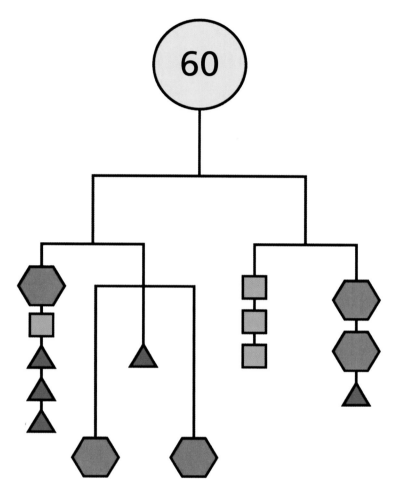

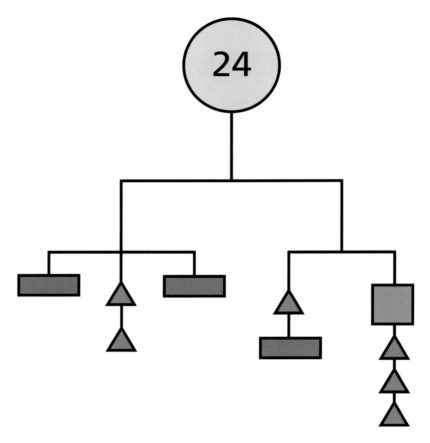

Mobile Puzzle 3

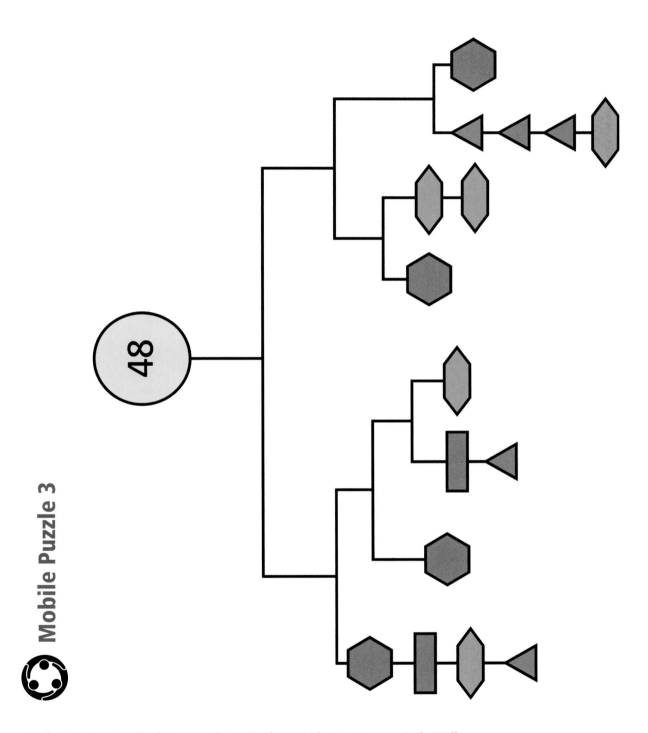

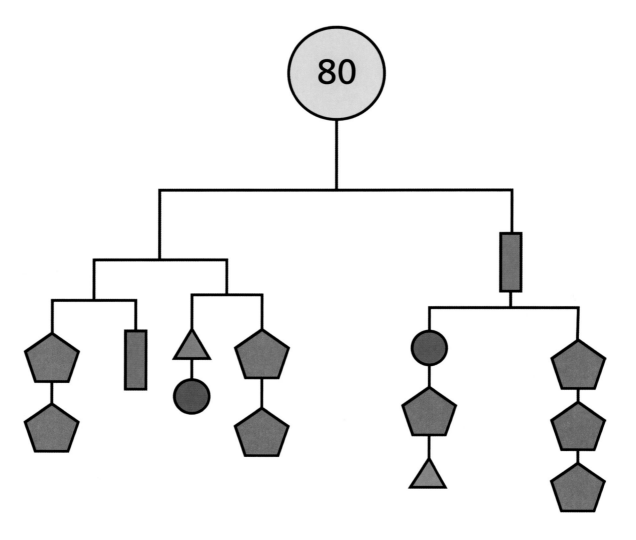

Radial Patterns

Snapshot

Students investigate the growth of radial patterns and how to represent the relationship between the cases in the pattern and the number of tiles needed to construct it.

> **Connection to CCSS**
> 6.EE.2, 6.EE.5, 6.EE.6, 6.EE.7, 6.RP.3a,b

Agenda

Activity	Time	Description/Prompt	Materials
Launch	10 min	Show students the Radial Pattern sheet and ask them how they see the pattern growing. Allow students to turn and talk to generate ideas.	Radial Pattern sheet, to display
Explore	30+ min	Partners investigate how the radial pattern grows and how they can use this pattern of growth to predict how many tiles would be needed to build case 5, 10, or beyond. Students develop ways of representing the relationship between the case number and the number of tiles of each shape needed to build it.	• Radial Pattern sheet, one per partnership • Make available: pattern blocks and isometric dot paper (see appendix)
Discuss	15–20 min	Discuss the ways students saw growth and the relationships they identified. Discuss how they might predict the number of tiles needed for any case and how they could represent that prediction using symbols.	• Radial Pattern sheet, to display • Chart and markers
Explore	30–40 min	Partners design their own radial patterns and record the first five cases. They investigate the relationships between the number of tiles and the case number, and create a poster to show what they found.	• Pattern blocks, isometric dot paper (see appendix), chart, and markers, for each partnership
Discuss	15–20 min	Do a gallery walk of the patterns students have created. Discuss any patterns that look the same, but where the relationships were represented in a very different way, and vice versa.	

To the Teacher

In this activity, we extend students' work with representing relationships by exploring radial patterns. Radial patterns begin with a central element and grow out from the center, radiating in all directions in some regular or predictable way. These patterns present students the opportunity to connect this tiling work to ratios or rates as we did in the Visualize activity of Big Idea 4. In those tiling patterns, the relationships fit together repeatedly in all directions infinitely. These radial patterns have an algebraic relationship that includes the ratio of different shapes to one another, built around a constant core. For instance, in the radial pattern we have provided, the hexagon in the center remains constant, while the trapezoids and squares increase at a rate of 3 each per case and the parallelograms increase at a rate of 6 per case. Students may see this as a ratio of 3 to 6 between trapezoids or squares and parallelograms. Representing these relationships with symbols and connecting the multiplier of 3 or 6 to rate is a critical idea that will ultimately connect slope to rate of change.

Activity

Launch

Launch the activity by showing students the Radial Pattern sheet on the document camera. Tell students that this is a pattern, with the first case on the left, growing toward the right. Ask, How is the pattern growing? How do you see it? Give students a chance to turn and talk to a partner to generate some ideas before heading off to work on the investigation.

Explore

In partners, students investigate the following questions:

- How is the pattern growing? How do you see that growth?
- How can you predict how many of each tile you would need for case 5? Case 10? Any case?
- How could you describe the relationship between the case number and the number of tiles of each shape needed? How can you represent this relationship using symbols?

Provide partners with a copy of the Radial Pattern sheet so that they can mark up the pattern, and make available pattern blocks and isometric dot paper (see appendix) so that they can build additional cases to test their ideas.

Discuss

Gather students together to discuss the following questions:

- What relationships did you notice?
- How can you predict the number of each tile you need for each case?
- What symbols or equations could be used to express these relationships? Why do these ways make sense?

Record on a chart the patterns and relationships students found and the ways they represented these using symbols. Come to agreement about the relationships students found and the different ways we can describe and name those relationships in words, pictures, and symbols. It may also make sense to mark up the Radial Pattern sheet with the ways students saw the pattern growing.

Explore

Invite students to design their own radial pattern, one that grows predictably from the center outward. Provide each group with pattern blocks and isometric dot paper (see appendix) for recording. Ask the groups to determine how their radial pattern will grow and then to construct and draw at least the first five cases in the pattern.

Partners investigate the relationships between the number of tiles needed for any case and develop ways of expressing these relationships using symbols. Each group creates a poster of their radial pattern to share with the class, which includes the first five cases, the relationships among the number of tiles and the case number, and any ways they found to use symbols to represent these relationships.

Discuss

Ask partners to post their charts around the room, and hold a gallery walk of the patterns students created. As students walk, ask them to consider the following questions:

- Can you find any patterns that look similar but where the groups represented the relationships in very different ways?

- Can you find any patterns where the relationships between the tiles and cases look similar but the radial patterns look different?
- What is interesting about the collection of patterns we made?

After students have had a chance to explore others' patterns, discuss what students found during their gallery walk and what they are wondering now.

Look-Fors

- **Are students developing radial patterns that grow predictably?** Students may be tempted to build a pattern outward from the center but to do so in ways that simply fill in the space as it grows. For instance, they may first add squares all around, then blue parallelograms, then trapezoids and brown parallelograms, then hexagons, and so on. While it may be radial and there is a pattern, such a creation is not predictable. The goal is for students to create a pattern that will extend predictably, and then to be able to use that predictability to make projections and representations. If you notice this unpredictable way of constructing radial patterns, ask students, How do you know what will come in the next case? What is the pattern you are using to build from one case to the next? If students don't have such a pattern, you might ask, How could you make a pattern where you can describe with words how to build from one case to the next?

- **How are students representing growth symbolically?** In this third activity related to representing relations symbolically, students have seen many different ways that they might express patterns, equivalence, or other relationships. Point out to students the connections between ways they are representing patterns and how they have done so in the previous activities. If students struggle to represent these patterns of growth, you might ask, How have you represented relationships before? What tools or ideas from other activities might help you here? Students may also represent the relationships in fragmented ways, saying that you take the case number and multiply it by 3 to get the number of squares, or symbolically something equivalent to $3c = s$. This documents one of the relationships in the pattern but not all. This is completely fine at this stage, and students are not expected to string all the relationships together into a larger equation. However, if anyone does, be sure to spend some time discussing this strategy as a class.

- **Do students see connections between a pattern's growth and rates or ratios?** As students are describing growth, notice the language they use and how it is connected to rates. For instance, students may say that "for each case you add 3 more" or "there are 3 squares per case." These kinds of ways of describing growth are rates, and you might choose to revoice their thinking by saying, "So, they are growing at a rate of 3 squares per case?" Highlight connections to rates or ratios that students seem to be making, even if those connections are not stated explicitly, as in the previous examples. You may even want to draw attention to these connections by asking about them in the discussion, How are these patterns connected to rates?

Reflect

How did representing patterns with symbols change how you saw them?

Radial Pattern

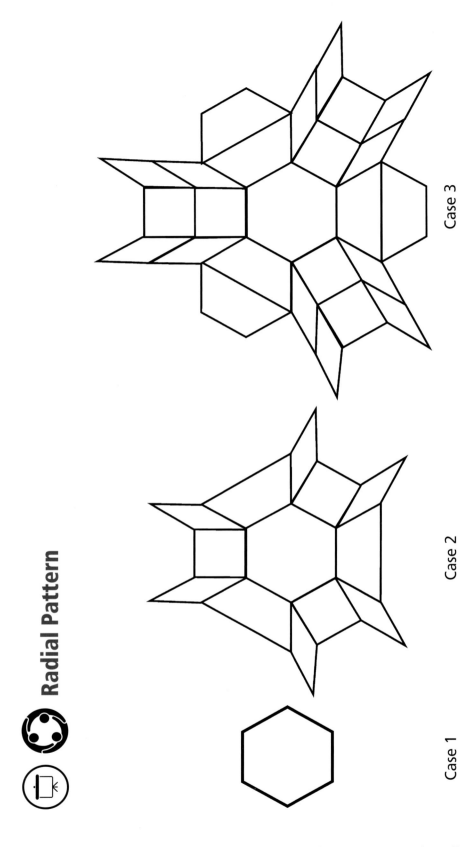

Case 1

Case 2

Case 3

BIG IDEA 8

Generalizing

The big idea that is at the center of this set of activities—generalizing—is an action that could represent all of mathematics. When teachers share methods with students, they are showing them something that is general—an idea that always works. For example, we know that multiplying a natural number by 10 results in a zero being added to the number. The problem that arises in many mathematics classrooms is that teachers show a general idea, one intended to help students focus on the underlying concept, but students think it is a specific method they should memorize. The same problem can come up when teachers show any method—for example, the multiplication algorithm or a method for working out ratio. A good way to show new ideas is to share that something general is happening—something that always happens—and teach students that their role in mathematics is always to work out what is particular in a situation and what is general. Each activity in this set is conceptually interesting and offers students occasions to study numbers and patterns, which is valuable in its own right. The activities have also been designed to give opportunities for students to think: What is particular and what is general? This question is at the center of the work of mathematicians, who study patterns to make general statements that ultimately lead to mathematical proofs.

In the Visualize activity, students are presented with a display of data and asked what it represents. This is a great occasion for students to struggle, as it is not obvious what the data display represents, but it is something students will be able to work out through exploration and investigation. When the display is presented to the class, students will probably have lots of ideas and conjectures about what they think the data in the pattern represents. The line plot actually shows the number of factors for each number. We are really excited about this activity, and we think students will embrace the challenge of the number mystery. In this activity, help students produce general statements and consider together how generalizable they are. For example, they may say that odd numbers have shorter stacks. Is that a generalizable statement? Is it always true? It is good to ask students why their observations exist, to help them think about the structure of numbers and reason about them.

In the Play activity, we present the game Pennies and Paperclips. This activity comes from a wonderful website and collection of activities called Discovering the Art of Mathematics, and it is a game that I use often with my undergraduate students. It is a lovely example of a low-floor, high-ceiling task: it has a low floor—anyone can access it and play the game—but it extends to very high levels and cool generalizations. In a sixth-grade classroom we do not expect students to come up with formal mathematical proofs that relate to the patterns, but they can come up with conjectures and patterns that are generalizable. Can they work out situations when Pennies always wins? Or Paperclips always wins? Would these generalizations hold on different sizes of boards?

In the Investigate activity, we share a toothpick squares puzzle. In this activity, students build 2×2 and 4×4 toothpick squares, and we ask them to investigate any patterns they notice and record them on chart paper for a gallery walk later. This activity provides a really good opportunity for showing a generalization through color coding. Bringing color to mathematics is always worthwhile, both to highlight particular aspects of a mathematical idea and to bring mathematics to life. Many people know that color can be helpful, but they may not have used color to show how a pattern grows and to show generalization, as we highlight in the task, so this is a good opportunity for students to learn this approach. After students have engaged in a gallery walk, they can discuss as a class how their generalizations might work for finding out how many toothpicks there would be in any case.

Jo Boaler

Generalizing Number Patterns

Snapshot

Students explore making generalizations about numerical patterns presented graphically, to build an expansive understanding of what generalizations can be.

Connection to CCSS
6.SP.1, 6.SP.5b

Agenda

Activity	Time	Description/Prompt	Materials
Launch	10 min	Show students the Number Mystery Line Plot sheet and ask, What do you think this graph shows? What do you notice about the graph that might help you figure it out? Collect some observations.	Number Mystery Line Plot sheet, to display
Explore	20 min	Partners explore the Number Mystery Line Plot sheet to collect observations and develop a conjecture about what the graph represents. Students use their conjectures to predict additional data and add it to the line plot.	Number Mystery Line Plot sheet, one per partnership
Discuss	20 min	Discuss students' conjectures about what the line plot shows and evidence to support or refute these ideas. Come to consensus that the graph shows the number of factors of each whole number, and add data to the line plot for 17–20.	Number Mystery Line Plot, to display
Explore	30 min	Partners explore patterns in the data and make general statements about what they notice. They investigate whether these general statements hold true when extending the graph and what new general statements they can make with this additional data.	• Number Mystery Line Plot sheet, one per partnership • Colors • Make available: tape and additional paper

Activity	Time	Description/Prompt	Materials
Discuss	20 min	Collects students' general statements about the patterns in the data into a Generalizations about Factors chart, and name these statements as *generalizations*. Ask students to provide supporting evidence for these claims, or counterexamples to refute them. Come to consensus about which the class believes to be true.	Chart and markers
Extend	30+ min	Partners develop their own number mystery graphs that show something about numbers without indicating just what they display. Groups swap mystery graphs to see whether they can find patterns and identify what the graph shows.	Make available: grid paper (see appendix), rulers, and colors

(Continued)

To the Teacher

In this activity, we begin our exploration of generalizing by focusing on a number pattern presented visually in a line plot.

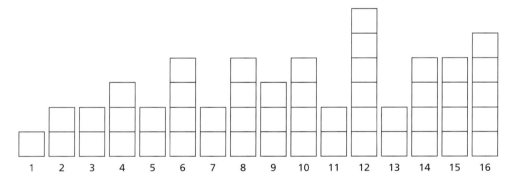

What number pattern does this line plot represent?

Whole numbers are shown across the horizontal axis. We challenge students to first make observations about this data and then try to figure out what this line plot shows. In a similar vein, we challenge you to try this with colleagues before you ask students to do so. Such an experience will give you insight into the ways students may be struggling to track down just what this data shows.

Upon looking at the graph, you and students will notice that the data appears to grow, but irregularly. The pattern is certainly not linear. It does not grow regularly, as with the radial patterns students investigated in Big Idea 7. In fact, what is shown is not a pattern of growth at all, but a reflection on the numbers' own properties. This is a graph of the number of factors of whole numbers.

We've left the boxes within the line plot open so that students can choose to write or color inside them to help document the patterns they see, or the reason behind those patterns. For instance, if students were to jot the factors inside these boxes, they would see that all of the numbers with stacks of two boxes have just 1 and themselves. They would also see that the first (or last) box is always 1, and every number has 1 as a factor. This could lead to a generalization such as "no number has zero factors."

Activity

Launch

Launch the activity by showing students the Number Mystery Line Plot in the document camera. Ask, What do you think this graph shows? What do you notice about the graph that might help you figure it out? Give students a chance to turn and talk to a partner. Invite students to share observations about the data that might help the class figure out what the graph shows—not their conjectures about what the graph represents. Be sure to ask students to hold on to their conjectures for later; at this stage you want to hear observations. Annotate a few on the line plot.

Explore

Working in partners, students explore a copy of the Number Mystery Line Plot sheet and use their observations of the data to try to figure out what the graph represents. Ask students to develop a conjecture with evidence to support that idea.

Once students have a conjecture, ask, If your conjecture were true, what would the next few values on the line plot look like? Ask students to add their predicted data to the graph.

If students struggle to develop a conjecture, ask them to start collecting evidence that will be useful either in supporting or refuting others' conjectures.

Discuss

Gather students together to discuss the question, What does this line plot show? Ask groups to pose their conjectures and provide evidence. All groups can contribute additional supporting evidence or a counterexample which shows that the conjecture is not true. Use the class's observations to come to consensus about what the line plot shows.

Ask, What would the next few values on the line plot look like using this conjecture? Together add data for 17–20 to the line plot. You might invite students to cross out the Number Mystery title of the line plot and give it an accurate name, such as Number of Factors. Tell students that in the next part of this activity, they are going to be trying to make general statements about the graph, the numbers, and the data.

Explore

Partners explore the following questions:

- What patterns do you see in the data?
- What general statements can you make based on this data? (Invite students to color-code or mark up the graph to make these visible.)

Students collect their general statements about the data and can test them by continuing to extend the line plot. Provide students with additional paper and tape to make their line plots as long as they want. Students explore the following questions:

- Do your general statements continue to hold true as you extend the graph?
- What new statements can you make with more data to look at?

Discuss

Gather students together and collect groups' general statements about the factors of numbers as represented in the line plot. Tell students that these general statements are called *generalizations*. Record each statement on a chart called Generalizations about Factors. Then invite the class to share supporting evidence for this generalization or a counterexample which shows that the statement either is not true or needs to be revised. All groups should be involved in providing evidence for any generalization. Students can contribute evidence using their entire line plot, however much they have extended it.

Come to agreement about which generalizations seem to hold true based on the data the class has. Discuss the following questions:

- What do these generalizations make you wonder?
- How far might we need to extend the graph to be confident in the claims?

Extend

Students can create their own graphs of number data without showing what that data represents. Provide groups with grid paper (see appendix), rulers, and colors. Once students have developed a graph, groups can swap number mysteries with one another. Students explore, Can you figure out what the line plot shows? What is your evidence? Each group develops a conjecture and evidence and presents it to the group who created the graph to find out whether they are correct.

Look-Fors

- **Are students testing ideas for the Number Mystery Line Plot that focus on number properties?** Students have seen data that is collected to show variation among a sample in Big Idea 6, such as the data of hurricane frequency by category. The data in this activity is different, because it is based on the properties of the numbers themselves. While there is variation along the graph, any graph that plots the factors of whole numbers will be identical to this one. For students to interpret the graph, they need to think about what they know and can find out about the numbers themselves. Students must ask questions about the trends in the data, if any, and how those connect back to number properties. To help students attend to numbers, you might ask, What do you know about these number across the horizontal axis? What patterns do you see? How do those connect to what you know about these numbers? You may focus students on one number or a few numbers in particular to support students in generating ideas.

- **Are students' generalizations general?** Moving from observations to generalization is a leap. Students may make an observation like, "Most of the odd numbers have shorter stacks than the even numbers." But this is not yet a generalization. Observations that include language like *most, some, few, rarely, almost all, tend to*, and so on hint at a pattern but acknowledge that the pattern is not generalizable. Students may struggle with moving from these observations to identifying patterns that hold true across all numbers. You might ask students to think about why their observations may exist, which could support them in reasoning about what may be general about them. Further, some generalizations can have exceptions. For instance, students can make the generalization that "all prime numbers are odd, except for 2." This is a valid generalization because no matter how far they extend the graph, no additional even primes will exist.

- **Do students extend the line plot accurately?** Once students have a shared understanding of what the line plot shows, they will need to extend the graph to continue to explore and test their observations and generalizations. If students make errors in counting the number of factors for a given whole number, this will shift the statements that they can make about the data. Attend to students' extended graphs and ask them questions about how they constructed the data. If students are struggling with testing their ideas on the extended graph, you may suggest that they check their data to be sure that it is accurate before they discard generalizations.

Reflect

What did looking for generalizations help you notice?

Number Mystery Line Plot

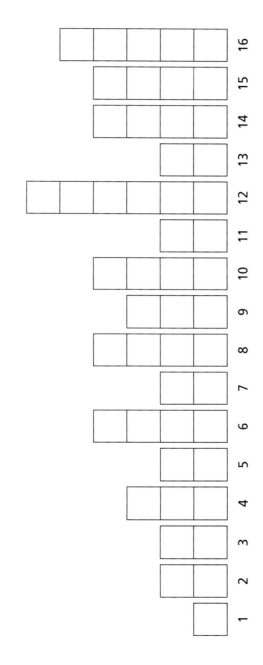

Generalizing Strategy

Snapshot

We explore generalizing strategies by playing the game Pennies and Paperclips and developing statements about how players can win.

Connection to CCSS
6.EE.9

Agenda

Activity	Time	Description/Prompt	Materials
Launch	10–15 min	Show students how to play Pennies and Paperclips and ensure they understand the rules.	• Pennies and Paperclips Game Board sheet, to display • Two pennies and several paperclips
Play	20–30 min	Partners play Pennies and Paperclips several times, with each partner getting an opportunity to be the Pennies player and the Paperclips player.	• Pennies and Paperclips Game Board sheet, one per partnership • Two pennies and several paperclips, per partnership
Explore	20+ min	Partners develop statements about how Pennies can win and how Paperclips can win. They may test these statements by continuing to play the game.	• Pennies and Paperclips Game Board sheet, one per partnership • Two pennies and several paperclips, per partnership
Discuss	15+ min	Discuss students' conjectures about how Pennies can win and how Paperclips can win. Record students' ideas on a chart and ask them to provide some evidence.	• Pennies and Paperclips Game Board sheet, to display • Two pennies and several paperclips • Chart and markers

Activity	Time	Description/Prompt	Materials
Play	20–30 min	Partners choose one or more conjectures to test by playing the game. For each statement they test, students record the results of their game on the Pennies and Paperclips Evidence sheet.	• Pennies and Paperclips Game Board sheet, one per partnership • Two pennies and several paperclips, per partnership • Pennies and Paperclips Evidence sheet, multiple copies per partnership
Discuss	20 min	Students discuss the conjectures they explored and offer evidence to support or refute these generalizations. Partners offer any new additional general statements to be added to the chart and evidence to support these. The class considers how much evidence is enough to declare a generalization true.	• Pennies and Paperclips Game Board sheet, to display • Two pennies and several paperclips • Chart and markers

To the Teacher

This activity is based on one developed by the mathematicians at Discovering the Art of Mathematics, an NSF-supported project whose goal is to develop approaches to teaching mathematics to liberal arts students at the college level. In their activity, they focus on proof (Fleron, 2013), but here we use the game of Pennies and Paperclips to engage students with generalizing strategy. Because generalization so often focuses on developing abstract and symbolic representations for patterns, students rarely get opportunities to connect the work they do in games with generalizing. Here, we ask students to play a game repeatedly with the goal of developing statements about effective strategies for winning.

As students start to develop ideas about the patterns within the game and how Pennies or Paperclips might win, the statements they make will likely be hesitant. Embrace this first-draft thinking and their risk-taking. While we encourage you to press students for reasoning, they are unlikely to yet have enough evidence for their ideas. Ask them questions about what they need to explore in order to gather more evidence or test their initial ideas, and then give them time to go back to the game to do just that. The more that students play, refine their statements, and collect evidence to support or refute them, the closer they move toward generalizing—without ever using symbols. This iterative exploration could take several days or continue as an ongoing exploration after two days of work as a class.

We strongly encourage you to play this game yourself repeatedly, in both the Pennies and Paperclips roles, to see how students will gain insight into the patterns within the game. Gather a few colleagues together and have a Pennies and Paperclips party and see what you discover.

Activity

Launch

Launch the activity by showing students on a document camera how to play Pennies and Paperclips. Be sure students understand the rules of play and how to win. Tell students that today they are going to explore this game and try to learn how Pennies can win and how Paperclips can win.

Play

In partners, students play Pennies and Paperclips several times. Provide pairs of students with the Pennies and Paperclips Game Board sheet, two pennies, and several paperclips. Each partner should get the opportunity to be both Pennies and Paperclips.

Game Directions

- One player is Pennies and the other player is Paperclips. Pennies receives two pennies, and Paperclips receives several paperclips. Place the game board where both players can see and reach it.
- Pennies places two pennies on any two squares on the board.
- Paperclips then tries to cover the rest of the board with paperclips. Each paperclip must be placed across two adjacent squares (squares side by side horizontally or vertically, but not diagonally). Only one paperclip can cover any square. No paperclip can cover a square with a penny on it.

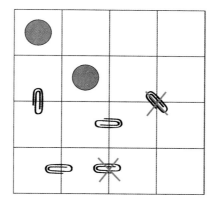

A game of Pennies and Paperclips showing three paperclips
placed correctly and two that are incorrect

- Winning: If Paperclips can cover all the remaining squares on the board, then Paperclips wins. If Paperclips cannot cover all the remaining squares, then Pennies wins.

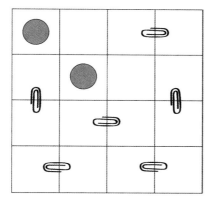

In this game, Pennies
wins, because Paperclips
did not cover all the
squares.

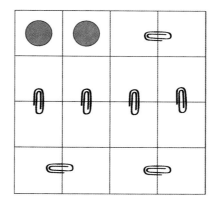

In this game, Paperclips
wins, because all squares
are covered.

Explore

After partners have had a chance to play several times, ask students to try to make some general statements about strategies for winning the game.

- How can Pennies win?
- How can Paperclips win?

Students may want to play the game as they develop these statements to test out their ideas. Ask students to record their ideas so that they are ready to share these with the class.

Discuss

Show a Pennies and Paperclips Game Board sheet on the document camera and have pennies and paperclips handy so that students can show their ideas. Discuss the general statements students can make to describe how Pennies wins and how Paperclips wins. Record these conjectures on a chart and ask students to show some evidence using the materials on the document camera. Students' ideas at this point are going to be in development and will probably sound like, "We think Pennies wins if . . ." These statements, along with some evidence—not full proofs—are what we are hoping to generate at this point. If students need more time to play to develop these ideas, send them out to continue work. Students may also present ideas that others disagree with. Celebrate these moments in which ideas and evidence come together.

Play

Ask students to choose and test one or more of the conjectures from the chart you created as a class during the discussion. Students will need to play the game several times with the specific goal of collecting additional evidence that this general statement is true or of finding a counterexample, a case when it does not hold true.

Students should use the Pennies and Paperclips Evidence sheet to record the trial they explored and the outcomes as evidence to share. Students jot at the top of the sheet the conjecture they are testing. Whether they find supporting evidence or a counterexample, each game they try is evidence.

Discuss

Gather students together to discuss each conjecture that students tested, using the following questions:

- What evidence did you find to support this general statement?
- Did anyone find a counterexample—a case when the statement did not hold true?
- Do we now believe that this general statement is true? How might we need to modify the statement?

Discuss any additional general statements students might now be able to add to the chart:

- What new strategies did you develop?
- What statements can we now make about winning the game based on your evidence?
- What are you still wondering?

Students may well want to return to playing the game to continue to test, develop, and refine general statements about winning this game. Encourage students to think carefully about how to make their statements precise and when they can say they are convinced that a statement is true. Ask students to consider, How much evidence is needed?

Look-Fors

- **Are students trying different game-play strategies systematically?** Initially, we invite students simply to play the game. But as the activity progresses, students should be focusing on exploring the conditions that lead to Pennies or Paperclips winning the game. To do so, they will need to think systematically as they consider different types of moves. For instance, they may categorize the initial placement of the pennies by their location relative to each other to investigate what happens when pennies are in the same row or column, when they are diagonal to one another, or neither. They may explore whether the color of the squares matters by asking, What happens when the pennies are on the same color, or on different colors? By thinking in these ways, rather than simply placing the pennies in different positions over and over, students can more systematically explore what might influence winning. Ask, What idea are you exploring now? You might notice something about their board and ask what happens now, such as, "I notice you put your pennies close together. Do you think that matters? Do you think it might help Pennies or Paperclips?"
- **How are students gathering evidence?** As students begin to develop ideas, they will need to have some evidence to share, even if that evidence begins with a single example. For students to share, they will need to record their thinking somehow so that they can remember precisely the positions of the pennies and paperclips they want to report on. If students are struggling to

hold on to their ideas, you may want to offer the Pennies and Paperclips Evidence sheets earlier in the lesson to support them. To push their thinking, after students have an idea and one example that supports it, ask, How can you test this idea with another example?

- **Are students looking for counterexamples?** When students have ideas, they want to find evidence to support them, but just as valuable are counterexamples. While it may be frustrating for students to find that one of their ideas does not always hold true, you can support them by highlighting the work they did to pursue evidence and discover that something that appeared to be true was, in fact, not. Encourage students to deliberately search for counterexamples by exploring extreme cases, or complex cases where multiple factors intersect. For instance, if students think that having pennies in the same row matters, then ask them to explore whether that is true in cases where the pennies are on the same or different colors or explore whether it matters if that row is at the top or in the middle of the board. Ask, Are there any cases where you're not sure whether your idea will work? How will you test those?

Reflect

How much evidence do you think you need before you can consider a generalization true?

Reference

Fleron, J. (2013, October 24). Pennies & paperclip proofs. Retrieved from https://www .artofmathematics.org/blogs/jfleron/pennies-paperclip-proofs

Pennies and Paperclips Game Board

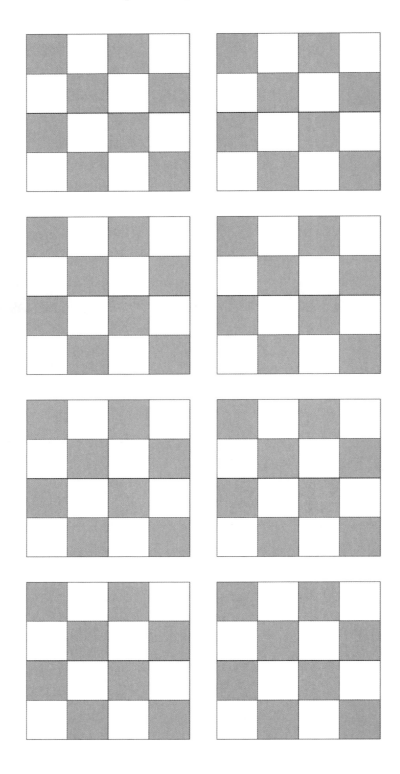

Generalizing Visual Patterns

Snapshot

Students investigate generalizing from visual patterns by exploring networks of toothpick squares and the number of toothpicks it takes to construct them.

Connection to CCSS
6.EE.4, 6.EE.9

Agenda

Activity	Time	Description/Prompt	Materials
Launch	10–15 min	Show the 3 × 3 Toothpick Square image and ask students, Without counting one by one, how many toothpicks do you think there are in this image? Discuss this question as in a number talk, and diagram, color-code, and record the ways students saw the toothpicks.	• 3 × 3 Toothpick Square sheet, multiple copies to display and mark up • Colors
Explore	30+ min	Partners or small groups construct 2 × 2 and 4 × 4 toothpick squares to investigate the patterns they notice in the number of toothpicks needed. Groups make generalizations about the relationship between the square size and the number of toothpicks needed and present their findings in a chart.	• Make available: toothpicks, dot paper (see appendix), colors, and tape. • Chart and markers, for each group
Discuss	20 min	Do a gallery walk of groups' work. Discuss similarities, differences, and connections among the groups' findings. Discuss the evidence for the generalizations the class has made and how these generalizations might help predict the number of toothpicks needed for larger squares.	

Activity	Time	Description/Prompt	Materials
Extend	60+ min	Students investigate how their generalizations change if the growing pattern changes. Select a new growing pattern or invite students to devise their own to investigate.	Make available: toothpicks, dot paper (see appendix), colors, and tape

(Continued)

To the Teacher

In this activity, we explore a classic problem about toothpick squares to invite students to make generalizations from a visual pattern. The standards relating to generalization in sixth grade focus on representing these relationships symbolically. While students may do that in this activity, particularly as they construct expressions to represent how they saw the number of toothpicks, they will also likely represent their generalization using diagrams, color coding, and words. We value all of these forms and believe that in building connections between them all, students have a more robust understanding of what it means to generalize, why it might be useful, and the many times they engage in this kind of mathematical thinking in the real world already.

The extension for this activity provides an interesting twist on this classic problem by asking students to compare their generalizations about toothpick squares to other growing patterns of toothpicks. These are not frequently explored, and students may discover intriguing ways that their understanding of toothpick squares is applicable to or in conflict with the growing patterns of toothpicks in other arrangements. You could conceivably spend multiple days investigating and comparing these different patterns and designing your own.

Activity

Launch

Launch the activity by showing students the 3×3 Toothpick Square image. Tell students that this is a square made out of toothpicks. Ask students, Without counting one by one, how many toothpicks do you think there are in this image? Give students a few moments to think, and ask students to give a private signal, such as a thumbs-up, when they have an answer, as one would in a number talk.

Invite students to share their answers and defend them by describing how they saw how many toothpicks make up the square. Color-code or mark up the different ways students saw the toothpicks and decomposed the image. Record any calculations student did, using expressions to show the complexity of students' thinking. For instance, if students saw four columns of three vertical toothpicks each and then three columns of four horizontal toothpicks each, you might record this as $(4 \times 3) + (3 \times 4)$.

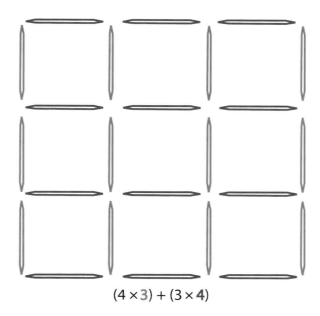

$(4 \times 3) + (3 \times 4)$

Come to agreement about how many toothpicks make up this image, and draw attention to the many different ways students saw the number of toothpicks.

Explore

In partners or small groups, students construct 2×2 and 4×4 toothpick squares, which represent those that come immediately before and after the 3×3 square in a growing sequence of toothpick squares. Provide students with toothpicks, dot paper (see appendix), colors or markers, tape, and a chart. Students investigate the following questions:

- How many toothpicks are needed to build each square?
- What patterns do you notice in the squares that help you figure this out without counting one by one?

- What general statements can you make about the number of toothpicks needed to build squares? Build as many more squares as you want in order to investigate and test your generalizations.
- How can your generalizations predict how many toothpicks would be needed to build any size square? Test your ideas by predicting the number of toothpicks in a larger square and then building it to see whether your prediction was accurate.

Each group constructs a chart to share what they have found and the generalizations they can make using their evidence.

Discuss

Ask groups to post their charts around the room, and hold a gallery walk. Ask students to consider the following questions as they compare charts:

- How are the different groups' findings similar or different?
- Do you notice any connections between the strategies different groups used?
- What does the class seem to agree on? What needs further investigation?

Discuss the observations that students made during the gallery walk, including the similarities, differences, and connections they observed. Discuss the following questions as a class:

- What generalizations do we feel confident in based on our data? Which generalizations need more evidence?
- How could we use our generalizations to predict how many toothpicks would be needed to build a square of any size?

Extend

Alter the growing pattern for the toothpick shape and invite students to investigate how the generalizations they can make will change or remain the same. Students could investigate any of the following:

- Rectangles where the length is one more than the width: 1×2, 2×3, 3×4, 4×5, . . .
- Staircase patterns of toothpicks, which add one more step as they grow

- Pyramid patterns that add one new layer as they grow
- Another growing pattern that students devise themselves

Look-Fors

- **How are students decomposing the toothpick squares to see structure?** While students can count these toothpicks one by one, doing so will obscure the structures that hold the toothpick squares together. As students construct, draw, and analyze other sizes of toothpick squares, watch how they find the number of toothpicks. Ask, What patterns in the square are you noticing? How are they constructed? How could this help you determine how many toothpicks a square is composed of? Extend these observations by asking, How do these patterns change when the square grows or shrinks? Students may, for example, decompose the square into vertical and horizontal toothpicks. You may want to ask, How are these related? What happens to the number of vertical toothpicks when the square grows? What about the horizontal toothpicks?

- **What connections are students making between the visual pattern, number, and symbolic representations?** One opportunity in this activity is for students to connect multiple representations of patterns to move toward generalizing. Ask students to show you the ways they are decomposing, diagramming, or color-coding their visual images of the toothpick squares. Ask students how they would describe these patterns, and then how they could represent these patterns with numbers or symbols. If students use numbers or symbols, ask questions about how these connect back to the images they have constructed. They may want to color-code their expressions to match the color-coded diagram, for instance, to make those connections clear.

- **Are students' generalizations general?** Students' observations about growth are likely to begin as quite specific. For instance, they may say that the 2×2 toothpick square has half the toothpicks of the 3×3 square. Such observations may be true, but they are not yet generally applicable to all cases. When students make observations about the changes in the numbers of toothpicks overall or in rows and columns, ask them, Do you think this will be true for all cases, or just in this case? How could you find out? Push students to notice and test iteratively to move progressively toward general statements. You might ask them why they think this relationship exists by saying, What is happening in the toothpick square that is leading to that change? The structures that underlie differences are where students are most likely to make general statements that hold true across cases.

Reflect

When do you think generalizations are useful? Why?

3 × 3 Toothpick Square

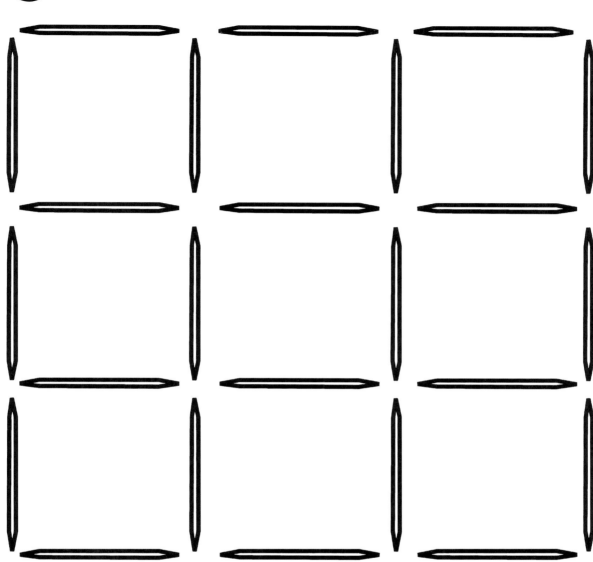

Appendix

Centimeter Grid Paper

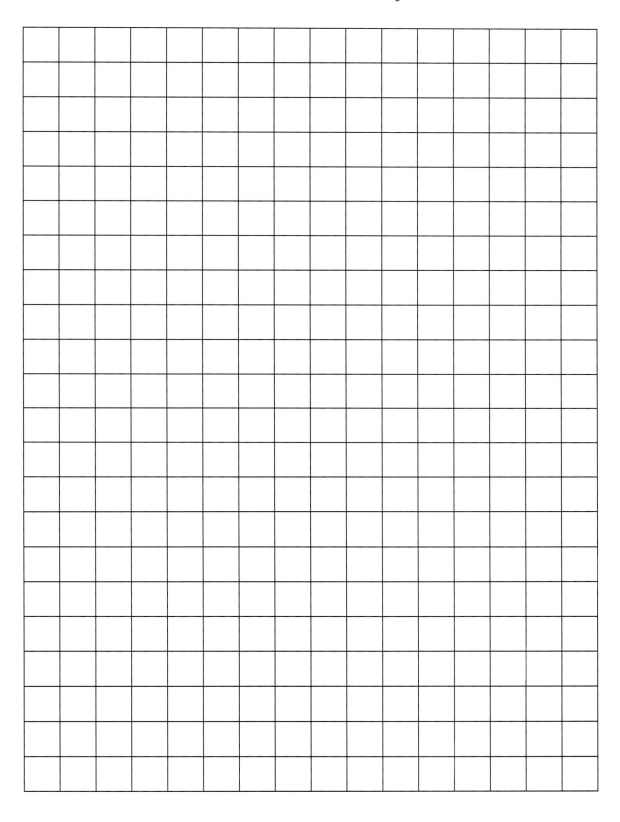

Grid Paper

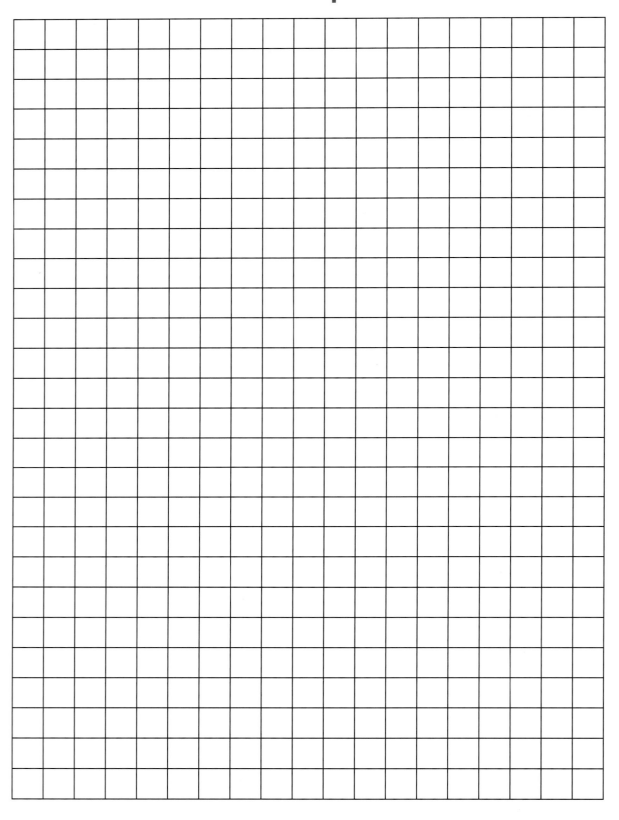

1" Grid Paper

Isometric Dot Paper

Dot Paper

About the Authors

Dr. Jo Boaler is a professor of mathematics education at Stanford University, and the cofounder of Youcubed. She is the author of the first MOOC on mathematics teaching and learning. Former roles have included being the Marie Curie Professor of Mathematics Education in England, a mathematics teacher in London comprehensive schools, and a lecturer and researcher at King's College, London. Her work has been published in the *Times,* the *Telegraph,* the *Wall Street Journal,* and many other news outlets. The BBC recently named Jo one of the eight educators "changing the face of education."

Jen Munson is a postdoctoral fellow in learning sciences at Northwestern University, a professional developer, and a former classroom teacher. She received her PhD from Stanford University. Her research focuses on how coaching can support teachers in growing their mathematics instructional practices and how teacher-student interactions influence equitable math learning. She is the author of *In the Moment: Conferring in the Elementary Math Classroom*, published by Heinemann.

 **Cathy Williams** is the cofounder and director of Youcubed. She completed an applied mathematics major at University of California, San Diego before becoming a high school math teacher for 18 years in San Diego County. After teaching, she became a county office coordinator and then district mathematics director. As part of her leadership work, Cathy has designed professional development and curriculum. Her district work in the Vista Unified School District won a California Golden Bell for instruction in 2013 for the K–12 Innovation Cohort in mathematics. In Vista, Cathy worked with Jo changing the way mathematics was taught across the district.

Acknowledgments

We thank Jill Marsal, our book agent, and the team at Wiley for their efforts to make these books what we'd imagined. We are also very grateful to our Youcubed army of teachers. Thanks to Robin Anderson for drawing the network diagram on our cover. Finally, we thank our children—and dogs!—for putting up with our absences from family life as we worked to bring our vision of mathematical mindset tasks to life.

Index